A New Theory of Organizational Ecology, and Its Implications for Educational Leadership

Also available from Bloomsbury

Leadership for Sustainability in Higher Education
by Janet Haddock-Fraser, Peter Rands and Stephen Scoffham
Sustainable School Leadership by Mike Bottery, Wong Ping-Man
and George Ngai
Pluralist Publics in Market Driven Education: Towards More Democracy in Educational Reform by Ruth Boyask
Teaching in Unequal Societies by John Russon
Preparation and Development of School Leaders in Africa edited by Pontso Moorosi and Tony Bush
Race, Education and Educational Leadership in England: An Integrated Analysis edited by Paul Miller and Christine Callender
System Leadership: Policy and Practice in the English Schools System by Susan Cousin
Understanding Educational Leadership: Critical Perspectives and Approaches edited by Steven J. Courtney, Helen M. Gunter, Richard Niesche and Tina Trujillo

A New Theory of Organizational Ecology, and Its Implications for Educational Leadership

Christopher M. Branson and Maureen Marra

BLOOMSBURY ACADEMIC
LONDON • NEW YORK • OXFORD • NEW DELHI • SYDNEY

BLOOMSBURY ACADEMIC
Bloomsbury Publishing Plc
50 Bedford Square, London, WC1B 3DP, UK
1385 Broadway, New York, NY 10018, USA
29 Earlsfort Terrace, Dublin 2, Ireland

BLOOMSBURY, BLOOMSBURY ACADEMIC and the Diana logo are trademarks of
Bloomsbury Publishing Plc

First published in Christopher M. Branson and Maureen Marra, 2022
This paperback edition published in 2023

Copyright © Christopher M. Branson and Maureen Marra, 2022

Christopher M. Branson and Maureen Marra have asserted their right under the Copyright, Designs and Patents Act, 1988, to be identified as Authors of this work.

Cover image © ihsanyildizli/iStock

All rights reserved. No part of this publication may be reproduced or transmitted in any form or by any means, electronic or mechanical, including photocopying, recording, or any information storage or retrieval system, without prior permission in writing from the publishers.

Bloomsbury Publishing Plc does not have any control over, or responsibility for, any third-party websites referred to or in this book. All internet addresses given in this book were correct at the time of going to press. The author and publisher regret any inconvenience caused if addresses have changed or sites have ceased to exist, but can accept no responsibility for any such changes.

A catalogue record for this book is available from the British Library.

Library of Congress Cataloging-in-Publication Data

Names: Branson, Christopher M., author. | Marra, Maureen, author.
Title: A new theory of organizational ecology, and its implications for educational leadership / Christopher M. Branson and Maureen Marra.
Description: London; New York: Bloomsbury Academic, 2021. | Includes bibliographical references and index.
Identifiers: LCCN 2021015179 (print) | LCCN 2021015180 (ebook) | ISBN 9781350159631 (hardback) | ISBN 9781350159648 (pdf) | ISBN 9781350159655 (epub)
Subjects: LCSH: Educational leadership–Cross-cultural studies. | Organizational behavior–Cross-cultural studies. | Organizational change–Cross-cultural studies.
Classification: LCC LB2806.B697 2021 (print) | LCC LB2806 (ebook) | DDC 371.2/011–dc23
LC record available at https://lccn.loc.gov/2021015179
LC ebook record available at https://lccn.loc.gov/2021015180

ISBN: HB: 978-1-3501-5963-1
PB: 978-1-3502-1515-3
ePDF: 978-1-3501-5964-8
eBook: 978-1-3501-5965-5

Typeset by Newgen KnowledgeWorks Pvt. Ltd., Chennai, India

To find out more about our authors and books visit
www.bloomsbury.com and sign up for our newsletters.

Contents

List of Illustrations   vi

Introduction: The Organization as an Ecosystem   1
1   Leading the Whole   11
2   Reconstructing Culture   31
3   Organizational Energy   67
4   Organizational Synergy: Teams Working Together   87
5   Creativity and Innovation   111
6   Simplifying Complexity   131
7   Leadership Wisdom   159
Conclusion: Applications and Implications   177

References   195
Index   205

Illustrations

Figures

I.1	A diagrammatic illustration of an organizational ecosystem	5
1.1	A diagrammatical illustration of an organizational ecosystem and its potential energy flow	14
2.1	An illustration of the phenomenology of an organization's culture	49
2.2	The people, the leader, and the culture—intertwined and inseparable	61
4.1	A diagrammatical illustration of the variable flow of energy (dotted and solid arrows) into and through a disconnected organization, and the subsequent reduced outcomes (grey arrows)	89
5.1a	A graphic illustration of dynamic equilibrium	113
5.1b	A graphic illustration of dynamic quasi-equilibrium	114
5.2	Disturbance and modulation in well-connected organizations and/or teams	116
6.1	A sociogram illustrating the personal professional connects across the law firm	155
7.1	A conceptual framework for the phenomenon of wisdom	165
7.2	An illustration of how the interplay of leadership wisdom and the Theory of Organizational Ecology underscores appropriate contemporary leadership practice	170
C.1	A diagrammatical illustration of the case school's organizational ecology	181
C.2	A model showing the constituent aspects of a team's culture that are integral to the achievement of cultural alignment	186
C.3	The organizational chart developed by the executive team as the explicit outcome from its cultural alignment process	190

Tables

I.1	The principles of organizational ecology	7
3.1	Cause and effect of blockages to the flow of information	76

Introduction: The Organization as an Ecosystem

The timing of this book is perfect! There is little doubt that organizations around the world, regardless of country or context, are on the threshold of unparalleled change. They are now beginning to be confronted by a plethora of pressures to change caused by global competition, heightened client wishes, rapid technological advancement, intensifying employee expectations, mounting operational accountabilities, and escalating resourcing costs—all of which are also in the context of the Covid-19 global pandemic. All these conditions are also occurring at the same time as organizations are heading into what has been referred to as Industry 4.0—the fourth stage of the Industrial Revolution—with its disquieting operational, employment, and social implications resulting from the integration of artificial intelligence, the internet-of-things, and machine learning dramatically changing the nature of work. But what makes this situation far more disturbing is that most of our organizational leaders are drastically underprepared to be able to confidently and successfully cope with the myriad of challenges that these changes are already demanding.

Indeed, contrary to the hope inherent in its name, our contemporary organization theory, Complex Adaptive Systems, seems to have little to offer in the way of direction and strategy. Although it purports to provide leaders with the means for successfully achieving organizational adaptation, it fails to do so when innovation and adaptation are so desperately needed. Hence, without an effective organizational theory to act as a leadership guide, organizations are like ships without a rudder. Some are luckily heading in the right direction, others are heading in the wrong direction, and some are finishing up "on the rocks."

Hence, it is into the maelstrom of organizational confusion and uncertainty that we are providing a new organization theory—the Theory of Organizational Ecology. We argue that this new theory not only achieves what Complex Adaptive Systems claimed but failed to provide but also much more. Essentially, as will be described in this book, the Theory of Organizational Ecology coherently unites our current leadership, culture, and organization theories, and does so in a powerfully understandable and implementable way.

However, in order to fully appreciate this power of the Theory of Organizational Ecology it is necessary to build its foundations from the bottom up by first looking at what is now recognized as not working in today's organizations.

What's Not Working?

At the very heart of this lack of organizational confidence and capacity is the issue of leadership lore. Leadership lore is flawed leadership axioms, sayings, anecdotes, or beliefs that are so pervasive in leadership thoughts and practices that they erroneously achieve the status of immutable facts underpinning mandatory practice. There is unequivocal research evidence showing that much of our current organizational leadership practice is more informed by lore than suitable contemporary theory. On a daily basis we are being swamped with leadership and organizational development articles and reports from the main global business management consultants and tertiary academic faculties. In nearly every case, these articles and reports recognize that something is not working well for organizations and so offer shiny new ideas supported by glossy images and graphs. Invariably, however, these fail to grasp the simple and most important factors that (1) there is a history of misunderstanding the real nature of leadership—that it is a relationship between the person in charge and the people who carry out the work, (2) managerialism can never create a healthy culture, and (3) organizations are abnormal socio-relational places for people. Regardless of what the future holds for organizations in the artificial intelligence and post–Covid-19 era, the simple basic fact is that people need leaders, not managers, to advance and thrive in this new era.

Hence, despite the availability of abundant research data showing that many of today's business leaders, along with their educational counterparts, are struggling to cope with the diversity and complexity of contemporary organizational and societal change, they remain fixated on applying a grossly outdated command, control, and management style of leadership. Therefore, we assert that the most alarming current organizational challenge is the multiplicity of out-of-date managerial practices and their accompanying socio-relational dysfunctions. These counterproductive practices result not in increased employee performance and productivity but rather in the development of employee individualism, exclusivity, competitiveness, discrimination, poor performance, and disconnection. Hence, organizations are now facing alarming levels of employee disengagement and organizational change failure. Numerous large-scale international studies show that employee disengagement hovers around 80 percent and organizational change failure is consistently above 70 percent.

It seems that in our apparently endless global need for solutions to organizational problems, a lucrative commodification of past leadership and organizational change lore is being constantly rejigged and promoted. As a result, not only has leadership theory lost its way but leadership practice is now often an expression of a confused, overcomplicated, and bewildered array of recycled versions of outdated management customs that never really worked anyway. Essentially, leadership has lost its compass and is floundering.

The Way Forward

We believe that there are two critically important factors that all of our current and past theorizing has ignored. First, our theories have never embraced the understanding that employees are socio-relational human beings driven by a set of intrinsic motivators including a desire to feel valued, to have positive relationships with others, to sense they truly belong to a team, and a deep wish to be contributing to a cause they believe in. Hence, healthy, supportive interpersonal relationships within and across teams and the organization provide the best environment for employees and leaders to thrive. It is only from the establishment and maintenance of such beneficial interpersonal relationships that goodwill, constructive collaborations, new ideas and innovations, and essential information can flow throughout the organization and beyond and, thereby, become the lifeblood of the organization.

Secondly, our current and past leadership and organizational theorizing has always invoked a differentiated and incomplete perspective. While it is true that there are copious amounts of current research-informed literature describing every conceivable aspect of leadership, these are invariably confined and separated. Some of the literature describes the nature of leadership, while others describe how to lead change, or how to manage organizational culture, or how to engage employees, or how to enhance performance, or how to develop effective teams, or how to encourage creativity and innovation, and so on. Who can blame a leader for becoming so overwhelmed and confused by this plethora of fragmented advice that they give up trying to understand it or apply it? For such leaders, it is far easier to act on leadership lore than it is to make sense of and enact the diversely differentiated demands associated with all such theories about leadership and organizations.

In contrast, this book provides the lens of the ecosystem to view the organization as a whole and to fully understand how it is that the people are the organization. Not the logo, the systems, or the buildings, but the people define the organization; and how their interaction in their workplace is solely dependent upon their relational connectedness with others and the organization. Hence, this book provides a coherent, interconnected, ecological description of what is now considered to be all the key parts of an organization and, thus, its culture and its leadership. As such, it describes a new organizational theory.

What Is an Organizational Ecosystem?

The very first issue to clarify is to define the terms, "ecology" and "ecosystem." An ecosystem is a community of living organisms (biotic component) interacting as a system with each other and in their environment (abiotic component). Organisms in an ecosystem maintain relationships and interactions between and among each other as well as their external environment for the purpose of obtaining basic life requirements like food, nutrients, water, and residence. This means that an ecosystem is a system or network of things that are interacting and relating to each other within a clearly discernible boundary defined in either physical or functional terms. Ecology is the study of these interactions and relationships in the ecosystem.

Thus, an organization viewed as an ecosystem implies that it is a clearly identifiable group of people interacting and relating to each other and their environment to collectively achieve a common goal. In other words, due to the myriad of interdependent activities required for it to be continually achieving its core purpose, the organization, itself, can be considered to be an ecosystem. However, if we wish to study the nature and function of the relationships among these organizational activities, then we are initiating an ecological exploration of the organization. Such an ecological exploration would, for example, endeavor to determine the way in which personnel and environmental interactions might be influencing the success of the organizational ecosystem. Simply stated, an organization can be considered to be an ecosystem because the combined contributions and activities of its employees are focused on achieving a common outcome, while the ecology of an organization seeks to describe how to improve the functioning of these contributions and activities and, thereby, increase the organizational output.

Hence, when we simply describe the critically important relational components of an organization, we are viewing it as an ecosystem, but when we are describing how these components interact and are either codependent or interdependent, we are providing an ecological perspective of the organization. Figure I.1 provides a diagrammatic illustration of an organization viewed as an ecosystem.

All the illustrations in this book have been created by the authors for the specific purpose of supporting the discussion provided throughout this book.

Although described in far more detail throughout the chapters of this book, suffice to say at this early point is that the manifestation of all of the relational components depicted in Figure I.1 develops from the type of leadership, the sense of belonging felt by each employee, the level of individual and team trust, the degree of commitment to cooperation and collaboration, the depth and breadth of information and knowledge sharing, the openness and support of creativity and innovation, and the nature of the organization's culture. When one or more of these integral relational components is compromised, or not what it should

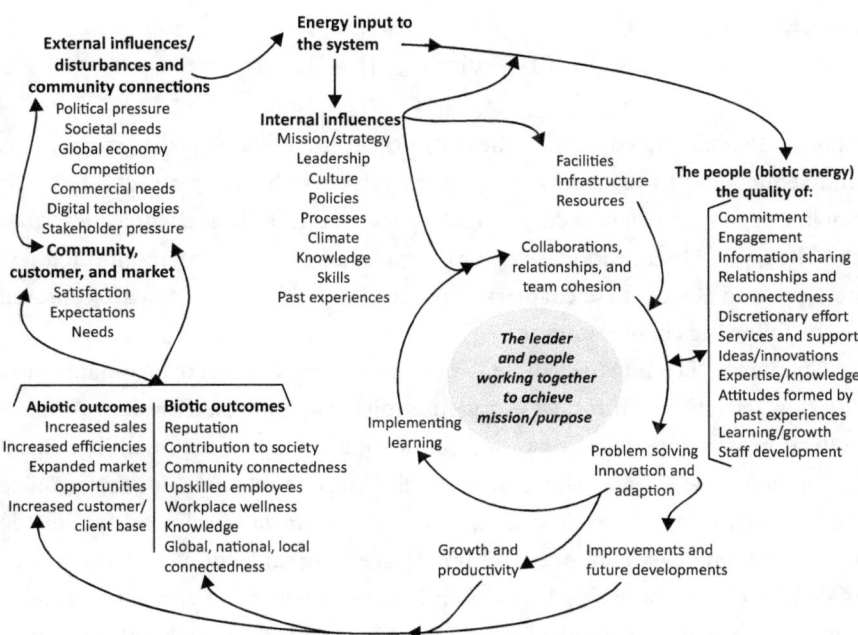

Figure I.1 A diagrammatic illustration of an organizational ecosystem.

be, then it is likely that the organization's overall performance will be merely the sum of its underperforming parts. When all of these relational components are maximized, the organization's overall performance is synergized—it becomes much greater than the sum of the performance of its parts.

But all truly worthwhile theories are grounded upon immutable principles. Hence, to this end we have adapted six universally accepted Laws of Ecology to form six principles of organizational ecology.

Principles of Organizational Ecology

In support of this view of an organization as an ecosystem we propose six principles of organizational ecology (see Table I.1), which are based on the Laws of Ecology initially proposed by Commoner (1971). These proposed principles of organizational ecology are generalizations of how employees and culture function and interact so as to create the ecosystem within and beyond the particular organization. This set of principles of organizational ecology is not mutually exclusive, but rather collectively reflect the complexity of organizations and the cultures within them.

An Overview of the Book

In order to maintain coherence, these six principles provide the discussion focus and sequencing for each chapter and, thereby, much of the structure of this book. Despite each chapter having its own focus, the book, as a whole, describes the Theory of Organizational Ecology because of the close interconnectedness between and across these chapters. This structure and sequencing are captured in the following chapter outlines.

Chapter 1, "Leading the Whole"—no organization or parts of an organization exist in isolation—introduces organizations as connected systems, not a collection of fragmented and isolated entities. Rather, they are mutually beneficial and interconnected internally and externally through relationships that provide the life-giving connected flow of energy to the organization. In reality, isolated teams and employees are often commonplace in organizations, a consequence of deficiencies in leadership theories and practices which are very much at odds with contemporary theoretical view that leadership is relational, not positional.

Table I.1 The principles of organizational ecology

Laws of Ecology	Principles of Organizational Ecology
No ecosystem exists in isolation. Everything is connected to everything else.	No organization or parts of an organization exist in isolation: Organizations are open systems in which the incoming energy creates desired strategic outcomes/outputs through pivotal relationships, connectedness and flow of information in both its external and internal environments.
Climate is a major influence on the structure and functioning of an ecosystem.	Organizational climate (how culture is experienced by the people) shapes the level of individual, team, and departmental capacity, performance, and productivity: Organizational culture is a collective of subcultures that may or may not be aligned to each other or to the core purpose of the organization. The organization's core purpose is achieved by the employees and not the strategy, and it is the organizational culture that determines how committed the employees are toward achieving the core purpose and the full potential of the organization. Unless the leader has the wisdom to constructively attend to the organization's culture it will trump the strategy and capacity, and employee performance and productivity will decline.
The flow, utilization, and storage of information are fundamental features of living systems.	Information and knowledge sharing are pivotal to organizational success: The creation, gathering, utilization, and sharing of information and knowledge in an organization are fundamental to its success as these are the mechanisms for facilitating organizational unification, learning, innovation, and the flow of energy. This energy must be able to move throughout the organization in order for it to address both the relationship needs as well as the production needs according to the organization's core purpose.
The strength and hospitality of the connections influence the flows of organisms, matter, and energy within and between ecosystems.	Organizational success is greater than the sum of its parts: Organizations are communities of departments, teams, and employees providing various contributions to the purpose of the organization. When these departments, teams, and individuals are all working together purposefully and collaboratively, the overall organizational output is enhanced significantly. It requires leaders with the wisdom to nurture organizational-wide interpersonal collaboration, and strong, purposeful teamwork, and to maximize the organization's productivity.
Nothing stays the same.	Organizational change is constant: Organizations exist in a dynamic metastable equilibrium whereby they must constantly change and adapt. Hence staying the same is not a strategy for success. Organizations that are able to readily cope with change have leaders who have the wisdom to draw employees' attention to the constancy of change and to continually build their capacity to learn, adapt, and thrive.

Laws of Ecology	Principles of Organizational Ecology
Everything has a purpose.	Each person counts: Each employee, regardless of their particular role, consumes as well as creates some of the organizational energy. Whether or not this energy is lost or flows on to be used by others depends upon the levels of engagement and performance of each individual employee. The most successful organizations have leaders with wisdom who are able to maximize the flow of energy throughout the organization because their relational approach brings out the best in each employee.

It is through such fundamental shifts in thinking that leaders can and do create connectivity within and between the parts of their organizations.

Chapter 2, "Reconstructing Culture"—organizational climate (how culture is experienced by the people) shapes the level of individual, team, and departmental capacity, performance, and productivity—explains the powerful role that culture plays in the workplace and the shortfalls in current approaches. Although culture is a naturally occurring and evolutionary phenomenon in human societies, understanding how to create positive cultures in organizations has largely remained elusive. This is problematic because it is the organizational culture that determines how people behave and interact and how committed they are toward achieving the core purpose and potential of their organization. The problem is magnified by the limitations of current models and the misguided beliefs that culture can be ignored or managed. This chapter provides a new, reconstructed model of organizational culture; one that better describes its complexity and how it can be understood and changed when necessary.

Chapter 3, "Organizational Energy"—information and knowledge sharing are pivotal to organizational success—elucidates that it is through the sharing of information and knowledge, such as creative ideas and innovations, that the organization learns and grows. This is the energy of the organization—it flows through relational connectivity and this flow can only manifest under a wise leader who creates and fosters the cultural matrix in which the people collaborate, innovate, share ideas, and work together. In the absence of such a culture, the flow of information and knowledge is blocked—which results in significant disengagement and disenchantment among employees. This ecological perspective of an organization not only unmistakably illustrates why information and knowledge sharing is incomparably vital for strengthening the growth and interconnectedness of the organization, but it also demonstrates how the leader is readily able to create the most conducive culture to maximize its effectiveness.

Chapter 4, "Organizational Synergy: Teams Working Together"—organizational success is greater than the sum of its parts—provides a view of the potential energy that an organization has in the connectivity of all its parts through trust-based relational collaborations working toward a common purpose. Organizations are often complex communities that can be composed of sections, departments, teams, and employees all providing various contributions to the core purpose of the organization but commonly working in isolation and disconnection. Connectivity between the parts does not happen automatically, rather it must be integral to the leader's role in deliberately creating organization-wide interpersonal collaboration and strong, purposeful teamwork to maximize and release the organization's energy for the achievement of its core purpose. This chapter first comprehensively describes the foundations of collaborative teamwork and then applies this information toward illustrating how leaders are readily able to develop a unified and collaborative culture within and across teams.

Chapter 5, "Creativity and Innovation"—organizational change is constant—emphasizes the view that nothing stays the same. It describes organizations as being in a state of dynamic quasi-equilibrium where change is both constant and disruptive. Organizations now exist in ever-changing environments and, therefore, need to be constantly adapting and innovating so as to grow and remain relevant. This requires organizational leaders and cultures that foster curiosity, creative thinking, and innovation to cope with the pace of change, particularly with sudden and abrupt change. Thus, this chapter argues that when organizational culture is understood from an ecosystem perspective, where the ongoing development of connectivity, trust, and high-quality relationships is paramount, then curiosity-driven innovative, creative, and divergent ideas will not only be readily recognized and acknowledged but also will be welcomed, supported, and put into practice.

Chapter 6, "Simplifying Complexity"— each person counts—describes how the Theory of Organizational Ecology must replace our current incomprehensible and ineffectual organizational theory of Complex Adaptive Systems. At the core of both of these theories is the shared principle that each employee counts in today's organizational environment. However, unlike the Complex Adaptive System's dependence upon exclusive, unfamiliar, and ineffectual terms to describe the manner by which the leader achieves this desired outcome, it is inherent in the normal everyday leadership practices as proffered by the Theory of Organizational Ecology. Also, as has been previously illustrated throughout this book, the Theory of Organizational Ecology, unlike that of the Complex Adaptive Systems theory, seamlessly unites leadership, culture, and organizational theories. For the very first time we now have coherence, harmony, and synchronicity among all three theories of leadership, culture, and organization through the application of the Theory of Organizational Ecology.

Chapter 7, "Leadership Wisdom"— leadership in an organizational ecosystem where wisdom surpasses rational knowledge—describes the essential role of wisdom in enabling a leader to create a relationally connected organization where the energy can flow unimpeded throughout the organization. As described and illustrated in this chapter, such leadership wisdom is derived from the analytical, practical, emotional, and intuitive intelligences of the person formed out of the knowledge gained from their past and ongoing work and life experiences and learning. Moreover, it is the perceived level of leadership wisdom by which a person is judged worthy to be both trusted and accepted as the leader. Specifically, this chapter shows how wise leadership is that which prioritizes trust, support, connectivity, collaboration, belonging, creativity, initiative, and networking. Given that these equate exactly with the leadership qualities described throughout this book it is unequivocally claimed that the application of the Theory of Organizational Ecology naturally and unmistakably develops leadership wisdom.

The final chapter, "Conclusion: Applications and Implications," provides both research data highlighting the readily achievable practical benefits of the Theory of Organizational Ecology and the essential theoretical and practical consequences of its usage.

1

Leading the Whole

Principle of Organizational Ecology #1: No Organization, or Parts of an Organization, Exists in Isolation

Introduction

The first ecological principle concerns the unity of systems and the parts within systems. In the natural world, the fragmentation of ecosystems has created isolated parts, which struggle to exist without connectivity to other ecosystems because in isolation they lose diversity and the ability to grow and renew. Similarly, no organization, or parts within an organization, can exist in isolation. Organizations are not isolated from society because they serve society in one way or another. Also, the people who work in the organization bring their society-formed values, beliefs, attitudes, and behaviors into their workplace with them. Society and organizations influence each other culturally, economically, and socially; they are interconnected and interdependent. An organization isolated from society would eventually cease to exist. It would have no purpose. For example, following the Covid-19 extended lockdown response period, many small fashion shops in Australia closed permanently because their clients had changed their social norms by preferring the efficiency and convenience of online shopping.

Internally, organizations are highly complex social systems regardless of their purpose and sector. With the exception of very small organizations, they are typically structured vertically and horizontally into parts—teams, departments, sections, faculties, branches, and levels of seniority. Each part has its own purpose and those within each part have their own role in achieving that purpose. In theory, each and every employee and all the parts are meant to be working in machine-like synchronicity to achieve the core purpose of the organization. In reality, this is usually far from ideal. Rather, the parts are separate entities often in competition with each other, seldom in collaboration, and frequently with teams and employees oblivious to the contribution their work makes to other teams and the organization. Thus, the organization fails to be a system because there is no connectivity between its parts. As such, the potential of the collective strength of the organization is lost because of the isolationism and protectionism of its constituent parts.

Alas, connectivity cannot be mandated. Rather, as in society at large, connectivity is created through relationships. Organizational relationships with external stakeholders are currently being paid far more attention than the internal connectivity among the employees and parts. Internal connectivity is founded upon a sense of belonging to a group with others and building relationships of friendship and reciprocity within the group. Also, connectivity between groups results from mutual collaborations, which further strengthens the organization's connectivity. Relationships cannot be mandated either; rather these are the outcome of the leader's capacity to create the required relational culture throughout the organization.

Therefore, if we want our organizations to be thoroughly organized—to be internally united, connected, and well synchronized as its name suggests—then it is essential that we see and study an organization as a whole and not as differentiated parts. Studying an organization as an ecosystem does precisely this.

Thus, the purpose of this chapter is threefold. First, it provides a brief description of an organizational ecosystem in order to emphasize the requisite role of relationships throughout such a system. This requirement is then shown as also being recognized as a crucial quality in contemporary leadership across all organizational contexts including business, not-for-profit, and education. Thus, it is argued that viewing organizations as an ecosystem is explicitly compatible with today's understanding of what constitutes best leadership practice. However, this chapter then highlights the discrepancies and delusions in our current leadership literature because these, on the one hand, stress the need for a relational approach to leadership but, on the other hand, describe essentially past, outdated, and ineffective ways for achieving this desired outcome. Therefore, the chapter concludes with a description of what a truly relational approach to leadership entails.

An Organizational Ecosystem

A natural ecosystem operates as an open system because it receives external energy (e.g., from the sun) and, by means of internal systems, it uses, transforms, stores, and distributes energy back out to its wider environment. Organizations can also be described in the same way where incoming energy (e.g., revenue and employee commitment) is transformed in order to produce resources, facilities, processes, required products, and upskilling of employees so as to achieve the organization's core purpose to the benefit of its clients and society. As noted by Scott (1981: 119–20),

> the interdependence of the organization and its environment receives primary attention in the open systems perspective. Rather than overlooking the environment ... the open systems model stresses the reciprocal ties that bind and interrelate the organization with those elements that surround and penetrate it. The environment is perceived to be the ultimate source of materials, energy, and information, all of which are vital to the continuation of the system.

Thus, this implies that, when an organization is conceived as an ecosystem its productivity and sustainability are dependent upon the presence of high-quality reciprocal ties too. Such reciprocal ties within the organization's system are the myriad of relationships that create and facilitate the interconnected flow of energy. Thus, from an ecosystem perspective, relationships are the pivotal determinant in the achievement of organizational success. It is the diversity of quality relationships that shapes the essential productive interconnectivity both within the organization and with its external environment and, ultimately, determines not only the organization's level of productivity and therefore its longevity but also creates a work environment where people thrive.

This understanding of an organization as an ecosystem, which acknowledges the pivotal influence of relationships in determining the capacity and continuity of the organization, is illustrated as an idealized organization in Figure 1.1. The arrows represent the organization's reciprocal ties—its pivotal relationships, learnings, innovations, and collaborations that facilitate the flow of information and knowledge—that provide the energy flow through an organization. Without the network of relationships throughout the organization, there is no mechanism for energy to flow. Also, where required relationships fail to form or are weak, then the energy flow is diminished or constrained not only in this section but also for the organization as a whole to a significant degree. Hence, the organization, the collective of the people, underperforms; people are no longer fully committed, no longer thriving.

What all of this implies is that, when viewed as an ecosystem, no organization or part or employee can effectively or sustainably exist in isolation. Each of its internal parts, sections, teams, and departments must be strongly

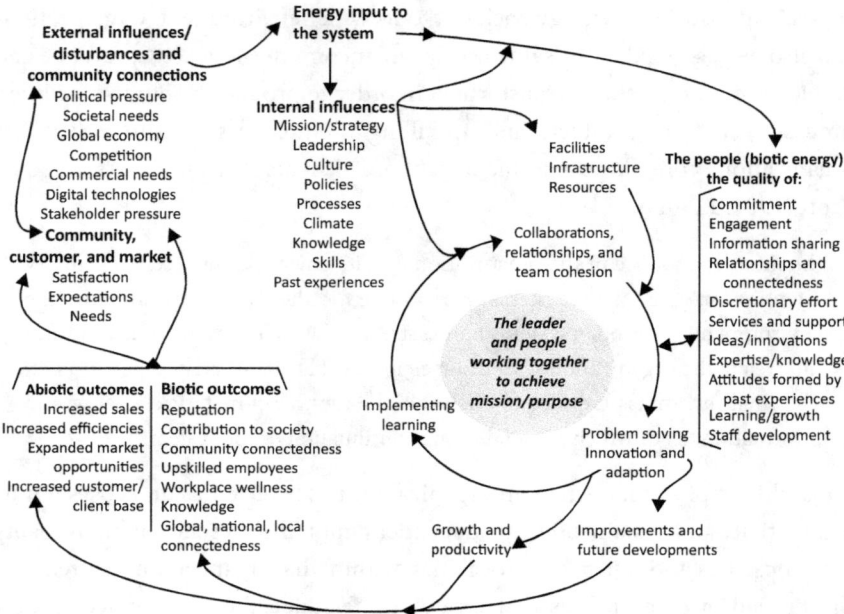

Figure 1.1 A diagrammatical illustration of an organizational ecosystem and its potential energy flow.

interdependently related just as the organization, itself, must be strongly interdependently related to its external influences. When one or more of these integral relational constituents is compromised, or not what it should be, then it is likely that the organization's overall performance will be merely the sum of its underperforming parts. When all of these relational constituents are maximized, the organization's overall performance is synergized—it becomes much greater than the sum of the performance of its parts. This model is discussed further in Chapter 4 where the importance of information and knowledge sharing is highlighted.

But is this foundational ecosystem implication, which emphasizes the primacy of relationships, incompatible with contemporary leadership theory? Quite the contrary, as will be shown in the remainder of this chapter.

Current Leadership Deficiencies and Delusions

It would be unwise if not foolhardy to ignore the following global organizational realities illustrating widespread and serious leadership deficiencies. First, in a continually changing educational and organizational environment, some 70 percent of change plans fail. In education, this serious leadership deficiency was first noted by Fullan in 1998 only to be reconfirmed by Hargreaves in 2005. Sadly, this regrettable outcome continues as a blight on today's school improvement processes. Arguably the most alarming research in this regard is that provided by the McKinsey company (see De Smet, Lavoie, and Hioe 2012), which involves a review of the degree of successful change strategies across not only all contexts (i.e., business, commerce, industry, education, etc.) but also during the past twenty-five years. This substantive research illustrates that this 70 percent failure rate is universal across contexts and has remained so throughout this timeframe. Despite the thousands of books and articles that have been written during this time describing how leaders can direct, control, and manage change, this advice has not made a difference. Although it is widely claimed that we are living during a time of unprecedented organizational change, it is unequivocally clear that our past leadership theories are largely unhelpful in preparing leaders for this challenge.

Secondly, at a time when high-quality performance is stridently sought, the level of employee disengagement around the world and across all contexts is an alarming 80 percent (Deloitte 2016). As expectations around accountability and levels of competition heighten the need for leaders to be able to maximize quality performance, this is impossible to achieve when 50 percent of employees are not engaged and 30 percent are actively disengaged. Such employees either come to work just to do the minimum or, if actively disengaged, they try various ways to undermine the work of others and the quality of the organization's output. Yet, for the past forty years or more leaders, often in association with their Human Resource Department personnel, have striven to implement command-and-control processes presumed to manage the performance of employees. These performance management beliefs and processes have been shown to be counterproductive and a complete waste of time for most employees. Indeed, the financial impact associated with these inept performance management processes has been calculated to have wasted organizations trillions of dollars annually.

What is of even greater concern is the realization that, if the majority of our leaders are struggling with successfully leading change and maximizing employee engagement, then soon they will be completely out of their depth as the world transitions from the third to the fourth stage of the Industrial Revolution—from an Industry 3.0 world influenced by electronics, computers, and automated manufacturing to Industry 4.0 world that will be influenced by cyber-physical systems in which real objects and virtual processes are interlinked.

Importantly for the role of leaders in this transition, getting to this fourth stage is not solely dependent upon technological developments because it is argued that particular sociocultural changes will be required too (Luppicini 2012). As artificial intelligence, the internet-of-things, and machine learning dramatically change the nature of work, it is argued that, for the longer-term sustainability of humankind, enhanced interpersonal sociability, cultural democracy, and moral integrity will become essential counterbalancing forces of an otherwise isolated and independent lifestyle. Thus, of particular interest here is the research study reported in the MIT Sloan Management Review (see Ready et al. 2020), which claims that only 9 percent of current organizations around the world have leaders with the necessary skills to successfully cope with the demands that will be generated by this transition. Our past ways of thinking about leadership will become much more deficient in the very near future.

Finally, there is a growing body of research now raising concerns about the capacity of leaders from the baby-boomer era being able to adequately lead those from more recent generations (see Anderson et al. 2017). It is argued that leadership practiced in its traditional forms is particularly unappealing and discouraging for those often labeled as millennials, people born between 1982 and 1999. Millennials are perceived as wanting new ideas, new behaviors, and new ways of looking at issues, which causes problems for leaders who have become too accustomed to being in control, too dependent on well-established policies and processes, too aligned with the need for predictability and certainty in regard to workplace performance, and too committed to a hierarchical administrative structure for organizational planning and decision-making. It is no wonder that schools and organizations around the world are struggling to entice millennials into leadership roles—they don't like what they see of leadership and so they don't wish to become this sort of leader.

Clearly, these serious issues cannot be overcome by our current ways of understanding leadership and organizational culture. So, what new perspectives are being promoted in our current research literature?

New Leadership Menus but the Same Old Recipes

The recent Price Waterhouse Coopers (PwC) Report (2020) titled, *Workforce for the Future: The Competing Forces Shaping 2030*, presents insights into how people think the workplace will evolve and how this will affect their employment prospects and future working lives. These insights were gathered from survey data involving approximately ten thousand participants from China, India, Germany, the United Kingdom, and the United States. This Report begins with the claim that we are living through a fundamental transformation in the way we work. Automation and thinking machines are replacing human tasks and jobs, thus changing the skills that organizations are looking for in their people. The crucial outcome generated by this Report is its capacity to forcefully illustrate and persuasively describe alternative organizational cultures and the effect these could have upon individuals, society, and the world. Hence, the unambiguous repercussion for a leader is the expectation that they should start right now to change their self, those they are leading, and their organization's culture in readiness for the future.

The fundamental implication for the organizational leader, as proposed by Blair Sheppard in this Report (4), is to "remember that intellectual complacency is not [your] friend and that learning—not just new things but new ways of thinking—is a life-long endeavor." More specifically, the three new messages to leaders provided in this Report are as follows:

1. Don't be constrained by what you are currently doing because you might need a more radically different leadership approach than the way you are leading right now;
2. Protect the people and not the jobs because you won't be able to protect jobs made redundant by technology, but you can ensure that the people in your organization are prepared best for the future; and
3. Build a positive vision about the future because workers are already anxious about their jobs due to automation; so start a mature conversation about the future.

However, what is absent in this Report is an attempt to provide current leaders with any detailed helpful advice as to how they are to begin to adapt their leadership understandings and practice in order to ensure they are able to adopt these new leadership responsibilities. It seems that the authors of the Report assume that just by simply knowing what leadership understandings and practices need to change will automatically result in leaders adopting these changes. The fact that so many organizational leaders are still using practices based upon understandings formed last century suggests that widespread changes to leadership practices can't be accomplished so simply.

A similar view is gained from the MIT Sloan article (2020), "Eight Management Ideas to Embrace in the 2020s," where it is argued that as technology and society continue to rapidly transform, it can also be overwhelming for leaders and organizations to think about what to tackle next. In response, this article utilizes both its ongoing research and the expertise of its contributing academics to provide insights into the specific knowledge, skills, and practices that will help leaders and organizations to "compete, thrive, and provide value for stakeholders in the years to come" (1). As a result of this research, the article promotes the following six key new qualities now required of organizational leaders:

1. Build agile, collaborative organizational cultures that encourage networking and are no longer controlled by traditional hierarchical managerial, communication, or change processes;
2. Effectively embrace emotions at work—which means learning how to give more useful, less hurtful feedback, to help all workers to feel a sense of belonging, and to better communicate and explain important decisions;
3. Understand and prepare for AI's impact by understanding how AI will augment and enhance the work they are doing;
4. Adopt a learning approach to difference and diversity so as to promote the understanding that each person has much to offer toward the ongoing success of the organization;
5. Strike a balance between human and machine capital to prevent a potential slide toward the devaluation of the human interface and a socially detrimental increase in inequality; and
6. Develop a hybrid extended learning organization by ensuring that the organization's focus is on continuous deep and autonomous organizational learning to maintain an appropriate balance between human and machine contributions, and to ensure governance and leadership practices remain ethical and socially acceptable.

Here, again, there is no guidance for leaders in how they might learn to improve their practices in order to eventually produce these desired outcomes. Indeed, most of the MIT Sloan 2020 articles that were published since the above article have concentrated on point 3—preparing the leader's AI knowledge and skills. We strongly argue that such professional learning will faulter greatly unless the leader is, first, provided with the knowledge, skills, and confidence to change their organization's culture, which contemporary worldwide research clearly shows that most leaders do not currently have. Thus, it is prudent to examine the most current published business information that focuses on organizational culture.

First, we must turn our attention to the *Harvard Business Review* article, "When Data Creates Competitive Advantage … And When It Doesn't" (see

Hagui and Wright 2020), which begins by posing the view that an organization's culture can actively support or discourage an organization's success. Moreover, the authors draw upon international research to claim that our current ways for examining, understanding, and altering culture "have significant shortcomings" (94). In particular, they argue that the values and beliefs that people say are important to them are often not reflected in how they actually behave. Moreover, it is suggested that any surveys used to explore an organization's culture often provide static, or at best episodic, snapshots of organizations and are limited by the researchers' tendency to assume that distinctive and idiosyncratic cultures can be neatly categorized into a few common types. In other words, the culture of each organization is uniquely structured by the exclusive and distinctive combination of its array of cultural artifacts. Any examination of an organization's culture thus requires a process that is able to surface personal interpretations and meanings associated with these specific artifacts that include values, beliefs, norms, allegiances, and so on.

Hence, it is extremely surprising to read how the article then proceeds to promote a software program that uses "big-data processing to mine the ubiquitous 'digital traces' of culture in electronic communications, such as emails, Slack messages, and Glassdoor reviews. By studying the language employees use in these communications, we can measure how culture actually influences their thoughts and behavior at work" (Hagui and Wright 2020: 95). There is no attempt to illustrate how a leader can better explore and understand their organization's culture.

Surprisingly, a slightly similar concern applies to the MIT Sloan article (2019), "A New Era for Culture, Change, and Leadership," which was structured as a conversation between Edgar Schein, the preeminent organizational culture researcher and author, and his son, Peter Schein, who is now working closely with his father to further develop new understandings of organizational culture. The essential new understanding promoted in this article is that "with the world in flux, organizations and the people within them need close relationships to thrive" (1). More specifically, the conversation highlights the current prominence of "level 1 relationships," which are described as tending to be distant and transactional so that people *learn to play various roles* in order to get along with others and to manage their daily affairs. Importantly, Edgar Schein highlights that there is a clear managerial culture that typically supports, if not encourages, this type of relationship even though "the distance between and even within roles makes it very easy for employees at all levels to avoid open communication and harbor distrust. Not speaking up becomes easier and safer when career competition is culturally taken for granted in a rigidly designed hierarchical system. This leaves the organization vulnerable to deficits in quality, safety, customer satisfaction, and innovation" (3). Thus the conversation moves on to promote the establishment of an organizational culture that encourages "level 2 relationships." This form of organizational culture is manifested when employees and managers form closer connections to create better communication and more trust. In level 2 relationships, people choose to treat each other as whole human beings, not just role occupants, which collapses the psychological distance even across hierarchical boundaries—as when a leader forms a personal relationship with an employee and thereby finds out what is really going on in the organization.

With respect to the nature and practice of leadership, this conversation posits that it has now become essential for us to think of leadership "as the creation and implementation of a new and better way of doing something ... [whereby] ... all members of the organization will have to feel psychologically safe to speak up when things are not working and to exercise autonomy when they see a new and better way of getting something done" (4). However, when seeking to describe what this might imply in more detail, the conversation illustrates certain generalities rather than specifics. For example, leaders are urged to adopt a Holacracy-informed approach that encourages dynamic, ad hoc, self-managed teams and networks in order to "*unshackle innovation from traditional command-and-control norms.*" Also promoted is the use of software that can connect goals and aspirations of all individuals in a work group, or an organization as a whole, to the key strategic imperatives of the organization. It is posited that such software ensures that everyone benefits from knowing where everyone else stands. "We may come to appreciate that the alchemy here is in connecting the technical benefits of visibility, predictability, and accountability with the socio benefits of involvement and engagement" (6). What is most surprising with this commendation is that it seems to contradict the very intention of the focus of this conversation, which is the importance of interpersonal relationships in the culture of an organization. Describing a way in which leaders can work with the people through mutually beneficial relationships to ensure performance and engagement are maximized and in alignment with the organization's strategic imperatives would be far more in keeping with the focus of the conversation than is the promotion of data-gathering software supposedly achieving the same outcome.

What is so surprising about this conversation is that it does not include any detailed information about what are the fundamental values, beliefs, and attitudes upon which level 2 relationships are formed, and how it might be possible for the leader to personally nurture these while also encouraging a commitment to these in others as well. Thus, what is missing from this discussion is elaboration about what would be the key elements of an organization's existing culture that would need to be explored and possibly adjusted in order to move the interpersonal relationships from level 1 to level 2 across all roles. Indeed, there is an implied assumption that the leader, themselves, already has the knowledge and capacity to not only personally make this change but also to be able to enable others to achieve it as well.

The essentialness of drawing attention to the organization's relationships, both external and internal, was clearly highlighted also in Deloitte's 2019 *Global Human Capital Trends Report*. Here it was highlighted that organizations are now increasingly being judged on the basis of relationships among employees, with their clients, and with their communities, as well as their impact on society at large. Specifically, this Report describes the unequivocal need for today's organizations to be concentrating on improving both its ecosystem (external focus) and its symphonic systems (its internal culture of connectivity, collaboration, and integration). Importantly, on page 39 of this Report it is reasoned that it is paramount for the organization to have a culture, the structure, and the management processes to cultivate what is now required for success. In general, this Report urges organizations to create cultures that promote transparency, trust, and respect, that have leaders who act as a collaborative team rather than from self-interest, and that has a working environment which readily copes with uncertainty and change. However, despite this being a 112-page document these principles remain aspirational as there is no attempt to provide any further detail as to what and how the leader is to enact them.

A similar criticism can be raised about the current educational research literature. For example, in Michael Fullan's (2019) most recent publication, *Nuance: Why Some Leaders Succeed and Others Fail*, he makes the claim that "society in general is worsening and that education in particular is less effective at its main role of producing better citizens" (ix). Hence, he calls for the need for a new kind of leader, a nuanced leader, "one who can get beneath the surface and help us understand and leverage deep change for the better" (ix). At the very core of Fullan's nuanced educational leader is a person who is willing and able to be fully present and engaged with all those they are leading—a leader who seeks to fully understand a situation, despite its complexity and unfamiliarity, by listening and learning about it from others, by building the capacity of others to deal with the situation, and by trusting others to resolve the situation with whatever help from the leader that is required. According to Fullan, such nuanced leaders are able to "unlock, mobilize, and create collective care" (42)—effective, purposeful, and successful teamwork—when it comes to the challenging task of resolving complex, unfamiliar, and problematic educational situations. Essentially, Fullan's nuanced leadership manifests through the positive relationship the leader has with each person they are leading. However, rather than delving deeper into the foundations upon which this positive relationship is formed, and why this is able to produce its effectiveness, Fullan provides a rich array of case descriptions of leaders, who appeared to be applying the principles of a nuanced leader, to clarify and endorse his claims.

Importantly, while there is a somewhat unified view of what leadership needs to now look and feel like, there also is a common flaw across each and every one of these key articles. Each in their own way seeks to describe how different the future of organizations will be and, therefore, urges the importance of adopting a new, more relational, approach to leadership in order to create a far more inclusive, connected, and collaborative organizational culture. Yet each one also fails to fully grasp the need to describe how to develop a relational approach to leadership or how this understanding of leadership can be seamlessly aligned with an understanding of the organization's culture. In the absence of such a seamless alignment most leaders will remain incapable of being able to adjust their organization's culture as required. Instead, these articles have reverted more toward fine-tuning or rebranding many existing leadership practices and organizational cultural concepts to give the appearance of providing new knowledge and skills, but these are unlikely to achieve the relational approach to leadership now being promoted. In other words, much of the current published literary advice to leaders can be classified as nothing more than new leadership menus from the same old recipes.

But rather than merely highlighting this widespread problem, we have provided a solution previously (Branson et al. 2018). The following section presents some insights from the book *Leadership in Higher Education from a Transrelational Perspective* in order to provide clarity about what a commitment to a predominately relational approach to leadership practice would imply.

A Relational Approach to Leadership

When leadership practice is first and foremost relational, this implies that it is specifically suited to the organization's unique context which includes its employees, its core purpose, its local community, its available resources, its history, and its culture. Leadership is contextual and not generic because it emerges out of a sincere interpersonal engagement of the leader with those to be led. However, its essential purpose is to engender relationships throughout the organization that seek to manifest a culture based upon the shared values of trust, openness, transparency, honesty, integrity, collegiality, and ethicalness. This is a culture in which all feel a sense of safety and security because they each feel that they can rely on each other in order to achieve their best. Through facilitating and supporting mutually beneficial relationships, the leader enables the organizational conditions to be created whereby those they are leading willingly and readily perform at their best. This, in turn, allows the leader to actually become the leader, and to continue to enact true leadership, which ensures the growth and sustainability of the organization. This is "transrelational" leadership, because leadership "is best understood as a transrelational phenomenon as its essence is to move others, the organization and the leader to another level of functioning by means of relationships" (Branson, Franken, and Penney 2016: 155).

Thus, the relational cornerstone of leadership is the reciprocal and dynamic interaction process between the formal leaders and those to be led. Leaders who are attuned to the pivotal relational dimension underpinning their leadership allow multiple futures and are open in terms of what these might be. Rather than controlling futures they cultivate conditions where others can produce innovations that lead to somewhat unpredictable yet largely productive future states. Their influence derives from their ability to allow rather than to direct and is grounded in people in the organization remaining engaged and connected. Through recognizing the importance of interactions as the ideal source of employee engagement, high performance, and innovation, these leaders build correlation: the emergence of a common or shared organizational vision and a recognizable widespread pattern of positive organizational behavior. Through this focus everyone in the organization can find meaning and purpose in whatever is unfolding.

In addition, these leaders enable the emergence of new ideas and behaviors that sustain and grow the organization by directing attention to what is important to note from contrasting the internal and external organizational environments. From this perspective, building collegiality, cooperation, and teamwork should not be seen as only part of leadership but, rather, be understood as its very essence.

Importantly, what this discussion highlights about the fundamental role of relationships in leadership is that "acceptance" and not "appointment" creates leadership. Being accepted as the leader is the bedrock for becoming a leader. Simply stated, the person must first be accepted as the leader before they can begin to behave as the leader so as to have the influence commonly associated with successful leadership. Furthermore, being accepted as the leader is solely dependent upon the establishment of widespread, socially positive, mutually beneficial, interpersonal relationships with those to be led. To this end, the very first step in becoming a leader is to show that you want to truly belong and to become a respected organizational member.

When first appointed, the potential leader must continually strive to be seen in words and deeds as a fully active member of the organization. The leader must be seen to belong in the organization whereby they appear relaxed and at ease in and around its employees, they show ongoing interest and enthusiasm about what is happening in the organization, they are able to readily and openly talk with the employees, and they show that they have the best interests of the employees and the organization continually in mind. Each of these required outcomes are crucially dependent upon the quality of the leader's relational capacity with each employee. Simply put, to become the leader the person must be seen to be sincerely involved in the joys and celebrations, the hopes and dreams, the challenges and difficulties, and the doubts and uncertainties of the employees and the organization.

For the leader to truly belong in the organization it is not solely about establishing the right relationship with those they are to lead. Rather, it concerns seeing the organization as people who have basic human needs, which include being valued, acknowledged, and worthy of being known by the leader. Once established, the actions of the leader must be seen as maintaining this relationship. Trust is at the heart of all relationships and trust is built upon predictability, consistency, and authenticity. Being trustworthy is about the leader willingly acting openly, honestly, and consistently. It is more than simply telling the truth. Trustworthiness in a leader means that they consistently display total congruence between who they say they are and what they do. In other words, how a leader is able to influence their group members must support and not undermine the relationship that binds them to the group. The leader's influence is by means of, and consistent with, the relationship and not distinct from it.

The second step in enacting a relational approach to leadership is to regularly affirm and champion the organization and its employees. Simply put, this responsibility is about affirming, praising, and celebrating the achievements and successes of individuals, teams, departments, and the organization both in formal and informal ways, on stage, or in corridors. This is about being able to see and appreciate all of the good things that are happening no matter how large or small the outcome. Importantly, it is about seeing how such achievements are slowly but surely achieving the vision and mission of the organization. A leader's influence thus does not come into play until after they are authentically established as a member of the group and, as a consequence, can readily and willingly champion, affirm, and promote the activities of the group, and its individual members, in various forums. To be able to truly champion the organization, or its employees, a leader must first be able to deeply understand and appreciate what is happening, which requires the leader to truly belong in the organization. But it is also about filtering and protecting the employees from unnecessary or unsuitable demands. This is about acknowledging and appreciating the current levels of commitment and engagement, and thereby understanding the incapacity of the employees to fully or partially take on any additional responsibilities thereby providing those being led with the greatest sense of trust in their leader.

Once a potential leader has established themselves as fully belonging to the organization, and has built relational trust through championing and affirming what is happening in the organization, they are then able to initiate the third step in enacting a relational approach to leadership, which is about growing individuals and the organization. This is about building on the organization's strengths and achievements in order to help the employees work better as individuals and teams. This involves implementing inclusive and constructive processes to foster an organization that is able to learn about how it achieves its goals and how this might be done more effectively. The employees are being encouraged to learn from each other and to network better together in order to improve current practices. In this way, the leadership is evolving as the organization is becoming more and more open to having its culture being more finely tuned to meeting its strategic vision.

The final step toward enacting a relational approach to leadership involves providing the means and the safe environment in which the employees can look to the future and acknowledge its implications—to see and discuss what needs to begin happening now in order to confidently meet future demands. Once all in the organization are working better together, and showing that they are determined to work better as individuals and in teams, the leader is then in a position to draw the attention of all to the changing nature and demands of their external environment. Rather than telling the employees what needs to happen, the leader draws attention to the future possible challenges for the organization in an open, honest, and inclusive manner, and seeks feedback from the employees as to what this might mean for the organization, what individually and collectively the employees now need to do in order to meet these challenges, and how it would be best to initiate these required developments. This is about engaging the people in creating, rather than simply completing, the necessary change strategies. It is about allowing all in the organization to be involved in designing and creating the future rather than having it thrust upon them with little understanding of why things need to change. People resist change when they cannot see and fully understand the purpose for the change. By engaging all within the organization to be mindful of what the future is likely to bring upon the organization, the leader is beginning any change process by clearly establishing its purpose in the minds and hearts of each and every employee.

Furthermore, in Chapter 7 of this book, it is comprehensively argued that what our current leadership literature provides is grossly deficient because it focuses on knowledge and not wisdom. Mostly, this literature focuses on telling the leader how they are to act; providing the knowledge of what constitutes sound leadership practice. The glaring weakness here is the assumed universality of the prescribed behavior—that the behavior can be applied regardless of the context and circumstances. It requires wisdom to distinguish what knowledge is relevant and applicable in any given situation. As emphasized in Chapter 7, in today's ever-changing, unfamiliar, and demanding organizational world, we need wise leaders and not simply knowledgeable ones. This is no less so in our schools and educational systems.

Implications for Educational Organizations

The principle that *no organization, or parts of an organization, exists in isolation* is, or should be, the basic assumption of a school for no school or educational system exists in isolation. Schools provide a uniquely essential service to the respective community, society, and nation through their fundamental purpose of fully developing the growth potential of their students. Hence, relationships are at the core of all activities, be these between staff and students, among the staff, the school, and its parents/care-providers, the school and its local community, the school and its educational authority, and the school's educational authority and its national government. Thus, no component of a school can or does exist in isolation. Simply put, each and every school is an integral component of an educational ecosystem in which the quality of relationships and connectivity across all levels is pivotal in achieving the school's success.

Consequently, as an integral component of an educational ecosystem the school's culture should be overseen by a principal mindful of, and committed to enacting, a transrelational approach to their leadership practice. This implies that they acknowledge that they must first become accepted as the leader—and they do that by being regularly, willingly, and actively involved in their school community. Importantly, being one of a group for a school principal means interacting with the staff, building trusting relationships with them, talking with them, understanding what is happening for them in their classrooms, and their additional roles. This allows the principal to understand workloads and pressures, achievements and effort, the learning needs of the teachers and assistants, where there are gaps in professional knowledge and capability and how these can be overcome, and how to affirm and promote the school. It also provides the platform for the principal for creating professional networks and connections so that new ideas can flow and be shared in order to generate continual professional growth and development. Such a relational principal has the wisdom to know how people interact and behave in a group, understands what makes people tick, and what keeps them connected and engaged in their community. The wise school leader knows that the best outcomes for students and the school community is achieved through the effort of the teachers—and the best school culture for this to happen naturally is that which is connected, caring, supportive, cooperative, and where all feel they belong and are valued.

However, the problem with this claim is that school principals are not the controllers of their own destiny. When working with school leaders we invariably find that they are time-poor when it comes to expecting them to be more involved in the daily affairs of their school. Sadly, the desire by governments, education ministries, educational authorities, and governing bodies for evaluation, verification, and accountability has resulted in schools being micromanaged by these external agencies. As a result, the leadership of the school community has become increasingly task-based and distracted due to the rising tide of externally imposed demands upon the role. The ever-growing governance expectations and reporting demands in effect create a disruption to the development of the best learning and teaching environment because the principal is increasingly time-poor and task-based. The relationships between principals and governing agencies are now a power imbalance, with the loss of funding being the driver of the power over the principal for high levels of accountability. Many principals talk of "burnout" and confess that they feel like they are between a rock and a hard place. Many are leaving as a result.

When schools are seen as an integral component of an educational ecosystem then what we expect of school leadership and school culture must be identical to that provided by all levels of the governing educational authorities in which the school exists. At present, individual schools, school leaders, and school teachers are being unfairly blamed for perceived poor student learning results when, in truth, they are not at fault. From the perspective of the Theory of Organizational Ecology, we cannot expect to see real and sustainable school improvements until such time that governing educational authorities adopt a commensurate relational, connected, cooperative, and supportive role. In an educational system, as in any organization, the implementation of transrelational leadership must start from the very top. This is where wise leadership is so desperately needed.

Concluding Comments

The aim of this chapter was, first, to provide further insight into the concept of an organization as an ecosystem. Here, the fundamental criterion in adopting this concept is the acknowledgment that the organization and each of its parts cannot exist in isolation. All pervasive, dynamic connectivity or relationships are central and inescapable to the understanding of an organization as an ecosystem. However, this requirement potentially raises a concern about the credibility of the concept if relationships are not recognized as being in any way significant within our current leadership and organizational theories.

Thus, this chapter then turned its attention to a wide array of contemporary business, organizational, and educational research literature to explore whether or not the issue of interpersonal relationships features in any significant way. This literature highlighted the presence of serious deficiencies and delusions in our leadership and organizational practices, which work against creating a connected organization of people thriving and committed to their work. On the one hand, this literature describes how there are pressing organizational needs associated with employee underperformance and disengagement, ineffective change and development, rapidly advancing technology-based workplace reforms, and a dearth of aspiring leaders. Furthermore, the literature describes the need for a more relationally based approach to leadership while addressing these major concerns. However, on the other hand, the literature fails to provide any explicit description of a relationally based approach to leadership. Rather, most of these sources defer to promoting lightly disguised past leadership practices as new ways. Therefore, in order to fill this void this chapter provides a brief excerpt from our previous book, *Leadership in Higher Education from a Transrelational Perspective* (Branson et al. 2018), that succinctly describes the practical actions and responsibilities of a leader who adopts an essentially relational approach to their leadership.

What this means is that, from a contemporary leadership theoretical perspective at least, there are no inconsistencies or incompatibilities with the concept of an organizational ecosystem. Indeed, the two appear harmonious and well matched because both perceive relationships as their crucial base. Nevertheless, we argue also that it is blatantly unconstructive to isolate the study of leadership from that of organizational culture. Leadership and culture are inseparable and interwoven—how we understand leadership must compliment how we understand culture. This being so, it behooves us to examine the phenomenon of organizational culture to see if it, too, supports the primacy of relationships in its nature and functioning. This is the task of Chapter 2.

2

Reconstructing Culture

Principle of Organizational Ecology #2: Organizational Climate (How Culture Is Experienced by the People) Shapes the Level of Individual, Team, and Departmental Capacity, Performance, and Productivity

Introduction

In advancing our understanding of an organization as an ecosystem it must be acknowledged that it is completely impossible to consider interpersonal relationships without simultaneously discussing culture. Wherever human relationships exist, there is a culture. Interesting though, the culture can either be the glue that bonds the relationships together or it can be the barrier that impedes the relationships from forming, functioning effectively, or continuing.

In general terms, culture is, and has always been, a human social ordering phenomenon that forms naturally and subconsciously when there is a coming together of people for presumed mutual benefit. In a modern context, culture is intuitively understood and felt in most situations such as family groups, sporting teams, social gathering, national pride, and community celebrations. But it is essential to realize that we did not invent culture last century. As a mechanism for guiding the sustainability of the human race, culture has worked very well throughout our evolutionary journey across millennia. From the very beginning of our hominin existence culture has provided the norms—the social rules—for promoting acceptable social behavior, for the raising of children, and for the gathering and sharing of food. The focus of culture is collectivist where an individual's success is enhanced by belonging to a group and the success of the group is enhanced by the full contribution of its members. Belonging to a group means adopting its social expectations, such as collaboration and reciprocity, to ensure the success of the group.

Also, culture is shaped by the particular environmental conditions that the people exist in. For example, people living in desert or arctic or forest environments have very different pressures that the culture must embrace to ensure survival in the respective environments. Essentially, people work out the best ways to survive and then these become "hardwired" into the culture's norms and rules for the group. This hardwiring is the crux of the problem for organizational change. Whereas it helped ancient groups to survive, today it often hinders organizations seeking to change. This is the challenge for leaders. If the leader cannot influence their organization's culture, they will become the victim of its power.

The need to be able to fully understand the nature and function of culture raises a potential challenge to seeing organizations as ecosystems. If, as we have previously argued, an organizational ecosystem is founded upon the interdependent relationships of its employees then this indisputably links it to the culture of the organization. But if culture cannot be readily understood then so too would any concept linked to it be not understood, including that of the organization as an ecosystem. Hence, in order to advance our proposed Theory of Organizational Ecology, it necessitates the need to offer a means by which culture can not only be easily understood but also that it can be easily altered.

Therefore, the aim of this chapter is to overcome the current ambiguity and perplexity associated with understanding the nature and functionality of organizational culture. The first step toward achieving this end is to acknowledge both the positive and negative power of organizational culture as recorded in research literature thereby highlighting its absolute significance. Then, as the chapter delves deeper into the nature of organizational culture, it presents some of the different ways it has been defined and theorized along with an explanation of the inherent deficiencies in our current mainstream theory. Consequently, this is followed by a description of the idiosyncratic, abnormal nature of organizational culture as a prelude to comprehensively describing a reconstructed view of organizational culture that is both readily understandable and, therefore, straightforwardly changeable. As a reconstructed view, rather than an entirely new view, this understanding of organizational culture builds somewhat upon that which has gone before but then adds new insights and knowledge in order to overcome the current deficiencies and inaccuracies that account for its hitherto incomprehension. The chapter concludes by illustrating the ease with which this reconstructed view of organizational culture provides clarity and purpose to a leader wishing to change it.

The Power of Organizational Culture

A primary incentive for us to initially explore, and then develop, our theory of an organization as an ecosystem was the regularity in our research and consultancy work of finding leaders who were deliberately avoiding or were ignorant when it came to discussing their organizational culture and its impact. For many leaders, regardless of the context in which they were working, the nature and function of organizational culture, and its likely ramifications for the leadership aspirations and practice, remained a mystery. Even those leaders with theoretical knowledge about proposed constituent elements of organizational culture struggled to readily apply the knowledge in any coherent and beneficial way. While the theoretical models appeared to make sense, these did not seem to produce dependable and constructive insights for their organizational reality.

For these leaders, there seemed to be much more to be understood about organizational culture than what is currently available. In the minds of these leaders, theoretical knowledge deficiency resulted in pointlessness. Why bother with some theoretical concept if it doesn't clearly produce pragmatic benefits? However, despite these all-too-common observations, it is unwise to dismiss the importance of knowing more about organizational culture for, as forcefully proposed by Cameron and Quinn, "it is difficult to name even a single highly successful company, that does not have a distinctive, readily identifiable organizational culture" (2011: 5). Hence, the first step toward ensuring that leaders are committed to learning how to understand culture, in order to be able to adjust it if need be, is to highlight its unmistakable significance.

From a very general perspective, it is assumed that an organization's culture manifests as routine activities and practices within an organization, which are largely unconscious and automatic. Thus, the routines are considered to be indicative of the culture because these are founded upon taken-for-granted norms and customs that may not change very much over time. Importantly, however, extensive research has shown that these manifestations of an organization's culture have been shown to play a significant role in the organization's capacity to either nurture coworker collaboration, information exchange, knowledge sharing, client satisfaction, trust and mutuality with key stakeholders, innovative productivity, and output quality, or undermine, diminish, and limit these factors that enhance an organization's success. In short, these are the outcomes of the cultural norms—essentially what the employees do and how they go about doing what they do. Unsurprisingly then, Cameron and Quinn claim that "successful companies have developed something special that supersedes corporate strategy, market presence, and technological advantages. Although strategy, market presence, and technology are clearly important, highly successful firms have capitalized on the power that resides in developing and managing a unique corporate culture" (2011: 6).

In addition to this view of how positively influential culture can be at the organization-level, research has shown it to have an impact at the individual employee level too with respect to employee morale, commitment, productivity, physical health, and emotional well-being. Therefore, culture has been studied as a conceptual tool for helping organizations to improve the morale, motivation, commitment, loyalty, productivity, and profitability of their employees.

Arguably, however, the most widely researched and, therefore, the most documented account of the impact of organizational culture is its effect on organizational development and change strategies. Again, according to Cameron and Quinn, "without another kind of fundamental change, namely, a change in organizational culture, there is little hope of enduring improvement in organizational performance" (2011: 12). Regardless of context, it is now widely claimed through research that approximately 70 percent of planned organizational change fails. Moreover, the most frequently cited reason given for failure was a disregard for the influence of the organization's culture. In other words, failure to change the organization's culture doomed any other planned organizational change. Although the change process may have been thoroughly planned, the reasons for its implementation comprehensively described, and the change strategy executed with enthusiasm and vigor, if the fundamental culture of the organization—its values and norms, ways of thinking, leadership styles, paradigms, approaches to problem solving—remains the same, success may well prove elusive. Hence, the business literature idiom "culture trumps strategy every time."

There are two main cultural reasons provided for this high level of change failure. First, the existing culture could be marked by a predominance of employees with a closed mindset revealed in their dedicated commitment to past customary and somewhat ritualistic practices. Such a commitment to these customary practices demonstrates that the culture does not encourage change and is static rather than evolving, which may have supported hunter-gatherer groups in past times but is out of sync with the faster pace of change required in a contemporary organization. In such an organization, if the leader attempts to introduce a change strategy without simultaneously aligning the culture to the new strategy, because the values and norms stay constant, the organization quickly returns to the status quo.

Secondly the organizational culture can affect how the employees interpret and perceive the leader's description and justifications for the need to change. Those employees who remain unconvinced for the need to change will most likely resist the change initiatives. They will resist if they cannot see the compelling case for change; one that is based on a changed environmental factor and/or a new purpose of the work, both of which are at the core of the group's cultural norms. As an example, below is a case in point taken from our consultancy work:

> A new leader arrived to lead a team that had been working together for around two decades. The team members were well entrenched in how they went about their work and how they interacted with each other and the outside world. They had a history of self-management and self-reliance—an outcome resulting from performance neglect following years of laisse faire leadership. However, they were at a point where their work habits and expectations had become out-of-date and out-of-touch. Essentially, their norms were 20 years old and simply no longer viable in a digital world. The new leader was tasked with modifying the team. The team was speechless and dazed on hearing about the proposed changes to their work practices. They barely spoke to their new leader for three days; the uncertainty and fear was overwhelming them. But the leader spent time with each person—working with them to work out how they could perform their tasks differently and influencing their thinking as well. It took many weeks before they had confidence in themselves and their new leader, and, in doing so, found new norms, new ways of doing things. Within one year they were highly proficient in their work and fully enjoying their new existence. Essentially they eventually saw the need to change and developed a new set of "norms" to guide their new way of going about their work.
>
> Key points: (1) the environment eventually forced change on the team and (2) a leader simply outlining a new plan would not have brought about any significant change. Each employee needed to understand and accept the essential reason for the change and needed to have personal confidence in their own capacity to achieve it. In this case, both of these outcomes were better achieved one-on-one with the leader and each employee. By personally modelling a new relational culture, the leader not only radically changed employee performance but also, simultaneously, drastically altered the organizational culture.

Simply put, an organization's culture is a key factor that has either a positive or a negative impact on any change strategy and failing to take it into consideration can lead to undesired outcomes and employee resistance to change. This is because personality types, personal preferences, and behavioral habits rarely change quickly and/or significantly. Furthermore, failed attempts to change often produce cynicism, frustration, loss of trust, and a deterioration in morale among employees. Hence, where attention to culture is ignored an organization may be worse off than if the change strategy had not been attempted in the first place. Modifying organizational culture, in other words, is a key to the successful implementation of major improvement strategies as well as adaptation to the increasing highly competitive and ever-changing environment faced by modern organizations.

In addition to organizational change and development, there are two other key organizational characteristics that are considered to be heavily influenced by culture—reputation and knowledge sharing that, if poor, leads to organizational toxicity. According to research (see, e.g., Homburg and Pflesser 2000; Moorman 1995), an organization's culture has a direct impact upon its reputation among clients and stakeholders. Similarly, Wei and Morgan (2004) found that organizations with a strong supportive internal culture are more likely to establish strong connections and communication with key clients and stakeholders, which, in turn, strongly supports its external reputation.

Secondly, knowledge is now recognized as a key factor in determining organizational success or failure. It is now considered essential that an organization's culture maximizes rather than constrains knowledge sharing so it can remain innovative and competitive (see Chapter 5 for further elaboration). The research by Donate and Guadamillas (2010) shows that various organizational cultures have distinctive influences upon internal knowledge-sharing initiatives. For instance, certain cultural symptoms such as fear of failure, knowledge hoarding, and an undying commitment to the "tried and true" inhibit knowledge sharing in organizations (Michailova and Husted 2003), while research by Lemken, Kahler, and Rittenbruch (2000) suggests that a culture which favors knowledge sharing allows organizations to be adaptive to their surrounding environments.

Although much of this discussion has promoted the positive outcomes that can be gained by a conducive organizational culture, this discussion of its significance would be gravely incomplete if the far more damaging influence of organizational culture was not taken into consideration as well.

When Good Culture Goes Horribly Wrong

Although the majority of organizational culture research has concentrated on developing an understanding of the subject in order to improve employee performance and outputs, more recent attention has turned to the issue of toxicity within organizations. Initially such research focused on the inappropriate actions of individuals, but attention has now turned to focusing on the organizational norms and traits that seem to condone, if not promote, such actions (Van Rooij and Fine 2018). Both of these foci add important emphasis to this discussion by illustrating the potential pitfalls if a leader chooses to discount the substantial effect of the internal culture upon an organization.

There are five conditions that can turn culture into a toxic force for people, for the team, and for the organization. First, organizational toxicity has been shown to be aligned with individual actions—the leader and the employee. From a leadership perspective, Lipmen-Blumen proposes that "toxic leaders are those individuals, who by dint of their destructive behaviors and dysfunctional personal qualities generate a serious and enduring poisonous effect on the individuals, families, organizations, communities, and even entire societies they lead" (2005: 2). In such cases, Schein (2010) is correct in saying that the leader's values are reflected in the organization's culture. A toxic leader's grossly inappropriate values, as manifested in their destructive behaviors and dysfunctional personal qualities, create a destructive and dysfunctional organizational culture. A similar outcome is possible for those associated with a toxic individual employee. These are among the 20 percent of employees who are actively disengaged at work and who choose to "sabotage the workplace because they aren't just unhappy at work—they are resentful that their needs aren't being met and are acting out their unhappiness. Every day, these workers potentially undermine what their engaged co-workers accomplish" (Minnaar 2018: 1). This is the slow formation of a toxic organizational culture from the bottom-up, especially if the leader is unable to rectify it.

Rectifying such a problem necessitates seeing and acknowledging the presence of toxic cultural characteristics within the organization and being totally committed to remedying them. As Van Rooij and Fine (2018) posit, an employee who chooses to regularly act in an unacceptable way needs more than just personal motivation to do so; they also need an accommodating environment that allows them to get away with doing it. This is not simply suggesting that the leader is "blind" to such behavior and its consequences but also that the organizational structures, policies, processes, and rewards may provide such inclined employees with easier opportunities to act inappropriately. Here the organization's own norms and practices have come to undermine proper practice by not stopping or rectifying inappropriate behavior. Left unchecked, these practices result in organizational normalization of deviant behavior and, ultimately, "a collectively constructed cultural reality, incorporated into the worldview of the group" (Van Rooij and Fine 2018: 6).

The second condition that can turn culture into a toxic force is a potential outcome caused by the fact that workplaces are very abnormal socio-gathering situations. This is partly due to not only the diversity of people in an organization but also because relationships are imposed at work. For example, in most organizations the employees are not free to choose their own team, who they must associate with, or where they are located in an organization. They are automatically expected to fit in and to behave according to what they see others doing around them. Consequently, they may be required to work with people who behave in ways that are difficult to adjust to. This situation is a frequent outcome of organizational restructuring where restructuring reassembles groups of people into one team. This action is highly problematic because it essentially forces together two or more team cultures into one without any forethought about how the restructuring might play out in reality. Thus, the new culture can become a compilation of poorly matched subcultures that are often observed as cliques. Cliques can also form through individualism in the team where a dominant person is supported by subservient team members in the hope that their fortunes in the team will improve by aligning with an apparently upwardly mobile team member.

The third cause of toxic culture relates to organizations or teams where individualism is the norm. Individualism fosters competition, which both hinders the relationships that bind teams and reduces the motivational drivers that inspire people to be the best they can be. Competition nurtures exclusion and ultimately results in the manifestation of disconnection, disengagement, and lost potential. As stated previously, culture is very much a collectivist survival strategy—its essence is teamwork. Under normal circumstances, there is no place for individualism in a team culture.

Sadly, the fourth condition that causes the development of a toxic culture is the ballooning emphasis upon a management-based workforce at the expense of employee numbers at the coalface. According to Joost (2018), the number of managers and administrators in the US workforce has more than doubled since 1983, while employment in all other categories has grown by only 40 percent. Unfortunately, we remain largely invested in managerialism, which appears to be a force out of control whereby managerialism begets more and more managerialism. In a managerial-dominated workplace, the answer to most organizational problems seems to be that there is a need for more managers. Command, control, and manage will fix every problem. If management isn't working, then one must micromanage. No wonder many organizational cultures have grown toxic and the percentage of disengaged workers around the world has reached 87 percent. The naked truth of the matter is that managerialism and a healthy organizational culture are unlikely bedfellows.

Last, but certainly not least, a toxic culture will form where there is a breakdown in the social fabric within the organization, causing a loss of trust and respect for the leader and the organization. When employees know what should be happening is different from what others are actually doing, they expect the leader to do something about it. A toxic organizational culture will invariably form if many employees believe that ineffective responses are being made by the leader toward disruptive, antisocial, and dysfunctional behavior among some employees. In other words, a leader wishing to ensure that such an outcome does not occur in their organization needs to comprehensively know and understand their organization's culture so that the actual problem and not just the symptom is overcome.

What this section has clearly described is that, to be successful, organizations require a truly supportive culture, but this doesn't automatically occur. The onus is on the leader to make it so. This view is persuasively demonstrated by Edgar Schein (2010), arguably one of the most prolific and influential organizational culture researchers and writers, when he urges the need for leaders to be ever alert to the influence of their organization's culture upon all that is happening so that they can rectify it if it becomes unhelpful or dysfunctional. This demands that the leader has, and can confidently utilize, an ample understanding of the nature and function of organizational culture. But we argue that such an understanding may yet not be readily available because our current theories and definitions remain wanting, as will be shown in the following sections.

Definitions and Current Theoretical Understandings

A monumental stumbling block for anyone currently wanting to understand organizational culture is the lack of any universally accepted definition or theoretical description. In simple terms, the nature of organizational culture remains somewhat of a mystery. However, this does not mean that there have been few attempts to define it or describe it; quite the contrary.

For example, Cameron and Quinn (2011) claim there to be more than 150 definitions of culture from the simple, such as "the way we do things around here" to the far more complex, some of which are now provided. Martin defined culture as "the glue that holds a group together through a sharing of patterns of meaning. The culture focuses on the values, beliefs, and expectations that members come to share" (2002: 227). Hofstede, on the other hand, conceptualized culture as "the collective programming of the mind which distinguishes the members of one human group from another" (1991: 262). However, Pettigrew (1979) defined culture as a system of publicly and collectively accepted meanings operating for a given group at a given time while, according to Brown, culture refers to "the patterns of beliefs, values and learned ways of coping with experience that have developed during the course of an organization's history and which tend to manifest in the material arrangements and behavior of its members" (1998: 9). Deshpande and Webster define organizational culture as "the pattern of shared values and beliefs that help members of an organization understand why things happen and thus teach them the behavioral norms in the organization" (1989: 4). Finally, Schein argues that culture is "a pattern of shared basic assumptions learned by a group as it solved its problems of external adaptation and internal integration, which has worked well enough to be considered valid and, therefore, to be taught to new members as the correct way to perceive, think, and feel in relation to those problems" (2010: 16). Even in this extremely short list of possible definitions, there are widespread views and understandings. Thus, this calls for a deeper appreciation of what constitutes organizational culture.

There is agreement within the literature that there are two main disciplinary foundations upon which researchers have developed a theoretical perspective of organizational culture. The sociological foundation considers that organizations have a culture while the anthropological foundation considers that organizations are cultures (Cameron and Quinn 2011). Those writers who adopt the sociological foundation prefer a functional approach to understanding organizational culture where it is believed to emerge out of the collective behavior of all within the organization and is something that can be manipulated and changed. This leads to an analytical approach and a concern with being able to find objective elements of culture that can be measured in order to manage and control the culture. Hence, culture from this perspective can function as an agent of social control because it is believed to have the power to unconsciously determine and influence the attitudes and actions of employees. The early work of Schein (1985) reflects a commitment to this sociological perspective because he describes culture as a "concept," a generalized invention based on knowledge of particularly common phenomena. At that time, Schein described culture as a concept formed out of the common organizational phenomena inclusive of shared beliefs, values, and basic assumptions, which he then proposed could be strategically manipulated to create social stability and organizational success.

However, those who have adopted the anthropological foundation prefer a semiotic approach to understanding organizational culture where it is believed to emerge out of the individual interpretations and cognitions of those within the organization. This interpretation supports an approach that acknowledges the contribution of each person and a concern with understanding the culture from the subjective and objective views and justifications provided by those who live or work in it. Scholars who are driven by this perspective view culture as a natural part of societal groups and as socially constructed through day-to-day interpersonal interactions. Thus, culture is deemed to be a dependent variable formed as an automatic outcome of personal relationships so that it can be only described and explained rather than measured and controlled. Geertz (1973) is considered a leading advocate for viewing culture as emanating from the anthropological foundation. He emphasized the need for researchers to immerse themselves in the organizational context being explored in order to come to understand deeply the culture as described by those working in it. According to Geertz, a person "is an animal suspended in webs of significance [they themselves have] spun and culture [is one of] those webs, and the analysis of it [is] therefore not an experimental science in search of law but an interpretive one in search of meaning" (1973: 5).

Organizational Culture from a Sociological Perspective

To date, most writers have supported the sociological, functional approach whereby they have argued that culture is a socially constructed attribute of organizations that serves as the social glue binding the organization together. From this foundation they are then able to nominate certain key cultural characteristics, which are then collated into a proposed universal construct for classifying organizational culture. For example, Handy (1996) described four types of culture:

1. Power culture—where decision-making power is attributed to certain people.
2. Role culture—involves roles and responsibilities being delegated to staff who have the appropriate education, qualifications, and areas of interest.
3. Task culture—concerned with developing teams in which individual members have a common interest in overcoming challenges and achieving targets.
4. Person culture—describes a culture where staff consider themselves first before taking responsibility for the organization as a whole.

Rather than describing different types of culture, Johnson, Scholes, and Whittington (2008) present the concept of a more holistic and contextually specific organizational cultural web, which includes

1. Stories—events from the past that demonstrate what the organization perceives as exceptional behavior.
2. Rituals and routines—regularly ritualized behaviors either formally or informally performed and believed to portray essential values and beliefs.
3. Symbols—visual representations (e.g., logos and branding) of the organization's key features.
4. Organizational and power structures—depicting either those staff who can influence the formal decision-making processes or those staff who can informally influence the decision-making of other employees.
5. Control systems—policies and processes that have influence over elements such as finances, performance expectations, and rewards.

According to these authors, this cultural web provides a framework for not only considering the factors that influence an organization's culture but also for identifying areas of strength and weakness. In this way, it is argued that the cultural web can be used to identify an action plan for further cultural development incorporating measurable outcomes.

In his very early work, Schein (1985) provided a very similar sociological model in which he nominated the following three components:

1. Artifacts—the structure and the processes of an organization, which are visible but often not understood.

2. Espoused values—the publicly expressed strategies, goals, and philosophies of an organization.
3. Underlying assumptions—the often unconscious, ill-defined, and invisible shared values within an organization.

However, in his more recent literature Schein (2010: 15) argues that "we must avoid the superficial models of culture and build on the deeper, more complex anthropological models," which Schein then describes as being inclusive of

1. Observed behavioral regularities when people interact (e.g., language).
2. Group norms: The implicit standards and values that evolve in working groups.
3. Espoused values: The articulated publicly announced principles and values that the group claims to be trying to achieve.
4. Formal philosophy: The broad policies and ideological principles that guide a group's actions toward stockholders, employees, customers, and other stakeholders.
5. Rules of the game: The implicit, unwritten rules for getting along in the organization, "the ropes" that a newcomer must learn to become an accepted member, "the way we do things around here."
6. Climate: The feeling that is conveyed in a group by the physical layout and the way in which members of the organization interact with each other, or with other outsiders.
7. Embedded skills: The special competencies displayed by group members in accomplishing certain tasks passed onto newcomers to the team.
8. Habits of thinking, mental models, and/or linguistic paradigms: The shared cognitive frames that guide the perceptions, thoughts, and language used by the members of a group and are taught to new members in the early socialization process.
9. Shared meanings: The emergent understandings that are created by group members as they interact with each other.
10. Root metaphors or integrating symbols: The ways that groups evolve, to characterize themselves, that get embodied in buildings, office layouts, and other material artifacts of the group.
11. Formal rituals and celebrations: The ways in which a group celebrates key events that reflect important values or important "passages" by members such as promotion, completion of important projects, and milestones.

According to Schein, this wide array of key elements does not detract from the need to rely on the singular term, culture, because "the concept of culture implies structural stability, depth, breadth, and patterning or integration" (2010: 16).

Although in this revised description of organizational culture Schein has distanced his views from a purely sociological and functional foundation, we argue that he has not escaped entirely from it. Arguably, he still appears to be caught in the "cultural concept" trap. While this description of his interpretation of the cultural concept is now far broader, and far more inclusive of subjective, nonmeasurable elements than that which he initially provided in 1985, these still remain essentially differentiated and discrete. Hence, these elements appear independent and thereby somewhat concrete and fixed, which is in keeping with Schein's own acknowledgment that he is describing organizational culture as a concept. Ultimately though, such a description, despite its more comprehensive array of elements, maintains the confusion and ambiguity surrounding organizational culture and, therefore, adds to the reluctance of leaders to pursue trying to understand and work with their organization's culture. Thus, more needs to be known about organizational culture if this insupportable and detrimental situation is to be overcome.

Organizational Culture from an Anthropological Perspective

The very first step in overcoming this detrimental situation is to see organizational culture through an anthropological perspective. This necessitates acknowledging that organizational culture is not a concept; it is a phenomenon. It is essential to remember that culture, itself, is a phenomenon because it is a natural and not an artificially constructed part of our human existence. Culture always has been a natural part of human existence ever since hominins gathered in small tribes or clans for safety and sustainability.

This can be readily recognized today by conceding that people are highly culturally aware even though they might well be culturally ignorant. Whenever we enter a new social environment our senses are unconsciously seeking cues as to what is culturally acceptable as we try to fit in, as best we can and as quickly as possible. Yet, if asked to explicitly nominate exactly what cues we are looking for, it is highly likely that we would struggle to name them. Thus, on the one hand, often we are willingly influenced by largely covert and obscure cultural norms. But, on the other hand, we are only influenced by how we interpret the culture and not necessarily by how it is publicly proclaimed to be. If we recognize through the actions of others that things are done differently from how it is publicly proclaimed to happen then we are most likely to act according to the observed behaviors rather than the official expectations. Whenever we are with others, culture is present and we are automatically, but often unconsciously, looking to align ourselves with how we see and understand it.

However, it is also important to recognize that culture is not a consistent or static phenomenon. Each nation has a unique culture; each family has a unique culture; and each social group has a unique culture because they each have their own specific environmental pressures and conditions they need to survive within, and they each have their own understandings of their reason for being—their history, purpose, work, and/or identity. But also, the culture of a nation, a family, a social group, or even a small group of friends changes over time. Hence, the phenomenon that we call organizational culture is not something entirely different but rather it is simply another example of a culture within a specific context. This means that organizational culture is not constituted by independent and fixed elements but rather it is the ongoing but evolving conglomerated outcome of personal, social, and organizational cultural commonalities and differences among the group of people who constitute the organization. It is essential to realize that each organization is a culture which is unique and idiosyncratic. This means that if we want to explicitly understand an organization's culture, we must understand its idiosyncrasy (see Chapter 8 for a case study describing how this can be readily achieved).

The Idiosyncrasy of an Organization's Culture

Two aspects of culture create difficulties for contemporary organizations. The first one is that culture has evolved since ancient times to serve as a stabilizing, survival mechanism for humans. However, because society is rapidly changing, organizations are increasingly required to change to stay relevant. Thus, the stabilizing factors of culture, the hardwired norms and rules, over time become at odds with the organization's strategic thinking. It is a constant tension between "the way we do things around here" or "the way we have always done things" and the need to innovate, renew, and change. Essentially, the purpose, the critical foundation of culture, has changed. Resistance to change is cultural and therefore is a leadership matter. It is a case of the team and organization renewing the underlying basic assumptions, values, and behavior to achieve a clearly defined new purpose. Again, there is literature describing such a process (Branson 2008) and a practical application of this is provided in Chapter 8 also.

The second idiosyncratic aspect of an organization's culture is, as previously stated, that it is not a normal gathering of people. Although an organization usually has a clearly stated core purpose, each employee comes to work with their own individualistic reason for being there. Each employee comes with their own knowledge, skills, past experiences, expectations, and aspirations, and assumes that they will not only be able to readily contribute to the ongoing success of the organization but, also, they will benefit personally and career-wise from doing so. Importantly, the primary reason that nearly every person accepts employment in an organization is for these personal benefits and not because they are, first and foremost, attracted by its culture.

Hence, it is near impossible to know a culture until one is an integral part of it. Unlike family culture, for example, to which we are born into and learn more about as we grow, we arrive into our organization's culture ignorant of its true functioning and complexity. Indeed, it is the familiar tune of the new recruit, having successfully passed muster at their interview, to arrive at the new job excited and full of ideas only to be slam dunked and constrained by the culture. Although another person might try to describe an organization's culture to you, this is only how they see it, interpret it, and interact with it—which could be quite different from how you might see, interpret, and interact with it. This means that a new employee's alignment with and commitment to the organization's culture is not necessarily a given outcome. It takes considerable time for such an outcome to be achieved because culture is not only an extremely complex phenomenon, such that there is a lot to learn, but also much of it resides in subliminal norms, which can only be learned from experiences rather than from anticipatory advice. Also, once the person has commenced their new employment it is quite possible that they are not able to fully or partially fit into the organization's culture. Thus, unlike friendship and social groups in which a person remains a willing member because the culture suits their needs, in any given organization there is likely to be a wide variation in the level of employee alignment with and commitment to the organization's culture.

In other words, it cannot be assumed that an organization's culture is a unifying force upon each and every employee. Unlike the situation when a person first meets with a potential new friend or chooses to join a social group for the first time where there are no obligations to continue to meet with this person or group, once a person accepts employment in an organization there are various pressures for them to remain. Key considerations for most employees are associated with maintaining expected income and career opportunities. Hence, while committing to an ongoing relationship with a potential friend or social group is strongly dependent upon one's sense of the suitability of the respective culture in meeting their personal needs, values, beliefs, and aspirations, this is not necessarily so when working for an organization. It is quite possible that an employee can sense a misalignment between their own needs, values, beliefs, and aspirations and those promoted within the culture of either or both the social/team groups within the organization and the organization's itself, but feel compelled to "stick it out" for personal rather than cultural commitments. But, because it is extremely difficult for a person to fully enact cultural expectations when they feel detached from it, it is likely they will choose to act selectively and variably in alignment with the culture or to disengage from it completely.

In addition to this personal level of cultural engagement within an organization, particularly at the local or team level, there is also likely to be a social one. Undoubtedly, an employee's work within the organization will provide them with opportunities to join both social and organizational groups. As described comprehensively in Chapter 4, these social groups and organizational teams will naturally develop their own unique cultures, which may or may not be closely aligned with the desired or actual culture of the organization. Thus, again, the willingness of an individual to join any existing social group within the organization, or their readiness to be a fully committed and engaged member of an organizational team, will be strongly influenced by how closely the social group's culture or the organizational team's culture aligns with their personal expectations as determined by their own needs, values, beliefs, and aspirations. However, regardless of the fit between personal and team culture, in a workplace situation, people's personal life commitments can make it nigh impossible to fully engage in the social aspects of their team culture and so such employees are likely to contribute less than their 100 percent to the team.

Finally, there is the interaction between the employee and the organization's culture. It is generally accepted that an organization's culture is founded on its values, beliefs, and implicit assumptions. However, although the concept of "organizational values" regularly appears in research literature, it must be remembered that values only reside in people. In other words, a value will only become an organizational value if more than 50 percent of employees willingly and regularly employ this value (Branson 2007). Just because a leader says that certain values are their organization's values this doesn't make them so. The actual organization's values are those that the majority of employees automatically apply to their work each day, which may or may not align with the personal values of a new employee. On the one hand, where there is a positive alignment, the employee will develop a stronger attachment to the organization and their engagement and performance will be maximized. They will be self-motivated and enthusiastic about their work. On the other hand, should a negative alignment occur, the employee will begin to feel out of place and undervalued. They will feel that they can't contribute or, worse, don't want to contribute because their work is not acknowledged or appreciated. Hence their engagement and performance can suffer.

It is for these reasons that we propose that organizational culture is idiosyncratic thereby rendering many generic cultural assumptions as irrelevant. This demands the need for a new or reconstructed view of what constitutes an organization's culture and an explanation of how it functions.

The Foundations of a Reconstructed View of Organizational Culture

From a theoretical perspective, our reconstructed view of organizational culture can be seen to embrace an anthropological foundation because it explains how the culture emerges out of the everyday individual and personal aspirations, interpretations, and cognitions of those within the organization. Moreover, this view conceives organizational culture as a phenomenological, and not a conceptual, entity. Thus, any description and modeling of the formative processes for organizational culture must capture the interdependencies of the naturally inherent cultural phenomena rather than merely present an image of basically independent, concrete, and fixed elements. As stated previously, we argue that what we experience as an organization's culture is, in fact, not a singular, pure, independent entity but rather the felt outcome from the weaving together, the conglomeration, of different levels of cultural phenomena. Figure 2.1 illustrates this understanding.

As the title of Figure 2.1 indicates, it is an illustration, rather than a model, of some of the key phenomena that weave together to form what is experienced as an organization's culture. As an illustration, the aim of Figure 2.1 is to guide understanding so that a leader can then work with their culture. It is not about providing a leader with a plan for how to control the culture. As is discussed below, understanding culture is about understanding the people begetting the culture. Thus, working with the culture is about working with the people. Changing the culture involves the leader helping the people to know why the

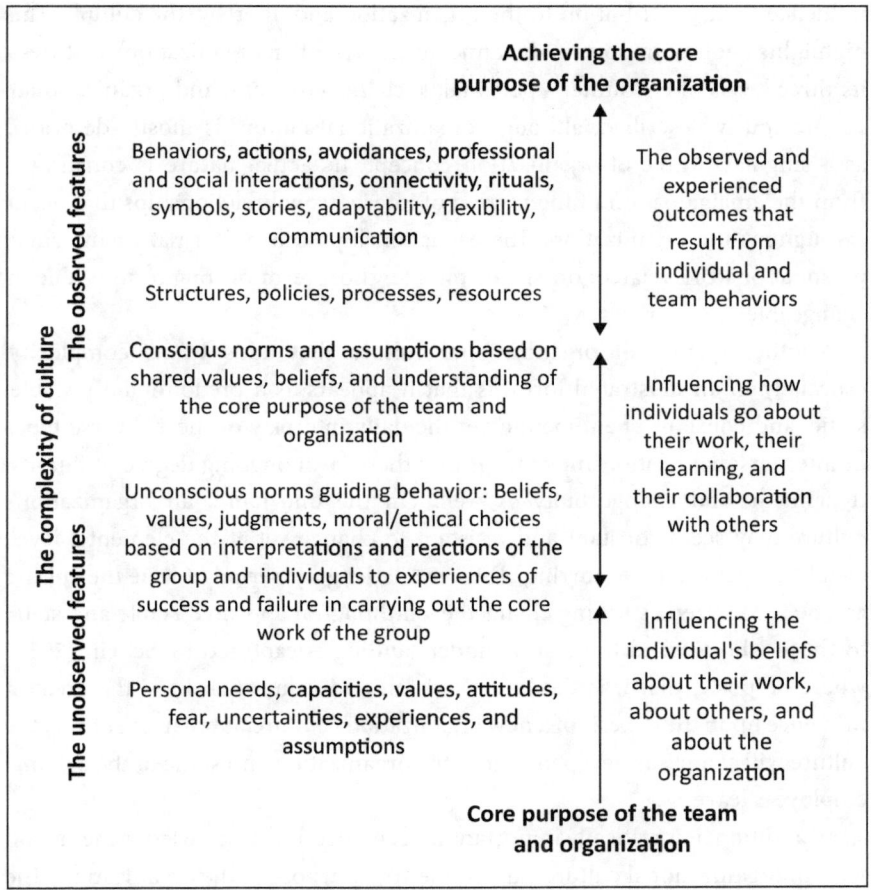

Figure 2.1 An illustration of the phenomenology of an organization's culture.

culture needs to change and then supporting them in how they bring about the change. However, the inherent difficulty with trying to illustrate organizational culture is its multi-stratified nature.

Culture is not formed in a linear fashion and so it is extremely problematic to implement a simplistic cause-effect rationalization. This understanding is indicated by the observed-unobserved continuum. While culture is experienced at the tangible, observable level much of its formation occurs at the unobservable level where its genesis is most often happening unconsciously in the individual minds of the employees. Even when an employee becomes conscious of their innermost thoughts about the organization, and their role within it, they might choose to not disclose their thoughts, yet these will still influence their contribution to the organization and, thereby, the culture. This highlights another important dynamic dimension of an organization's culture—its three levels of encounter—personal, social/group/team, and organizational. As previously described, although organizational culture is mostly described as a singular, whole-of-organization concept, its actual nature is constituted from the amalgamation of the myriad of interpersonal relationships that occur throughout the organization. These relationships can be formal or informal, personal or work related, on-site or off-site, short term or long term, stable or changeable.

Another quality of organizational culture that adds to its complexity, especially in an illustrated form, is that it appears as a predominantly stable, static, and constant phenomenon yet the daily interplay of these diverse types of interpersonal relationships means that there is an ongoing degree of fluidity, dynamism, and changeability as well. On the one hand, an organization's culture may seem constant and resistant to change yet at the elemental level, small changes can be occurring. Thus, over a lengthy period of time the culture can be recognized as having changed even though it appeared stable and static to those who worked there. This understanding is captured by Schein (2010) where he posits that it is the leader's vision and values that have the greatest influence upon the genesis of a new organization's culture but that, over time, the culture will change as new people join the organization and some of the original employees leave.

In addition, it is critically important to recognize and acknowledge the reason why an organizational culture exists—the core purpose of the organization. The establishment and continuation of an organizational culture is made manifest by the degree to which all associated with the organization are committed to its core purpose. Although the ideal is for each and every person associated with the organization to be fully committed to maximizing the achievement of the organization's core purpose, this is not an automatic outcome. Organizational research literature highlights how the nature of an organization's culture can lie somewhere along a unity-fragmentation continuum (Kujala, Lehtimäki, and Pučėtaitė 2016). Here, unity is often associated with completeness and harmony, while fragmentation is considered to be a state of incompleteness and deficiency.

Arguably, the perennial problem with our current attempts to understand organizational culture is that a top-down approach is used. Here the assumption is that organizational culture is an independent, antecedent construct that applies some form of influential control over all associated with the organization. Furthermore, the belief is that this influential control is consistent and universal in its impact across the organization—each person is similarly influenced and responds accordingly. Thus, the "holy grail" of organizational culture research has mainly focused on determining its constituent elements so that the leader can gain complete control of not only the culture but also, by inference, the thoughts and actions of all they are leading. Despite the ongoing lack of success of this approach, its appealing simplicity and desirability largely remains. We argue, to understand organizational culture confidently, one needs to seek a "bottom-up" perspective, to see how an individual person engages with the culture from whence they first begin working in an organization and to understand how deeply they feel they belong to the organization.

Belonging as the Cornerstone of Organizational Culture

If the manifestation of an organization's culture is directly aligned with the intensity of relational connectivity among employees, then this is about how well each employee achieves a sense of belonging. People are only truly connected with others when they feel a deep and sincere sense that they belong to the group. Hagerty and colleagues defined this sense of belonging as "the experience of personal involvement in a system or environment so that persons feel themselves to be an integral part of that system or environment" (Hagerty et al. 1992: 173). Similarly, Cockshaw and colleagues (1993) proposed that belongingness is "the extent to which individuals feel personally accepted, respected, included, and supported by others in their social environment" (81). According to social psychology, this need to seek belongingness comes from our basic survival instinct. From an evolutionary perspective, humans have developed a subconscious acknowledgment of being relatively frail and defenceless individuals, and so we automatically seek to overcome this vulnerability by living and working closely with others. Thus, this inherent human need for belonging is accepted as being one of the most powerful sources of personal motivation. Indeed, this need for belonging is so important to us that social psychology research has shown that its absence in peoples' lives can lead to depression, sadness, and lowered self-esteem and self-confidence.

This acknowledgment of the motivational power of belonging has led to an extensive array of research toward better understanding its nature and function. For example, various research studies have confirmed that individuals with a strong sense of belonging are more likely to experience good physical and mental health outcomes and achieve higher levels of performance. Further research has shown how belongingness promotes meaningfulness within an individual because it creates a personal positivity through being able to help others, being appreciated and validated by others, gaining access to required resources, and having influence over one's environment. Hence, Moynihan, Igou, and van Tilburg argue that "one of the great benefits that feelings of belongingness offer is that they serve as a key source of perceived meaning in life" and add that "meaning in life substantiates the relationship between free will beliefs and belongingness" (2017: 55). That is, free will enables people to restrain their impulses so as to gain acceptance and approval from others, which in turn promotes feelings of belongingness and thereby meaningfulness.

Meaningful work is something each and every employee seeks. As proposed by noted psychiatrist, Viktor Frankl (1959), the innate human quest for meaning is so strong that, even in the most appalling circumstances, people seek out a meaning, a purpose, in their life. More recently, researchers have shown meaningfulness to be more important to employees than any other aspect of work, including pay and rewards, opportunities for promotion, or working conditions. Meaningful work can be highly motivational, leading to improved performance, commitment, and satisfaction.

It is for this reason we claim that any attempt to develop a working knowledge of organizational culture must begin at the individual level—but not at the level of what the individual is doing or not doing, rather how they are thinking. How are they interpreting their workplace environment in order to create personal meaning and purpose? It is at this individual employee level that we can begin to see how culture is formed.

The Individual as the Foundational Level of Organizational Culture

As briefly mentioned above, when a person first joins an organization they arrive with certain expectations and aspirations about the organization, and its core purpose, and what benefits they might potentially gain from their contribution. Also, at this point, they are willingly seeking to be seen to be "fitting in," which means they are adopting organizational cultural mores according to their sensory perception of them.

However, it is vitally important to realize that their initial workplace expectations and aspirations are not based upon superficial or inconsequential personal beliefs and opinions. Rather, these are formed in their self-concept, which can be described as the composite of powerful ideas, feelings, and attitudes people have about themselves (Branson 2007, 2014). It is the image, the belief, the picture that the person has of their self and what they can become. It enables the person to be able to differentiate themselves from others and to distinguish their own individuality with respect to what they see of others. Moreover, the person's self-concept controls how they see, interpret, and react to their environment because they are driven to fulfilling their self-concept. In other words, their self-concept governs their personal needs, values, attitudes, expectations, and assumptions. A key aspect of a worker's self-concept is the image or picture they have of themselves as an employee now and in the future, which then induces largely inviolate personal needs, values, beliefs, attitudes, expectations, and assumptions about what they wish to do in the organization, how they would wish to do it, and how they would like to be supported by their leader and the organization toward achieving their self-concept.

Although described here definitively, in reality some of these personal phenomena may be unconsciously held but this does not diminish their influence. For example, most people are unaware of their personal values; values are subliminal influences upon the person (Branson 2007, 2014). Personal values are mostly an unconscious personal standard that guides actions, influences attitudes toward objects, and affects perceptions of reality. A person's values underpin their ideology, their presentations of their self to others, their evaluations, their justifications, their judgments, their comparisons of their self with others, and their attempts to influence others. Indeed, it is difficult for a person to think of themselves apart from their values despite often being unaware of their actual values. Every decision a person makes is based on their values, whether they are consciously aware of it or not.

Although the person may not be conscious of their values, they will be aware of the consequential outcomes generated by them, yet these are mostly not readily disclosed to others. While the person might be fully aware of how they see themselves engaging and growing as an employee in the organization, it is likely that they are not able to immediately nominate the value(s) underpinning this image and the beliefs and assumptions it entails. Thus, the person might be open about how they like to perform their workplace roles, and even what their future workplace roles might look like, but they are far less likely to be open about their innermost beliefs and assumptions upon which these judgments are based. Hence, the unconscious or undisclosed existence of these personal phenomena dramatically increases their resilience and steadfastness. In some cases, a person's unconscious and undisclosed phenomena pertaining to their workplace role can be so resilient and steadfast that their own judgment about the quality of their work, and their future work-related aspirations are, in the opinions of their co-employees, clearly and decidedly at odds with their current level of performance.

Be that as it may, once the person has commenced their role within the organization these fundamental personal phenomena are slowly but surely compared with the perceived potential outcomes being afforded by the organization. The person begins to interpret and judge their workplace experiences relative to their personal beliefs, expectations, and aspirations. Crucially, these interpretations and judgments are idiosyncratic but there are some general trends which surely alert a leader to aspects of the culture that can become problematic. For example, in the Gallup article, "Perspective on Building a High-Development Culture through Your Employee Engagement Strategy," it is argued that "the demands and desires of today's employees have changed as well. People are looking for more than just a paycheck. They want purpose and meaning from their work. They want to be known for what makes them unique. And they want relationships, particularly with a manager who can coach them to the next level" (2019: 3). Also, according to noted neuro-endocrinologist, Robert Sapolsky (2017), the three most critically important aspects of a culture that invariably influences a person's acceptance of it are fairness, indirect reciprocity, and avoidance of despotism. People want to know that the organizational culture will ensure that they will be treated fairly, justly, and equitably—that if they help a co-employee then they will be similarly helped by a co-employee or a leader if the need arises. Also, people expect that the organization's culture will keep them safe from all forms of intimidation and powermonger behavior.

By and large, very few individuals like to stand out from the crowd. As has already been noted, mostly people want to fit in and feel they belong. Thus, although the foundations of an employee's interaction with the organization's culture occur at the personal level, the desire to seek belonging means that they will look to join with others in formal and informal ways, if at all possible.

The Individual's Cultural Choices

Based upon the individual employee's interpretation and judgment of their workplace experiences relative to their own beliefs, expectations, and aspirations they make choices about their engagement with the culture. The employee participates as an agent within the culture. People's behavior is said to be agential because it has a specific purpose (Bandura 1997). People's behavior is not aimless and accidental but, rather, it is initiated in order to achieve desired outcomes. The person's behavior seeks to progressively bring about the realization of his or her self-concept (Branson 2007). In an organizational sense, the employee deliberately acts in accordance with their perceived level of alignment with the organizational culture. How they feel about the culture is reflected in their behaviors, actions, noncommitments, resistances, and avoidances, and these, in turn, influence the organization's culture. The more employees support the culture, the stronger the culture. Conversely, the more employees undermine the culture by not committing to desired actions, or by resisting planned changes or avoiding certain tasks and ceremonies, the weaker the culture.

If the employee judges that their needs are being fully met, then they will willingly and enthusiastically embrace and promote the culture along with all of its norms and behaviors. Where the employee senses that the organizational culture makes them feel welcomed, appreciated, and supported, they will be self-motivated to do their best and will respond with loyalty and commitment to the culture and, thereby, the leader and the organization. However, where the employee senses that the organizational culture does not make them feel welcomed, appreciated, and supported, because they deduce that their needs are not being met, they will begin to consider how they might respond. This could include deciding that they will initiate some overt actions to show their discontentment, or that they will choose to avoid or resist completing some responsibilities, or that they may begin to seek employment elsewhere.

But, for most employees their judgment about the organizational culture lies somewhere in between these two extremes. These individuals are content with some benefits they gain from the organization while, at the same time, are unhappy with other aspects of the organization, which they believe to be constraining, unfavorable, or undermining their requirements. Often these individuals choose to surreptitiously seek out other individuals who share the same negative opinions so as to validate and confirm their own negative beliefs and assumptions. Although this is common practice and may not cause undue concern, under certain conditions this situation can become problematic if left to fester and grow. In this case, encouraged by the awareness that their negative opinions and understandings have significance and merit, because other employees think the same, one or more employees can become emboldened toward acting in support of their negative beliefs and assumptions. They create self-justified reasons as to why they are vindicated in resisting some of the leader's requests or ignoring certain common policies and processes or restricting access to resources or spreading internal or external gossip about the organization's failings. In this situation, these employees have created a subculture that has the potential to adversely affect the organization's culture.

Fortunately, this form of informal group subculture is not universally common but formal group culture is. Today, most medium to large organizations at least depend on certain essential work being produced by teams. This means that the individual, along with all their personal needs as described above, are expected to work collaboratively with others in a formalized team in order to produce a desired organizational benefit. Thus, any discussion of organizational culture must explore the impact of formal group and team culture.

The Group and Team Culture

It is diabolically wrong, if not dangerous, for a leader to assume that a team's culture will automatically mirror that of the organization. A team's culture is the manifestation of the unconscious norms embraced by its members. These are captured and promoted by what is said by the team members about how the team "does its things." The unconscious norms determine the beliefs and attitudes supported by each team member about who the team connects with, how the team behaves during its meetings, which team member does which task, how the team member is to complete their assigned task, what are to be the team's achievements, and how the team intends to promote its activities. From these beliefs and attitudes arise the explicit outcomes—the team's conscious norms (team rules that can be openly described and stated) and commitments (agreed team responsibilities and activities)—which are then buffeted against the objective aspects of the organization's culture—its structures, policies, processes, and ceremonies. These have been described as the visible artifacts of an organization's culture (Schein 2010). Ideally, these are meant to reinforce the culture by directly influencing the actions of the employees. However, this is not necessarily the case. Most often the team's cultural characteristics provide it with the norms believed by the team members to best suit the team's success without any consideration of the organization's culture. Thus, a team's culture can become countercultural from the organization's perspective.

For example, Schein (2010) describes how, particularly in large organizations, there is a strong likelihood that subcultures will form in which its members will share values, beliefs, and assumptions beyond those promoted by the organization. He explains how these variant values, beliefs, and assumptions usually reflect the members' educational background and/or their specific functional role and experiences within the organization. Thus, as Schein further highlights, these role-based subcultures often experience difficulties when attempting to communicate with other such subcultures because each has different goals and very different views about what should be the organization's priorities, and so can become highly competitive and lose sight of the organization's purpose and values in favor of the subculture's purpose and values.

To emphasize this possibility, Schein (2010: 58) describes three regularly found generic subcultures of "operators" (e.g., the nurses or teachers or factory floor operators etc.) who produce the organization's actual product, "engineers" (e.g., human resource management staff, information technology staff, administrative staff etc.) who design and manage the functioning of the organization, and "top executives" (e.g., CEO, senior leadership team, governing board members etc.) who are the key decision-makers and financial overseers of the organization. Importantly, as Schein adds, rather than accepting that the success of the organization depends upon each group working fully and cooperatively with the other two, they tend to each assume that they, alone, deserve a far more important status than the others and so diminish their cooperation to that which is only essential. Relative power and authority are of far more concern than maintaining a healthy, united organizational culture. In particular, the engineers and executives can even consider that the operators, the people who are doing the actual work, are the problem when things are not looking all that bright for the organization. Sadly, this is an attitude that was first proposed by renowned social theorist Max Weber one hundred years ago when he posited that bureaucracy develops more perfectly the more it is "dehumanized" (Weber 1921: 937). In a healthy culture, under a relational leader where employees are connected and valued, these subcultures cannot exist because of the fundamental commitment to collaborative relationships, an openness to the sharing of information and knowledge, and a compelling drive to achieve a common purpose.

What this shows so dramatically is that, just as it can happen in an organization's department or section, whenever people join a team to work together for a common outcome, a subculture will form. The development of this subculture will be influenced more by how the respective team member's capabilities, personalities, past experiences, and personal expectations blend together than by the organization's culture. Ultimately, this blending process results in the formation of the team's unconscious norms, which basically describe "the way the team does its things." These norms form the nuts and bolts of the team's culture. Their manifestation arises out of the team's tried-and-tested practices and approaches that have proven to be successful over time. Once these norms have been established, the team's approach to carrying out aspects of its role becomes automatic because each team member knows their task and how to do it. However, while there are these procedural benefits once the team's culture has stabilized, it can also be a source of serious problems.

The first of these problems concerns the situation where a new employee, including possibly a new leader, needs to join the team. Invariably this person will join the team with new ideas, different work/life experiences, distinctive skills, and new ways of interacting. Unless the group culture is particularly inclusive, open, and adaptable, the way the new member decides to act and participate in the team's activities will be judged against the existing procedural norms. The new team member's behavior and interactions will be observed and judged by the continuing members as to whether or not the newcomer is fitting into the team's culture in an acceptable way. From a cultural perspective, any new way of doing things needs to be understood as good and right by the team, and then it will lead to a new way of doing things—thereby lead to new unconscious norms.

The second problem associated with a very mature team culture relates to its degree of flexibility and openness to change. In a culture where innovation and change are valued, newcomers and their new views and ideas are less threatening. Although the unconscious intention might well be to maintain the team's existing culture, where the new member is totally accepted, they could influence changes being made to some of the team's beliefs, interpretations, judgments, and decisions and, thereby, help in modifying the culture. However, if the team's culture is more focused on maintaining the status quo than being open to innovation and change, then a newcomer's fresh ideas will fall on deaf ears. In addition, the team members can openly display animosity and disregard towards the new team member. In a general sense, the team's reaction to the new member can be one of total acceptance, or unreserved rejection and thus isolation, or circumscribed acceptance along with the intention of modifying the new member's beliefs and opinions so that it eventually supports the existing culture.

Thus, it can be seen that while organizational culture is experienced as a seemingly singular phenomenon, its actual nature is quite the opposite. There are many things happening at individual employee and group or team levels that weave and collate together in order to form the culture as experienced by all. Hence, although this description of organizational culture has, by necessity, differentiated these key individual and group/team components, we again wish to emphasize that, in reality, these are all linked and woven together seamlessly. As we proposed at the outset of this chapter, organizational culture is the combined outcome, the felt reality, of a conglomeration of interdependent phenomena. Hence, organizational culture's currently perceived complexity and ambiguity.

To date, organizational culture is thought to be a complex and ambiguous concept because the plethora of attempts to conceptualize and model it has largely failed to produce practical benefits. Most leaders still either struggle to understand and work with their organization's culture or they avoid even trying to do so because their attempted application of current models doesn't seem to produce pragmatic benefits. We claim that this is not the case when organizational culture is understood in ecological terms as described above. As will now be described, this view offers a variety of quite simple yet highly manageable and effective ways that a leader can come to understand and influence their organization's culture.

Leadership Implications

First, it is essential to emphasize the unique insight that this reconstructed view of organizational culture provides. Previously, organizational culture has been portrayed as a far more inert, peripheral, and depersonalized concept. Although intrinsic elements were previously named, there was little in the way of describing how these interacted together in forming the culture. As a result, the organization's culture appeared as a mythical, obscure, indistinguishable, ether-like vapor that enveloped and affected all and sundry. Once formed it seemed to have an existence unaffected by the daily lives of those within its powers while, at the same time, dramatically and continually influencing these lives. Hence, knowing the elements of the culture did not provide an understanding of it and, consequently, left most leaders befuddled and incapable of adapting or changing an unhelpful organizational culture.

In contrast, this reconstructed view of organizational culture has illustrated its human and pragmatic origins, and how these influence an employee's willingness to align with and commit to the existing culture. By so doing, this view provides a simple but powerful way for a leader, or line manager, to monitor the organizational culture daily. This is not about trying to connect together and interpret inexplicit environmental characteristics but rather coming to deeply know the culture simply by regularly talking with the employees they are leading. There is no need for the leader to be an expert cultural analyzer; all it takes is for the leader to know how culture is formed and, therefore, be able to ask the right questions and seek the right information from employees on a regular basis. This means that it is not a mechanistic, formalized, periodic process of control but, rather, it is a humanistic, relational, daily way of leading. Moreover, this reconstructed view mandates that the leader needs to understand the organization's culture from its grassroots, from the phenomena upon which it is created, and not from its observable or espoused symptoms. It seeks honest, accurate, truthful, and insightful information from each employee about how they are experiencing and contributing to the culture either as an individual or as a team member.

Figure 2.2 illustrates the connectedness between the employees and the leader in the culture thereby showing their inseparability. Moreover, this figure identifies how and where the leader is able to influence the culture. The first crucial step for a leader, middle leader, or line manager is to create belonging for each person. As discussed above, a sense of belonging is critical for people, their well-being, and their commitment. Information about their work and how they are feeling comes from talking to the employees at the coalface, as individuals and as team members, and asking questions inclusive of the following: "Tell me about your work." "What do you do? How does your work contribute to the team and the organization?" These questions are critical because it is the perception and interpretation of each employee and team about what they consider to be the core purpose of the organization, and how they are able or not able to contribute to its achievement, that is the basis upon which culture forms.

Sadly, throughout our extensive consultancy work we have found widespread inconsistencies in many organizations in how employees understand the actual core purpose of the team and the organization. If employees don't understand the core purpose, then they clearly can't align their own work to it. If this happens, they immediately lose any tangible sense of meaning or purpose in their own work. This is a major cultural problem for organizations. As one person stated, having been asked the reason for their work, "I don't know. I just come into work every day and do it. I've been doing it for years and I hate it." Our investigation showed that her work provided essential support for a major process within the organization—yet she personally did not know the importance of her work. Meaning and purpose are critical because these not only synchronize effort but also act as key sources of intrinsic motivation.

The second crucial step for the leader is to ask if anything is stopping the employee from being the best they can be in their work. From this question, the leader can begin to understand the perceived barriers that seem to be inhibiting performance and the development of new ideas and improved practices (e.g.,

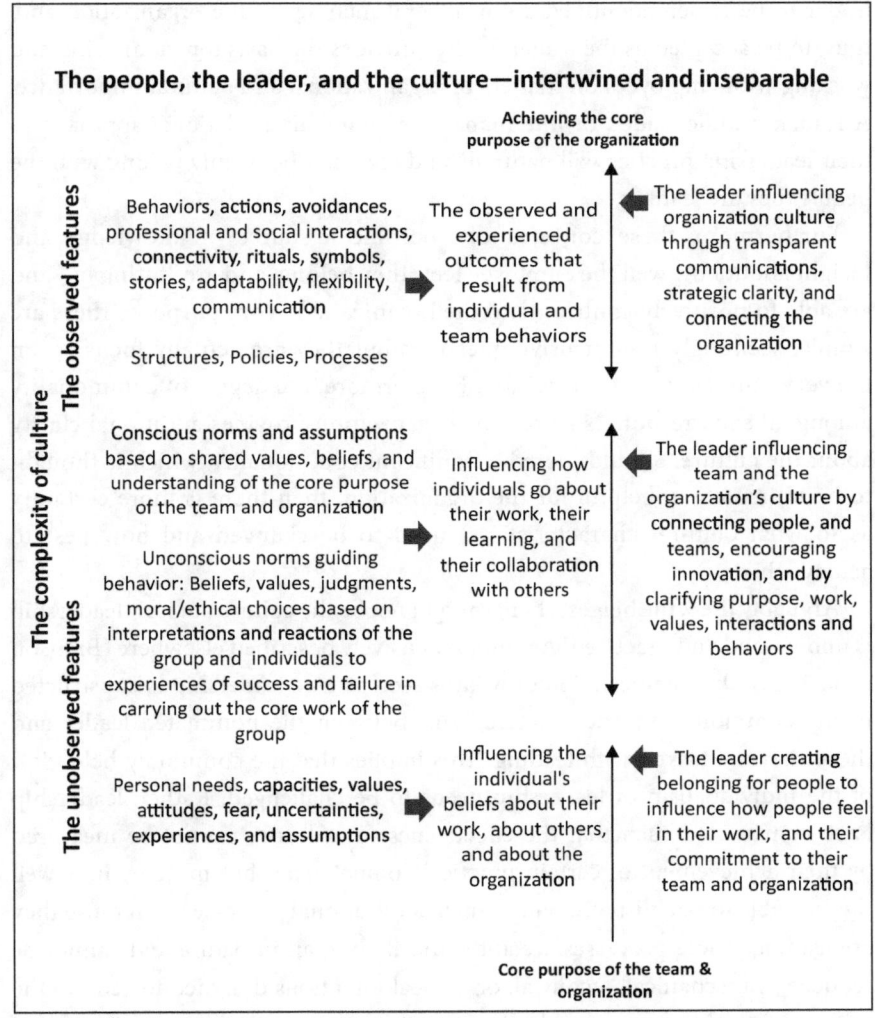

Figure 2.2 The people, the leader, and the culture—intertwined and inseparable.

support, knowledge, collaborations, and resources). The third question follows on from this information. "How can I help you with your work?" This is not only encouraging the employee to always be thinking and learning about their work, so as to be seeing solutions as well as problems, but also projects the leader as someone who is interested, inclusive, and supportive.

Such conversations provide the platform for the leader to learn the ropes, become known to staff and, thereby, to be in a position to constructively influence the organization's culture. It provides a very practical and achievable way for the leader to be closely identified as an integral member of the organization and, thus, to be accepted as the leader. It also provides the basis for monitoring and working with employees on matters of organizational and cultural importance. A leader, middle leader, or line manager acting with a relational approach to their leadership practice will naturally and regularly be openly talking with the people they are leading.

Furthermore, these conversations become a source of knowledge and insight about how well the employee feels they belong, and are "fitting in," and are able to positively contribute to the organization's core purpose. These are simple, seemingly nonintrusive questions but they are actually focusing on the very foundations of the culture. Furthermore, the degree of commonality among all such responses across the organization provides additional clarity about the culture. Should there be significant commonality, which is thought to be ultimately unhelpful for the organization, then there is more certainty as to what cultural characteristic(s) need to be changed and how best to achieve this.

Arguably then, the biggest change might not be the culture but how leadership is understood and practiced. As comprehensively described elsewhere (Branson et al. 2018), the manifestation of what is seen as true leadership is constructed in the common daily social interactions between the nominated leader and those they are tasked with leading. This implies that the commonly held view of the individualism of leadership needs to be challenged. Rather, leadership is co-constructed such that the effectiveness of a leader cannot be measured by their achievement of certain practical competencies but more by how well they are able to establish mutually beneficial relational processes with those they are leading. These processes are authentically human in nature and cannot be reduced to mechanical, technical, or clinical intentions designed to achieve the self-interests of the supposed leader. They are characterized by a social flow of interacting and connecting whereby organizations, groups, leaders, leadership, and so forth are constantly under construction and reconstruction.

What this all means is that a leader can only come to truly know their organization's culture, and thus have the appropriate insight into what needs to be changed and how to best achieve it, by relating closely with those to be led. But, also, they can only become the accepted and respected leader by developing mutually beneficial relationships with those to be led. Here, again, we are seeing the inseparability and the interwoven interdependency of organizational leadership and culture.

Implications for the Leadership of Schools

In many ways, the culture of a school has not changed during the past one hundred years. If such a thing as a time machine existed so that we could bring a doctor from the beginning of last century and place them in one of today's large, modern hospitals they would probably have no idea where they are, or how the hospital functions, or what they should do. But the same cannot be said about a teacher. A teacher transported through time from the beginning of last century would quickly realize where they are, be fairly familiar with how the modern school functions, and would soon be capable of starting to teach. Key features of the culture of schools have been noticeably stagnant despite dramatic changes in pedagogical knowledge and teacher practice. The problem is that knowledge and behavior do not change culture significantly, but culture has a huge impact on beliefs and behavior. Simply put, an unhelpful school culture will invariably act to minimize the professional practice of teachers despite any advancements in pedagogical knowledge. Hence, when invited to conduct cultural audits in schools (see the concluding chapter for a description of this process) we regularly find that it is the lingering presence of many elements of a vastly outdated, unhelpful, traditional school culture that is impeding school improvement attempts.

Sadly, this is not surprising given that, as described above, our way of understanding organizational culture has been seriously ineffective. In keeping with this deficient understanding of culture, schools have closely attended to establishing community values, defining vision and mission statements, comprehensively documenting position descriptions, clarifying administrative structures, developing guiding and unifying procedural policies and processes, consolidating their brands with professionally designed symbols and logos, and carefully orchestrating their important ceremonies and celebrations. But this has largely entrenched and stymied the culture rather than enabling it to fully support the ongoing professional evolution of teaching and learning.

Ignoring and leaving the culture of the school to struggle along as it always has is a recipe for division, competition, and conflict within and between the many parts of the school. For example, in our current outdated school culture, the underlying basic assumptions guiding the development of teaching and learning is often hampered by personal teacher fears and anxieties that never get heard—fears associated with professional reputation, lost career opportunities, interrupted friendships, personality misalignments, insufficient resources, inadequate support, misguided professional learning, and doubts about the credibility and validity of proposed changes. As described previously, when such beliefs and feelings remain suppressed and unspoken, they influence the behavior and commitment of the teacher and thereby impact upon the culture in a detrimental way. Unless such a school culture can be changed it can become toxic—highly competitive, noncooperative, divided, and individualistic—which, ultimately, has a negative impact on every person associated with the school, not least being the students.

If we are serious about facilitating school improvement, then we must change how we understand organizational culture to that described in this chapter. But it must be realized also that the culture of a school is a reflection of the leadership provided by the principal. Therefore, the school principal must first understand how their school's culture is being formed and then attend to the culture by setting an example and by deliberately refreshing the culture.

To be able to truly understand their school's culture means that the principal must jettison the ineffectual ways of the past and embrace the description offered by this Theory of Organizational Ecology as illustrated in Figures 2.1 and 2.2. These figures detail how the culture is formed and the roles the principal must play in establishing the best culture for the school. Here it is explained how the culture of the school is a collective of the culture existing in each team as it works toward achieving its fundamental purpose. Ignored by the leader, these team cultures are often without the required values and norms that guide the team toward achieving the greater good of the school. For example, when working with schools, we have found many examples of bullying, exclusion, and competition for resources based upon historical academic hierarchies even in school senior management teams such as that of the Heads of Subject Departments Committee. Unless addressed, the inappropriate behavior generated by the unhelpful team culture sets the pattern for the behavior throughout the rest of the school. Therefore, the second step for the principal is to refresh and align the culture of such influential teams with the greater purpose of the school.

Simply stated, for schools to be functioning as a whole rather than the sum of its parts requires the personal input of the principal in a process of cultural realignment. Importantly, this process must include a values alignment process (see concluding chapter for an example) if behavioral expectations are to be met. These behavioral expectations unify the entire school by naturally connecting all teams, departments, and individuals through relationships founded on trust and the open sharing of information. Moreover, the values alignment process must be inclusive of values that encourage support, belonging, care, cooperation, and a community orientation. However, this pivotal part of achieving a refreshed, aligned culture will only succeed if the principal and other senior leaders model such values. As previously stated, it is essential that the work and relationships of the principal are reflective of the desired school culture. It is a wise principal who finds the time to lead the culture rather than be consumed by managerial tasks. It is the wise leader who prioritizes creating a deeply connected school because they know that this maximizes the benefits for all, especially for the students and their learning.

Concluding Comments

The notion that an organization is its employees, and not its structures, polices, or buildings, is often lost on leaders. Indeed, the organization's core purpose is achieved by the employees and not the strategic plan. This being so, then it follows that, ultimately, the quality and extent of the organization's productivity is significantly determined by how each employee feels about coming to work, whether or not they feel they belong in the organization, and how they feel about working with the other employees they have to engage with. The more the employee is looking forward to being at work, and willing, engaging, and collaborating with their co-employees, the more productive they will be. How an employee feels about coming to work and how willing they are to collaborate with others are key indicators of their perception of the organization's climate—how they feel about the organization's culture. In other words, it is the organizational culture that determines how committed the employees are toward achieving the core purpose and capacity of the organization. *Culture is king—it determines the way employees perform their work.*

Thus, it behooves the leader to understand their organization's culture. Organizational culture is the fabric of the organization, the matrix that enables relationships to develop and the organizational energy to flow. Hence it controls the organizational nutrients that can either sustain or deplete leadership intentions, practices, and efforts to create connectivity. Thus, the bottom line for organizational leaders is that they need to know that the workplace environment, and how each employee is engaging with it, creates the culture. This means that leadership and culture are inseparable.

Moreover, our view is that organizational leadership and culture are not only inseparable but also entwined; they are mutually dependent. A leader cannot avoid the influence of the culture but, simultaneously, neither is the culture immune from the influence of the leader. Rather, organizational leadership and culture are unequivocally interwoven. During our years of working with business, health, community, and educational organizations we have seen instances where the work of very good leaders and middle leaders has been stymied by an entrenched resistant culture to the point where some have left their organization. Also, we have witnessed organizations where a very vibrant and productive culture has been slowly but surely decimated by a new but aloof, self-opinionated, micromanaging leader. Futility and failure are the fruits of a leader who fails to continually monitor and appropriately tinker with their organization's culture—although, in the past, this may not have been possible because the means was not apparent. This is no longer the case.

This chapter has not only described a readily understandable explanation of how organizational culture is formed but also a resultant and practically applicable means for how it can be changed. In doing so, this chapter has also developed consistent coherency between contemporary leadership theory and organizational culture theory. In other words, seeing an organization as an ecosystem is effortlessly able to seamlessly align our understandings of both leadership and organizational culture.

However, more needs to be discussed about organizations before the full worth of the ecosystem perspective can be realized. Here, the concept of energy cannot be ignored. In a natural ecosystem the critical component of the connectivity flow is the nutrients that pass energy from one entity to the next, ensuring the whole system is connected and healthy. An understanding of the nature and importance of energy is an essential constituent of any ecosystem, including that of an organization. Chapter 3 will take up this crucial task.

3

Organizational Energy

Principle of Organizational Ecology # 3: Information and Knowledge Sharing Are Pivotal to Organizational Success

Introduction

Consistent with the ecological law positing that natural ecosystems are complex systems in which the flow, utilization, and storage of energy is a fundamental feature (Commoner 1971), we argue that organizational ecosystems are also complex systems comprising individuals, teams, and departments joined by relationships and connections along which energy circulates for mutual benefits. Hence, central to the perspective of the organization as an ecosystem is the acknowledgment that an organization's relationships are its pathways for maximizing the achievement of its core business. The better its internal and external relationships are the more likely it will maximize the achievement of its core business. The connections and relationships create energy, vitality, adaptability, strength, robustness, and harmony in the workplace which, in turn, fosters compassion, support, productivity, growth, and well-being. Thus, the energy of an organization results from its connectivity, its relationships, and its collective knowing and learning that flow through the organization.

Critically, in a connected organization, people are united in a collective commitment to achieve the purpose of the organization. This is the energy of the organization—it is the source of the flow of energy throughout. It is derived from the combination of the shared understanding of the purpose of the organization and what the organization stands for. Such a shared understanding is founded upon the gathering, utilization, and sharing of information and knowledge fundamental to not only each employee's sense of trust in the organization's culture but also their belief in the organization's success. From the development of a pervasive shared understanding comes shared commitments, beliefs, and efforts leading to avenues for collaboration and the sharing of ideas, possibilities, creativity, and innovation. This flow of energy must extend throughout the organization to allow for employee engagement, high-quality performance, cooperative teamwork, organizational learning, and organizational growth and rejuvenation.

It is in this way that we propose that the energy flows through an organization in the form of information and knowledge, which reinforces beliefs and values and provides support for new ideas and continuing success. Importantly, the flow of information and knowledge must be able to move throughout the organization and the mechanism for realizing this is the relationships among employees and across teams throughout the organization because these relationships provide the prerequisite for both creating and reinforcing the connectivity.

In support of these claims, this chapter begins by illustrating the primacy of information within the day-to-day functioning of an organization. Mostly, our literature draws attention to the physical, directly observable, and measurable aspects of an organization—employee performance, administrative structure, defined policies and processes, position statements—when promoting better leadership practices. In contrast, we show that the more fundamentally key consideration is information. This understanding is heightened when the chapter briefly describes the problems that can arise in an organization when information is limited or blocked. Once the pivotal importance of information for an organization has been established, the chapter proceeds to narrow the focus of information to that which is of most benefit—workplace knowledge: knowing how work is performed and how this performance can be improved. Furthermore, as the chapter explains, the full benefits to be gained from workplace knowledge can only be wholly accomplished when it is willingly, smoothly, and widely shared. When the organizational culture supports such knowledge sharing, the organization becomes energized. Employees are optimistic, enthusiastic, and committed, and performances and outputs are maximized. The chapter concludes by asserting that the sharing of information and knowledge provides the essential energy to the organizational ecosystem.

The Primary Importance of Information

Humans actively seek, gather, share, and consume information to a degree unattained by any other organism. Yet, people tend to take the communication of information process for granted. Despite living in social communities and witnessing people communicating all day every day, we may not recognize clear patterns or trends in dynamic channels of communication. We generally assume that the communication between two or more people is no big deal. It just works. Mostly, it is assumed that the information provided exactly equates with the information received. However, the reality is very different—the process of communication is decidedly complex and prone to misunderstandings and misconceptions.

Effective communication is a connection between people that allows for the exchange of information such as thoughts, feelings, and ideas, with the intention of gaining mutual understanding. This exchange is evidenced when a speaker sends a message to which a listener responds. It seems simple, but it isn't. There are many factors that ultimately determine whether the transfer of information via a particular communication is likely to be successful or not. There are internal factors that affect each person participating in the communication process individually, interactional factors that affect how information is sent and received between two or more people, and external factors that affect the extent to which the physical environment is conducive to effective communication. Each of these communication processes require increasingly sophisticated information-gathering, sensemaking, decision-making, and problem-solving strategies by both the presenter and the listener. However, the better people know each other the more effective and accurate is the communication.

Ideally, the transfer of information in an organization begins with the leader being the exemplar of regular, honest, and clear communication concerning the matters of organizational interest and activity. With the leader role-modeling the flow of information, communication throughout the organization is more likely to focus on matters pertaining to achieving the purpose of the organization such as successes, ideas, opportunities, problem-solving, developments, new external pressures or opportunities, new staff, and new skills. Essentially, this cannot be done well without getting to know people and teams in the organization, both socially and professionally. From the workplace performance perspective, people need to know what others in the organization are doing so they can see the connections with their own work and can see collaborative opportunities where possible. These relationships are critical for the organization because in knowing how the parts fit together, information about ideas and innovations can be distributed to other relevant parts of the organization. The challenge is for everyone to know what others are doing, particularly other employees who share the same workspace. Thus, it behooves team leaders and organizational leaders to cultivate interpersonal connections so that the information can flow freely and widely.

However, the receiving and interpreting of information is highly complex and influenced by both the person providing the information and the person receiving it, depending on a multitude of preconditions and perceptions of both parties. According to Lawton (2017), in his *New Scientist* feature article, if the information we receive does not match up to our personal knowledge and feelings, we confabulate—make up a story so that the information makes sense to us. The interpretation part of the brain integrates information from different parts of the brain and creates narratives to make sense of our world. "It rationalizes decisions we make based on subconscious processing that is not accessible to our conscious mind. And it fills in the gaps when information coming from the outside does not fit with our expectations" (Lawton 2017: 35). Simply put, in organizations, if employees are not kept fully informed, they will confabulate to overcome the uncertainty created by the paucity of information. Rather than building unity of purpose and practice, any deficient communication from the leader creates apprehension and suspicion among employees, which is counterproductive toward relationship connectivity. In other words, information and its effective transfer play pivotal roles in organizations. Moreover, information transfer impacts the receiver in different ways, including emotionally.

Information and Its Emotional Impact

What is highlighted by the previous discussion about the influence of information upon an individual is that information possesses the capacity to induce emotional reactions, which can be counterproductive. Relational interactions and emotions are reciprocally associated; the information provided via relational interactions elicits emotional responses that color the way we experience and evaluate the information and, consequently, our future interactions with the other person (Methor, Melwani, and Rothman 2017). Workplace relationships research demonstrates that discrete emotional expressions afford differentiated information to others about a person's beliefs, intentions, and feelings, which enables the others to make sense of their interaction with the person. For example, an individual's expression of contempt in a workplace relationship is a signal of disapproval, condescension, and exclusion; this expression leads the other person to infer that they should avoid or disengage from the relationship. Similarly, expressed anger signals coldness and potential aggression, suggesting others ought to move away, and expressed ambivalence can signal a lack of morality, suggesting to others that they should not trust the expresser. By contrast, expressing sadness signals warmth and a call for help, drawing others closer. Indeed, emotions such as sadness, gratitude, and appreciation have been shown to be important for the successful maintenance of relationships because these emotions signal cooperative and prosocial intentions.

Also, emotional information evokes complementary and reciprocal emotions in others that help individuals respond to significant workplace events (Methor, Melwani, and Rothman 2017). Because emotions can be contagious, expressions by one person can unconsciously spread to the others stimulating similar emotional states. Expressions of excitement can lead others to feel excited as well. One's expressions of anger or happiness in face-to-face negotiations have been shown to elicit similar emotions in those present. Other research suggests that emotional expressions can consistently evoke complementary but different emotions in others. For example, expressions of distress might elicit sympathy-related responses in others, and expressions of anger can elicit fear responses in others. In turn, these emotions will then influence the recipient's relationship-oriented attitudes and behaviors, such as the extent to which they cooperate and help others.

Based upon the information a person has gathered over time and across a chain of relational interactions, these emotional responses aggregate to form a summary of whether they assess a relationship as positive, negative, ambivalent, or indifferent. Positive workplace relationships are marked by pleasant interpersonal interactions and emotions and involve a genuine sense of relatedness and mutuality where both parties improve and enrich each other's experiences. These include workplace friendships, leader–employee relationships, mutual developmental relationships, high-quality connections, strong ties, and communal relationships. Furthermore, theorists propose that positive relationships are considered intimate, flexible, and resilient, are marked by feelings of positive affect and heightened vitality, are free of calculative or instrumental norms, and can withstand strain even when faced with demanding circumstances.

In contrast, according to contemporary research, the gathering of information by a person that leads specifically to purely negative relationships is rare in the workplace as it currently represents only 2–8 percent of interpersonal outcomes (Methor, Melwani, and Rothman 2017). Here, negative relationships are described as including difficult relationships, adversarial ties, toxic relationships, exploitative relationships, and enemies. Individuals in negative relationships have an enduring and recurring set of negative feelings and intentions toward each other and have interactions characterized by conflict, criticism, jealousy, rejection, and interference that are generally detrimental to the development of any form of a relationship. Often, these relationships are mutual and persistent, have a negative tone, and are likely to spiral downward when faced with difficult situations.

Another way to explore the influence of emotions within workplace relationships is provided by research focusing on the information gathered by lonely employees who have been unable to develop positive relationships with their co-employees. Within this research, loneliness is defined as "an aversive psychological state due to a person's perception of lacking satisfactory social relationships" (Lam and Lau 2012: 4266). The perceived number of workplace relationships is a contributing factor to feeling lonely: an employee will feel lonely when there are too few co-employees around them, as opposed to the crowded feeling when an employee is surrounded by too many co-employees. However, the perceived quality of workplace relationships may be more important than the number. As the desired number of workplace relationships varies among employees, loneliness has also been understood as the perception that one's existing interpersonal relationships do not meet one's expectations. Other scholars describe loneliness as painful feelings and emotional distress due to insufficient or unsatisfactory social connections or relationships.

Interestingly, research has also found that, rather than seeking new workplace relationships, a lonely employee usually adopts a passive approach of avoidance. When facing stress, lonely people are often likely to respond with pessimism and avoidance—a passive coping strategy that carries its own costs (Lam and Lau 2012). Normally, an employee who senses a lack of belonging and inclusion with others will attempt to behave in such a way so as to restore some form of social connection. On the other hand, research on social exclusion also suggests that when the information gained by an employee of any undesirable workplace relationship is essentially external—that is, unreasonable and unsavory opinions provided by others rather than being personally constructed—the isolated employee can react antagonistically by engaging in aggressive and harmful behaviors. But truly lonely employees are not able to react positively or antagonistically due to a deficit in their social skills. Lonely employees remain acutely aware of all forms of relational information but are too anxious to reestablish connections during interpersonal interactions. Thus, emotional distress is very common among lonely employees.

Within this workplace loneliness research, it has been found that, without satisfactory co-employee relationships, employees are more likely to perceive low social support in the organization. Perception of strong organizational support is conducive for employees to perform effectively at work and to reciprocate with discretionary behaviors. Also, when employees experience poor social relationships, they are less likely to feel they belong and identify with the organization. Prior research suggests that employees expect to seek affiliation and identification with organizations. Failure to do so reduces employee's organizational commitment and increases their intention to seek employment elsewhere.

Finally, because co-employees exchange critical work-related resources and information through formal and informal relationships, without a sufficient exchange of resources, lonely employees are less likely to perform their jobs effectively. In other words, information in all its forms plays a pivotal role in organizations from the individual employee's perspective but it also plays a pivotal role from a general organizational perspective.

The Pivotal Role of Information in Organizations

Given the acknowledged importance of employee relationships in the Theory of Organization Ecology, it is crucial to understand the way in which communication and information transfer influences these relationships. As discussed above, employees make decisions about who they wish to support and work more closely with based upon information gathered from many tangible and intangible forms of communication, especially when this concerns the relationships they have with their leader and/or supervisor and team members. Indeed, research shows that when another person's behavior appears as being inconsistent with one's own expectations, we reduce the inconsistency by changing our beliefs and attitudes about them so that the beliefs and attitudes reinforce our judgment about the inappropriateness of what we see as being discrepant behavior. For example, if an employee judges a leader's actions to be inappropriate leadership behavior then it is highly likely that they will not accept them as their leader and will, whenever possible, believe they are not compelled to fully comply with any of this leader's directives. This means that the employee is being influenced by information they are gathering about their leader in addition to that which the leader is deliberately providing to them.

While the leader might believe they are communicating all the right things that will reinforce their position and vision, the employee is being influenced by other information which undermines the very impression and motivation that the leader is striving to create in those they are leading. Hence, it is essential that a leader is fully aware of the sources of information that their employees are gathering and how this might be affecting not only their willingness to relate openly with their leader but also their organizational commitment, engagement, and performance.

Therefore, leaders should note that decades of research show people favor information that is consistent with their own conclusions, stereotypes, and decisions. This preference for consistent, as opposed to inconsistent, information is often referred to as a confirmation bias. From a functional perspective, this means that once an employee has established a poor impression of their designated leader or supervisor, they will continually seek confirming evidence to support this poor impression. It is extremely difficult for a leader to regain the trust, and thereby the full commitment, of an employee once they have created such a poor impression. It is imperative, then, for the leader to be ever conscious of the relational impression they are likely creating in the minds of those they are responsible for leading. It is essential that the leader is mindful of what information about the quality of their relationships and leadership is being received by each and every employee they are striving to lead.

Importantly, this information has less to do with what the leader actually says and far more to do with what others see the leader doing in comparison to what the leader has said. Human communication is based on a dynamic information exchange of both verbal and nonverbal information. Indeed, studies have shown how nonverbal communication carries between 65 percent and 93 percent more impact than the actual words spoken, especially when the message involves emotional meaning and attitudes. As the philosopher Friedrich Nietzsche claims, "all credibility, all good conscience, all evidence of truth come only from the senses" (1966: sec. 134, 278). How others sense or perceive the leader significantly impacts their acceptance, and thereby their success, as an organizational leader. Nonverbal information includes all the communication between people that does not have a direct verbal translation. This includes body movements, body orientation, nuances of the voice, facial expressions, details of dress, and choice and movement of objects that communicate. Time and space can also be perceived as having nonverbal information. Simply put, nonverbal information includes all the ways a leader might present and express their views, apart from the actual words they speak.

Thus, this nonverbal information is critically important in the workplace because perception is reality. When a leader sends a mismatched message—where nonverbal and verbal messages are incongruent—those receiving the message almost always believe the predominant nonverbal message over the verbal one. In other words, *how* the leader says something, and how they generally relate to those they are leading, has far more impact than *what* the leader says. Cognitive consistency is one of the most fundamental principles of social information processing. It plays a key role in almost all areas of social cognition, including persuasion, motivated reasoning, prejudice, and decision-making.

Cognitive consistency emphasizes that people have a desire to maintain consistent cognitions about other people. More recently, there has been a growing consensus that interpersonal cognitive consistency is a driving force in group behavior. The basic tenet is that, for a group to function well, group members need to be "on the same page," and to agree on how things should be done. In particular, interpersonal cognitive consistency plays a prominent role during group decision-making. Here individuals need to converge on one of several choice options. In line with this idea, there is evidence that the degree to which group members accept shared task information facilitates teamwork and effective group decision-making, thereby providing support for the idea that an important leadership outcome is to get a shared understanding about important team and organizational issues (as discussed more elaborately in Chapter 4).

Another way to recognize the pivotal role played by information in an organization and, therefore, the importance that a leader must give to it, is to examine what can happen when the flow of information is significantly diminished or blocked.

The Organizational Impact of Information Blockage

In toxic cultures, the flow of information is blocked because relationships are compromised, undermined, and diminished. Without strong, trusting relationships, information flow becomes blocked or sabotaged as are the relationships and connections within organizations (e.g., Figure 2.1) and beyond. The flow of information can be blocked in three ways: (1) information starvation, (2) information deafness, and (3) information strangulation and hoarding, as described in Table 3.1.

These information blockages are a consequence of the nature of the organization's culture impacting not only on how each employee feels about

Table 3.1 Cause and effect of blockages to the flow of information

Blockages of Information Flow	Examples of Causes	Effects on Information Flow
Starvation	Hierarchical secrecy caused by noncommunicative leadership, senior-level competition/cliques, and decision-making not occurring at the right level.	Confabulation—the production of false information: gossip, speculation, and rumor. The development of "us and them" cultural cliques creating competition and secrecy.
	Isolationism, individualism, and a lack of trust between the departments, teams, and the employees.	The organizational output becomes reduced to the sum of its non-unified, less effective parts. Secrecy—employees become far less willing to share information for fear of being disadvantaged or ignored.
Deafness	Micromanagement: Employees having no say in how their work is to be performed.	Disengaged employees become less committed to trying to do their best, leading to disinterest or avoidance in sharing information.
	Toxic culture leading to infighting, unfairness, competitiveness, disassociation, and isolation.	Can ultimately result in counterproductive behaviors such as attacks on others, falsifying facts, or spreading lies and conspiracies.
Strangulation and hoarding	Retribution where information becomes perceived as a source of power in the absence of recognition and influence. Individuals holding onto information for personal benefits including power, importance, and self-protection.	People do not get the information they need to do their work or to fully know what's happening. The hoarder increases self-interest and self-preservation.

the organization, as a whole, but also about how committed to and productive they are in their various roles. They are also very commonplace in teams and organizations. There are endless examples of hierarchical secrecy in organizations where the employees are not informed, particularly on matters that directly impact them. Similarly, information starvation is at plague proportions in organizations where management practices insist upon a "need-to-know" basis. However, strangulation is arguably the most covert blockage to the flow of information and the most commonplace. Typically, it presents as one person, due to their particular role or the key relationships they have been able to form, seeming to know everything that is going on in the workplace but keeping this information to themselves so that it can be used to maximize a future personal gain. Typically, these employees are not gossipers but rather hold onto information for reasons pertaining to their own security and for exerting power over others.

In order to heighten acknowledgment of the pivotal role played by information in an organization it is vital to consider a far more specific and, thus, instrumental form of information—workplace knowledge.

Information as Workplace Knowledge

According to Drucker (1993), knowledge is now recognized as a key factor in determining organizational success or failure. Knowledge can be broadly classified into two types: explicit and tacit. Explicit knowledge is that which can be articulated and stored independently and is constructible, expressible, and easily communicated. This form of knowledge can be gained from details, policies, formalized processes, facts, figures, statistics, literature, expertise, instructions, advice, guidelines, directions, counseling, notices, and documentation. However, information is more than facts, figures, and things that can be spoken, written, talked about, filed, analyzed, printed, or found online. This is tacit knowledge, which is inarticulable and intuitive, and is part of an individual's cognitive thoughts and perception. Importantly, a growing number of studies suggest that nonverbal communication has far more impact despite its increased complexity. For example, face-to-face communication between two people can include an exchange of up to ten thousand nonverbal cues in less than one minute (Gleeson 2017). Such nonverbal phenomena provide knowledge that helps to regulate communications such as guiding the relevance, appropriateness, sequencing, and depth of discussion in a group (Mandal 2014). These insights stress the importance in an organizational context for the leader to be attending to the influence of both forms of knowledge. In the past, most attention has been given to the explicit sources of knowledge delivery with little attention to the more powerful tacit sources.

Moreover, for information and knowledge to flow freely, people need to feel that they have a voice, that they will be heard, and that their opinions and knowledge will be considered and respected. For this to happen in an organization, the relationships between employees, teams, and leaders need to be trusting and respectful. People need to know that open knowledge sharing is practiced and encouraged in all aspects of the organization. Everyone involved in a particular issue should be included in problem-solving and decision-making from which the diversity and richness of work-life experiences of members are able to be accessed for contributing toward arriving at the best outcomes. In this way, knowledge is innovative and energizing. Where change is involved, employees have been well informed and included, thereby creating ownership of the change and eliminating suspicion, confabulation, gossip, and resistance. Simply put, how knowledge is shared throughout the organization is a crucially important consideration.

The Importance of Knowledge Sharing

It is essential to recognize that the exploration of employee knowledge is neither a simple nor incidental task. Humans aren't robots or automatons—they don't act like a preprogrammed machine. We don't just do as we are told or, for that matter, do things the way others might expect us to do them. We are self-determined. We seek autonomy. We each have our own skills and experience from which we see the world and go about our work. We wish to do things our way. In other words, we strive to weave our existing knowledge with that provided by others in order to choose how to respond to a given responsibility, task, challenge, or situation. Thus, within the confines of an organization, the challenge for the leader with regard to unifying each and every employee's work toward achieving the desired outcome is exceedingly complex because it requires the organization's capacity to reach an acceptable balance between uniformity and autonomy.

Micromanagement won't achieve uniformity because employees resent it and will strive wherever and whenever possible to undermine its directives. But absolute freedom and autonomy won't work either because the work output usually requires interdependency and the sharing of knowledge. Thus, the work that one employee completes influences the work that other employees then need to complete. This is the collective effort; it's the flow of energy in the team.

No one person, not even the leader, has all the knowledge required to solve every problem now faced by organizations. Hence, knowledge sharing is an unequivocal organizational necessity. Each employee needs to know the vision and purpose of the organization, and how their work contributes to achieving these outcomes. Also, each employee needs to know how their particular role and work contributes to the roles and work of others. Moreover, each employee needs to know how the work of others, which influences their own work, is to be completed to ensure a seamless alignment with their work. In addition, it is now widely accepted that, in today's complex organizational environment, leaders need to be deliberately seeking to be influenced in their decision-making by the knowledge possessed among their employees.

Arguably then, knowledge sharing is not just a necessity but rather it is the very heart of an organization. Without knowledge sharing an organization cannot function and, therefore, cannot exist. Thus, by inference, the success of an organization is directly related to the effectiveness of the knowledge sharing throughout the organization. It is through the capacity of the organization to widely and comprehensively share knowledge that its energy is able to flow smoothly and effectively. For leaders wishing to maximize the success of their organization, they need to gain a much deeper grasp of how well knowledge is being shared within their organization. Therefore, we argue that leaders need to understand the concept of organizational energy, and its derivatives, in order to better understand and acknowledge the importance of knowledge sharing.

Energy within an Organization

Information is fundamental to living systems (O'Connor et al. 2019: 3), and it is integral to how organizations function. Essentially, people are a key energy source in an organization. It is through people that information, especially in the form of workplace knowledge, can be readily transported throughout the organization via interpersonal connectivity and relationships. In this way knowledge manifests as the energy that flows through the organization from which innovation, organizational learning, growth, and improvement are made possible. This energy fuels and drives the understandings that employees have of their organizational culture as well as of each other regarding expectations of work and behaviors, urgencies, and priorities, and the rationale for the purpose of their work and the effort that is required.

The term, energy, has its origins in physics where it is used to describe the capacity of an object to do work. Mostly, it refers to a particular characteristic of a moving physical object to do "work" by causing a tangible impact on its environment. In an organization, the energy is also tangible in the achievements of the organization. Energy in an organization is its vitality, adaptability, strength, and robustness all of which are created, transformed, and boosted through connectivity throughout the organization.

At a very simple level, the application of the concept of energy to organizational life is acceptable because it is about "work." We are employed by an organization to do work. The work of an organization is to achieve its mission. Employees ideally work together to benefit the organization's productivity. Thus, it can be claimed that an organization's energy is its capacity to do its work, to achieve its mission. Also, to this end, this energy can be found in many different forms within an organization. Working together collectively to achieve a particular goal and to be acknowledged for the effort is in itself a source of energy for employees. So, too, is the remarkable ability of people to build a commitment to the cause through the belongingness, friendships, and care for the people they work with. Wars have been won unexpectedly on the ability of humans to unite for a cause. This is the energy that people release when they are collectively committed to a common goal. Just as energy in the natural world can exist in different forms depending on the particular circumstances of the object providing the source energy, the same can be said about an organization. Each and every organization has many different but necessary roles and responsibilities that attract employees with vastly different knowledge and skills, thereby creating a wide array of energies that the organization can use to complete its work.

In an organizational context, this generic understanding is given more substance when it is applied to the concept of motivation. According to Deci and Ryan (2008), intrinsic motivation is an internal drive that inspires us to behave in certain ways in keeping with our core values, our interests, our ambitions, and our personal sense of morality. These authors extend our understanding of intrinsic motivation by describing how it is formed from our wish to seek competence, autonomy, and relatedness. Competence is defined as our innate desire to learn, achieve, understand, and contribute to our environment. Autonomy is our wish to be able to not only act decisively according to our own free will but also to willingly and without restrictions persevere toward ultimate success. Relatedness highlights our instinctive yearning to find meaning and purpose in what we are doing by seeing how what we do, and how we work with others, is of significant benefit. Of particular note is the claim by Deci and Ryan that, unlike controlled external motivation that drains energy, autonomous internal motivation is a source of personal "exhilaration and energy" (2008: 184). This also shows how energy, in an organizational context, isn't just about the capacity of a person to perform their best but also to be a source of energy. We can become inspired and energized by the abundant enthusiasm, conviction, and performance of another.

Hence, each employee matters (see Chapter 6) because each person has a unique skill set, life experience, and an energy that they bring to their workplace. Bringing out the best in an employee allows them to reach their full potential, which is a win-win for the organization and the employee. It not only ensures that they are fully engaged and satisfied in their job but also creates opportunities for the organization to benefit from the employee's skills, experiences, growth, and creative thinking, and the positive energies that result. We often acknowledge that the level of a sporting team's energy, spirit, and performance can be lifted by the addition of a new coach or a new key player. In such circumstances, it is not simply that the new coach or player has excellent knowledge and skills but also that they are keen to help the team to perform better. They want the team to be more successful for the benefit of others as well as themselves, through their contribution. Similarly, in an organizational context, each employee feels that they want to contribute toward ensuring the organization's success. But this desire is more than the person's existing knowledge, skills, and experiences because it also includes their own career aspirations. People initially choose to be employed by a particular organization because they see a personal purpose for doing so. Psychology highlights how we each seek "self-determination"; we have the capacity and a desire to make our own choices and to control our own life. Thus, it is claimed that our sense of self-determination is a vital part of our psychological well-being. We have an intrinsic motivation to be the best that we can. If this is possible, then not only is the employee energized but others around them, who gain some benefit from their work, can gain additional energy too.

The concept of energy in an organizational context highlights the essential need for favorable connectivity between individuals and among team members working together in the organization. In a group sense, our level and sense of energy is significantly dependent upon the positive influence we perceive we are having on others. On the one hand, if we sense that our knowledge and skills have greatly helped others, especially if they have acknowledged and affirmed this to be so, then we are indeed likely to be energized and elated. On the other hand, if we are working in isolation from everyone else, it is likely to be far more difficult to reach the same levels of energy and elatedness, even though we might think we have done a good job. Simply stated, although we can each bring some energy to our organizational work, it requires the existence of favorable interpersonal connectivity—mutually beneficial relationships—in order to maximize its potential. Unlike the physical world in which different forms of energy can exist relatively independently, the work within an organization requires interpersonal cooperation and teamwork. In the organizational context, each of these different forms of organizational energy—administration, clerical, finance, leadership, professional, technology, maintenance, and so on—needs to be woven seamlessly together if the organization is to maximize its productivity.

As noted earlier, energy in the form of information and knowledge sharing can be withheld or misdirected as is summarized in Table 3.1. However, probably the major contributor to the loss of energy in organizations is disengagement. Indeed, Gallup (see Hartner 2017) estimates global costs of disengagement at several trillion dollars in lost productivity annually. Alongside poor performance and resistance to change, disengagement often manifests in organizations as withholding knowledge and information—effectively starving the organization of the energy it needs to ensure that its core business can be completed most effectively. The organization, as a whole, will underperform.

Such losses also occur when the leader is underperforming or performing in a way that is not considered acceptable to many of the employees. In this situation, so much energy is lost before it actually reaches down to support the everyday activities of the employees. If there is interpersonal conflict and noncooperation within the team, or if the individual becomes far too demanding and self-centered, then the organizational energy they are consuming will be far greater than the energy they are putting back into the organization. As a result, all those other employees that are depending on the outputs generated by this team or individual will gain far less energy—meaning that their work will be compromised as well.

In short, the flow of information and knowledge is a driver of the energy throughout an organization, and that can only happen through the degree of relational connectivity among all the employees. Moreover, the quality, diversity, and comprehensiveness of the organization's relationships directly influence the accuracy, power, distribution, and impact of the information and knowledge as it flows around the organization. The quality of the relationships within an organization influences the level and breadth of impact of the flow of information and knowledge, and thereby the amount of organizational energy throughout the organization.

Implications for Education

Through our work in higher education environments we became aware of a situation that exemplifies the key insight provided by this chapter. The particular institution in question had appointed two new professors to different discipline areas within the one faculty. The standard procedure at this university was that, on commencing an appointment, a new professor was provided with a $25,000 professional account. One professor assumed an individualistic perspective and spent the allocation on gaining an array of the most up-to-date technology equipment and software as well as on funding attendance at two international conferences. Over time, this professor became quite isolated from those working in the same department and had little influence and impact on colleagues. Indeed, colleagues tended to avoid contact both professionally and socially, and very few professional activities ensued. The potential energy to be gained from the professional account and the professor's presence in the department was mostly lost. Within two years, there was little to show that the appointment and the financial incentive had achieved anything other than disengagement, disillusionment, and disregard among the professor's professional colleagues.

The other professor chose a far more collective stance whereby the professional account was used to establish and support two distinctively different pilot research projects. Each project had a different research team, but each team included both experienced and early career researchers. One of the projects aligned with an international research program while the other focused on a local educational issue. Both projects achieved great success with numerous coauthored professional outputs and copresented national and international conference presentations. Needless to say, the energy among colleagues in this department was now tangible and inspiring. There were high levels of professional and social collegiality. Also, the university gained so much more from its initial investment than it had assumed. The personnel and financial energy provided by the university at the time of the appointment was significantly magnified through the personal and professional commitment of this professor, the quality of the relationships among the professor and department colleagues, the willingness of the department personnel to work together with purpose and commitment, and the commitment of all involved to share information and knowledge locally, nationally, and internationally.

Educational organizations are fundamentally about the sharing of knowledge and information for the growth and development of their students. Teaching and learning are social activities and as such information naturally flows as it must for knowledge to grow. The richer the information flow, the richer the teaching and learning experience. However, despite this imperative link between information and knowledge, often educational organizations—from schools to tertiary institutions—suffer blockages to the flow of information and creativity. As a consequence, the educational outcomes at all levels are being significantly diminished as the capacity of the organization is limited and therefore unable to fully meet the needs of its students. Instead of the collective need—the core purpose of the school or university—being met, it is being replaced by certain individual or group needs. Consequently, information is stifled, and suspicion and isolationism become the norm—causing a number of staff to leave or become disengaged and disconnected. Such staff keep their ideas to themselves and go about their work from a no-risk, task-based perspective. The sad reality for educators is that they are typically deeply committed to their teaching and their students—qualities that do not fit well in a disconnected, isolationist work environment. Thus, what all educational organizations require so that they can fully meet the needs of their students is for their leaders to have the wisdom, capacity, and commitment to create the organizational culture that is safe and inclusive, that is based on trusting relational connections, and one in which all staff share information in order to energize the organization to become a rich learning environment for all—leaders, staff, and students.

Concluding Comments

As described earlier, connectivity is fundamental to the health and sustainability of a natural ecosystem. Not only is each organism connected to other organisms in the ecosystem, but each connection enables the smooth flow of nutritional energy to each and every organism. Each relationship releases new energy, potential and new information. Each connection provides a crucial function toward maintaining the ecosystem. The same can be said of an organizational ecosystem too. But in this case the connection is not so much a physical component but rather the sharing of information. It is the sharing of information in its various forms that links together the work of each and every employee toward achieving the core purpose of the organization. It is through the sharing of information and knowledge that an organization becomes a unified system. And the excellence of the unification, the health of the system, depends on the quality of the flow of information throughout the organization.

Thus, the important message of this chapter is its emphasis on the critical role played by information and knowledge within the culture of an organization. Although the sharing of information is a common, natural, everyday human trait, within an organizational context it takes on far greater significance. While the potential effect and influence of verbal and nonverbal, tangible and intangible, explicit and tacit information on a person is the same no matter where it occurs, in the workplace the normal response can be constrained, suppressed, or modified by other mitigating criteria such as financial stability, career options, social connections, and travel proximity. You can't just walk away from a job, but you can walk away from another person or group. Thus, the person's observable response to some workplace information may appear far more compliant than it truly is. While the person's immediately observable behavior might convey a seemingly positive response, their more personally significant internal, unobservable values and beliefs could be quite negative. Consequently, over time this person will seek ways in which these values and beliefs can be explicitly realized by some form of defiant, resistant, or undermining action. In this way, an employee can have quite a marked impact not only on those working around them but also on the organization—depending on the degree to which, and the regularity by which, the person acts out any such behaviors.

Clearly, information and knowledge sharing are pivotal to organizational success. Leaders must understand the importance of how extensively employees are influenced by the way information and knowledge are shared throughout their organization, and how this plays a crucial role in the organization's success. It is essential for a leader to realize that the manner and pace of the flow of information throughout their organization is an explicit indication of the health of its culture.

However, a leader's capacity to monitor and enhance the flow of information throughout their organization is made far more complicated as the size of the organization grows. Clearly it is much easier for a leader to achieve this task in small organizations where they are in regular personal contact with each and every employee and often in the vicinity of most interpersonal interactions among employees. But, as the size of an organization grows, and its administrative structure becomes more stratified, there is far less opportunity for the leader to have such a pervasive influence. Most organizational structures include teams, departments, or sections in order to facilitate practical and logistical benefits. At the same time, there can be an erroneous subconscious assumption that the structure automatically creates effective communication channels and ensures the smooth and accurate transfer of essential information. Regrettably, the opposite is far more likely. Such structures can stifle, suppress, or block the flow of information to the lower levels of the organization. Therefore, the issues associated with information and knowledge sharing, and the impact of these on employee performance and organizational success, are magnified. It is to these issues that Chapter 4 turns.

4

Organizational Synergy: Teams Working Together

Principle of Organizational Ecology #4: An Organization's Success Is Greater than the Sum of Its Parts

Introduction

What is explicit in Principle #4 is the realization that the successful achievement of an organization's core purpose directly depends upon the development of a totally united organization. Organizational unity and, thus, synergy are not givens. Highly effectual interpersonal, intra-team, inter-team, and interdepartmental connectivity and collaborative relationships do not develop automatically. These need to be continually monitored and encouraged. If left to chance, then adverse social phenomena and behaviors are likely to eventuate, which will quickly diminish employee performance and organizational productivity.

Never before has such connectivity in organizations been more urgent than it has become in the past year. Although the Covid-19 pandemic very rapidly and effectively reshaped the socio-employment landscape, technology enabled organizations, sectors, and, indeed, populations to effectively adjust to the limitations of lockdowns and social-gathering restrictions. The long-term impact on the way we work is yet to play out over time. However, in places where restrictions are no longer in place, many employees are choosing to continue to work remotely for at least some of their working week. Working remotely, or away from office, is likely to continue to be driven by social factors, economic realities, and technological advancements. Thus, these employees will no longer cross paths, interact with, or work alongside others. Hence, the crucial necessity for information and knowledge sharing in such detached circumstances creates new leadership challenges.

In a workplace environment, in which all employees are physically present, a leader can mistakenly assume that everyone is united together. This is seldom achieved in organizations due to the application of essentially managerial processes that limit the development of the collectivist efforts required by a team. Such managerial processes are founded upon a poor appreciation of the essence of a team—the necessary culture of the team in order for it to function effectively, and the diversity of individual member responsibilities vital for team success. The challenges, then, for the leader are to fully and deliberately create the sense of the organization as a united team in all circumstances, including under exceptional circumstances requiring remote working and the absence of face-to-face interpersonal relationships. Thus, more than ever before, the leader needs to know what constitutes truly effective teamwork and how they can and must foster it. Interpersonal connectivity must be more deliberate, more focused on the collective effort, more inclusive, and far more relationally based right from the leader down through the rest of the organization.

Thus, this chapter provides practical insight into the potential cause of harmful disconnection and disunity in organizations and the way that it can be readily overcome. To this end, this chapter begins by illustrating how easy it is for organizations to become disunified and the detrimental impact that this can ultimately cause. This is a crucial insight because, as is then described, the utilization of teams as a dominant means for maximizing performance and productivity is now an unchallenged organizational practice. Given this prevalent use of teams, the chapter then proceeds to briefly examine what is required for maximizing a team's output. Here it is stressed how vital it is to attend not only to identifying and clarifying the team's task but also to equally address the genesis of teamwork—interpersonal connectivity, collaboration, and trust. Discussion then ensues regarding each of these basic characteristics of successful teamwork. The chapter concludes by applying these learnings to the presentation of the required leadership practices that appropriately support the establishment and continuation of effective and successful teams, and a united organization.

Disconnection and Disunity in Organizations

Organizations are complex systems comprising hierarchies of units or parts such as departments, teams, and individual employees all working to provide various essential contributions to the organization's core purpose. Typically, these parts are divided into broad functions or sections and more often than not, especially in large organizations, there are no ordinary everyday functional connections between them. Thus, in the absence of clear functional connectivity the organization is a collection of parts rather than a united whole. This is illustrated diagrammatically in Figure 4.1 as dotted arrows, which indicate diminished or absent connectivity throughout the organization.

In the absence of connectivity, the flow of energy via relationships in the form of shared information and knowledge cannot occur in a consistent or uniform way unlike that previously presented in Figure 2.1. As a result of diminished connectivity and energy flow, the effort people invest in their work is also diminished. As illustrated in Figure 4.1, this effort is the energy people contribute to the organization that manifests as the willingness of people to engage in their work, to share their information, to communicate ideas and expertise, to create relationships, and to be motivated to contribute toward the success of their team and organization.

The consequence of diminished effort is diminished results. Essentially, the greater the effort the better the results. Figure 4.1 shows the diminished

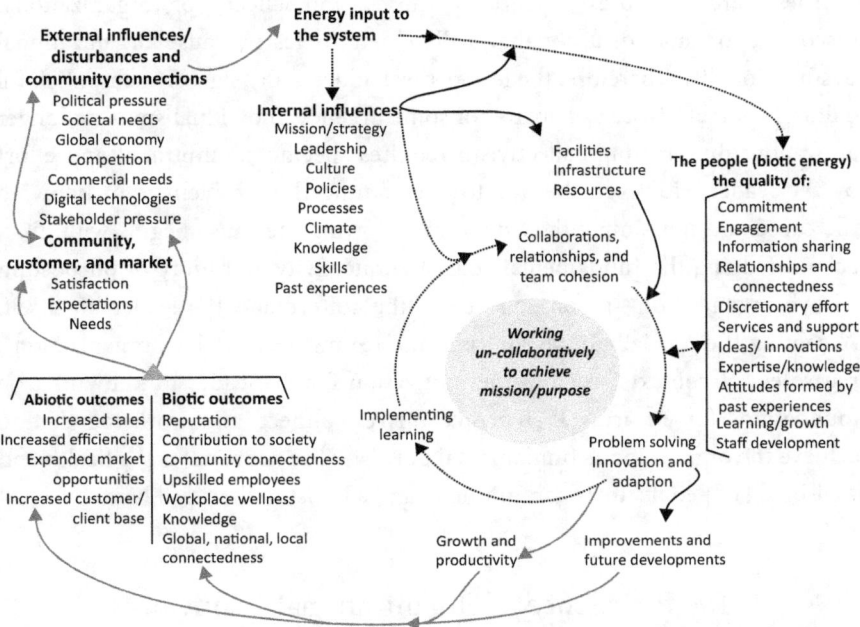

Figure 4.1 A diagrammatical illustration of the variable flow of energy (dotted and solid arrows) into and through a disconnected organization, and the subsequent reduced outcomes (grey arrows).

outcomes as pale arrows, impacting on the organization's ability to problem-solve, to learn and grow, and to create future developments. In turn, as illustrated by Figure 4.1, the organization's reputation is diminished, and this has a flow-on effect on external relationships and future opportunities. It is in this way that the disconnection between the parts in Figure 4.1 identifies where employee and team disengagement is likely to be occurring because there is a loss of energy that would otherwise have been available. Thus, the decreased energy in the ecosystem can only result in poorer organizational outcomes that can, ultimately, reduce the amount of future incoming energy.

Because organizations are artificially created social networks, a leader cannot assume, as explained in previous chapters, that each and every employee will naturally act in a civil, cooperative, friendly, and responsible way toward others in the workplace. Unlike a normally formed social friendship or relationship, employees won't necessarily develop a moral or even a professional obligation toward every other co-employee. Such an outcome takes time even if it does develop. The key insight, however, is that organizations need positively cooperative interpersonal relationships among its employees just as much as it does between each employee and the leader—and that is determined by trust.

These are ever-present serious causes and effects of organizational disconnection and disunity that will, if left to fester, cause organizational dysfunctionality. Therefore, the leader must address any sign of such unhelpful cultural characteristics as a matter of some urgency. Individualism is no longer an option. But creating collectivism requires specific commitment and effort by the leader. However, the key to overcoming this problem is in knowing the cause and not simply the symptom. Knowing the cause begins with, first, acknowledging the fundamental role of connectivity and unity of purpose in today's organization—a consequence of the culture and the leadership itself. Accepting the crucially important place of teamwork in today's organizations, regardless of context, provides the motivation for the leader to know its true foundations for ensuring that people thrive, connect, and work together to achieve the organization's fundamental purpose. The net result is the health and well-being of people, their commitment, and a boost in their productivity.

The Prevalence of Organizational Teamwork

In our current era of constant change, increasing technological complexity, socio-health restrictions, remote working, rapidly escalating levels of competition, and heightened stakeholder expectations, coupled with the rise of knowledge workers, the onus is now on organizations to evolve beyond the traditional ways of thinking and acting, and adopt new insights and new ways to perform in order to remain viable. Hence, ongoing organizational development is not an option; it is a necessity. Arguably, the most influential articulation of an organizational development process was that delineated by Peter Senge (1990) as the "Learning Organization." As defined (Senge et al. 1994: 3), a learning organization is one "where people continually expand their capacity to create the results they truly desire, where new and expansive patterns of thinking are nurtured, and where collective aspirations are set free." It is argued that a learning organization is one that promotes continual organizational renewal by weaving a set of core processes that nurture a positive propensity to learn, adapt, and change. Within his conception of a learning organization, Senge raised the importance of "team learning" as distinct from individualism and hierarchical control. Salas, Dickinson, Converse, and Tannenbaum defined an organizational team as "a distinguishable set of two or more people who interact, dynamically, interdependently, and adaptively toward a common and valued goal, objective, or mission" (1992: 4). The relevance of this definition echoes a crucial message through time and across socio-employment contexts. Now, more than ever, in the era of remote working, the concept of teams as learning, dynamic, interdependent, and adaptive is imperative for the success of organizations. Thus, team learning refers to the leadership action of providing employees with the opportunity and freedom to collaboratively devise, with other co-employees, new ways to increase the efficiency, quality, and productivity of their work.

Given that Senge's concept of a learning organization became the internationally acclaimed blueprint for how to achieve organizational improvement, teamwork has become ubiquitous for any organization seeking long-term success. In the light of the pressures on organizations in the 2020s, Senge's concept of a learning organization is arguably more important now than it was when he raised it three decades ago. This can be seen in data provided by Fay, West, and Patterson (2015) indicating that, in UK manufacturing, 65 percent of workforces are reported to be working in teams, while a US survey revealed that this figure is 48 percent across all sectors. Also, according to Deloitte's (2016) *Global Human Capital Trends* industry report, 45 percent of organizations are restructuring around teams and multi-team systems. More specifically, O'Neill and Salas (2018) highlight that teamwork is now widely applied in healthcare, space exploration, aviation, the oil and gas industry, the military, as well as in the corporate world. Nilsen and Curphy (2018) add to this by describing how their research found that 20 percent of their participants reported working in four or more teams at any one time within their respective organizations.

However, although the utilization of teamwork in organizations is now widely accepted and enacted, there has been little regard for how best to implement this cultural change. According to the research by O'Neill and Salas (2017), only 21 percent of leadership teams are performing at an outstanding level and 42 percent of organizational-level teams are performing poorly. Similarly, a McKinsey Report claimed that even at the top levels of an organization, developing an effective team is highly dependent on the soft interpersonal and relational skills of individual members. Importantly, this report concluded that "the soft stuff matters—and is hardest to get right" (Keller, Kruyt, and Malan 2010: 4). These data suggest that the ease of formation and the functioning effectiveness of a team are taken for granted. Perhaps leaders are lulled into neglecting such matters because they are surrounded by so many successful sporting, recreational, family, and social teams. They assume that cooperative and effective teamwork happens naturally whenever two or more people are brought together to complete a singular task. The reality is that teams in organizations are essential, they are here to stay, and leaders need to know a lot more about how to form and support them to be effective and successful.

The Team Approach Applied to Education

Unlike that witnessed in the corporate world, the move toward introducing a team approach in education has progressed far more slowly but it has taken root. The adoption of a team approach in school environments is fraught with difficulty mostly because the actual work of teachers is largely in isolated classrooms often with very limited professional interaction except within their own discipline or year groups. Hence, teams are often structurally defined for administrative and logistical ease rather than professional learning. Furthermore, teachers are time-poor, often working through lunch breaks and late into the day. Thus, the time spent with their professional peers is minimal compared with that in corporate organizations.

However, this traditional culture came to be questioned in the latter part of the twentieth century, which saw a growing international concern, particularly in Western nations, regarding the professional adequacy of their educational systems. The presumption was that the quality of education was deficient in preparing many students as future contributors to the national economy. Hence, governments began making educational systems, schools, and teachers far more accountable for how and what students learnt. Essentially, this was about expecting a dramatic improvement in teaching.

Consequently, questions arose concerning the individualized, isolated, and idiosyncratic culture of teaching both in terms of providing the best environment for improving teacher practices as well as enabling the adoption of any significant changes. It was argued that, left to their own resources, in which they did not know what they did not know, the individual teacher was not only unaware of how to improve their teaching but also they were far less inclined to see the need to change how they taught. It was into this sea of professional uncertainty, risk, and reluctance that a number of educational researchers began to promote the concept of a team approach to professional learning in education, which came to be known as the professional learning community. For example, Shirley Hord, an acclaimed professional learning community pioneer and authority, drew upon Peter Senge's work promoting a learning organization and defined a professional learning community as "a professional community of learners in which the teachers and its administrators continuously seek and share learning, and act on their learning. The goal of their actions is to enhance their effectiveness as professionals for the students' benefit; thus, this arrangement may also be termed communities of continuous inquiry and improvement" (1997: 1). However, interest and support for the concept remained sporadic until the early 2000s when its credibility began to gain a growing amount of research support.

For example, it was during this time that Stoll and colleagues asserted, "International evidence suggests that educational reform's progress depends on teachers' individual and collective capacity and its link with school-wide capacity for promoting pupil's learning. Building capacity is therefore critical. Capacity is a complex blend of motivation, skill, positive learning, organizational conditions and culture, and infrastructure support. The Professional Learning Community promises to achieve this aim" (2006: 1). The basic premise is a teacher can learn more about teaching that really improves student learning by cooperatively working with their colleagues in deconstructing, analyzing, and critiquing their own teaching practices, and that of others in the professional learning community, in order to create and construct new and enriching approaches for developing and encouraging student learning. A school-wide professional learning community was envisaged as a site of team-based teacher reflection on practice and collaboration in support of student learning. On site, teaching-centered, student-learning-focused, team-based professional learning was considered far more effective than the previous individualized, externally provided, generally focused methods.

During the ensuing years, research has shown that the development of team-based professional learning can have a wide array of very positive benefits for a school. For example, drawing on available research literature, Kalkan (2016) describes how working closely and collaboratively with teaching colleagues can positively affect student achievement, teacher morale, teacher effectiveness and job satisfaction, and school culture and climate. Furthermore, she highlights how this form of teaching teamwork has been shown to decrease teachers' isolation and loneliness while increasing their working capacity to ensure a productive student learning culture through improved quality of teaching. Kalkan adds that, in such a team-based approach to professional learning, teachers experience shared leadership, become aware of a distinct purpose, strengthen their commitment to the goals of the school and its mission, and strengthen their commitment to student learning.

But there is also ample research literature acknowledging the deficiencies of the team approach in education. Perhaps due to the previous history of unsuccessful strategies designed to improve teaching and learning, many schools and school systems jumped at introducing a professional learning community without first considering its true nature. Indeed, some educational jurisdictions went as far as to mandate the introduction of a professional learning community in each of its schools. Hence, many of these initiatives introduced a structural rather than cultural approach to creating a team-based professional learning culture. Teachers were grouped together usually based upon class or discipline similarities, meetings were scheduled, tasks were assigned, and outcomes prescribed. This was a management approach to the introduction of a professional learning community and, not surprisingly, largely failed to live up to expectations.

Why did these initiatives fail? These failed because <u>many</u> of these team-based professional learning initiatives focused too much on the accomplishment of predetermined aspects of teacher practice to the detriment of building the required deep interpersonal relationships. The key ingredients for the success of a professional learning community are trust, cooperation, openness, meaningfulness, and honesty. As Tschannen-Moran states, "professional learning communities are based on trust that teachers and principals will act with the best interests of students in mind by researching best practices and pursuing data to bolster decision making" (2004: 107–08). These are cultural elements that can't be externally imposed or created. It takes professional courage and resilience for a teacher to allow others to view, critique, and analyze their teaching practice. In these circumstances, a teacher can feel that their professional credibility and reputation are being challenged. Thus, the way in which the professional learning community is formed, the team culture that it ultimately nurtures, and the school culture in which the team operates must provide the participating teacher with a deep sense of safety, purpose, and benefit or else their commitment and ongoing engagement will be superficial and the outcome inconsequential.

What this means is, like that now being conceded in the organizational research literature as described above, the development of an effective school-wide and team-based professional learning culture is very dependent upon the quality of the teamwork. In other words, each organizational or school leader needs to take personal responsibility for fostering and supporting the quality of the interpersonal relationships within and between the various teams in their organization or school. Knowing how to do this begins with the leader comprehending what essential characteristics underpin interpersonal connectivity and cooperation within teams and across the organization.

The Nuts and Bolts of Teamwork

An effective team must be successful not only in completing its task but also in performing collaboratively as a team through being in unison in understanding the fundamental purpose of the work of the team and how it will achieve the best results. Teams are collectivist; individualism and the notion of a team are mutually exclusive. A group of individuals is not a team by any stretch of the imagination because a team functions on socio-relational phenomena such as reciprocity, collaboration, fairness, and support. A group of individuals, on the other hand, are competitive with each other as each focuses on achieving their own tasks rather than the team's purpose.

For teams to be successful, they not only need to specifically understand and believe in the purpose of their work but also be connected with each other so that the team learns, innovates, adapts, and grows together. Thus, success in achieving the team's purpose involves the performance of specific actions and responsibilities that team members need to complete in order to produce the expected practical outcomes of the team goals as aligned with the organization's core purpose. These actions and responsibilities represent the work-related activities that individuals or teams engage in as an essential function of their organizational role. However, the successful performance of these task-specific actions and responsibilities relies heavily on how well the team gels together. Here, attention to the team's performance focuses more on the collaborative behaviors and actions of both each individual and the team, as a whole, as influenced by beliefs, attitudes, knowledge, and openness.

Despite research urging the adoption of a contrary stance, most often it is the task side of a team's performance that gains the most attention from leaders. This research highlights how having an extensive knowledge of the task at hand, and all of the required work-related skills and knowledge present across all of the team members, doesn't guarantee team success. A team can fail to achieve its assigned tasks and responsibilities if its members cannot successfully share knowledge, coordinate behaviors, and trust one another. In fact, individuals who have extensive task-relevant expertise are still vulnerable to poor team outcomes if the team culture is inadequate and non-collaborative. In sum, "teamwork is an adaptive, dynamic, and episodic process that encompasses the thoughts, feelings, and behaviors among team members while they interact toward a common goal" (Salas et al. 2015: 600).

Connecting and collaborating to achieve a common purpose is not restricted to individuals within teams as it is also imperative that there is connectivity between teams as they work to contribute to the common purpose of the organization. Simply put, teams cannot be successful in isolation from each other and from the rest of the organization because, as shown in Figure 4.1, any degree of isolation strangles the flow of information and energy thereby reducing organizational productivity and growth. Isolated teams result in competition between teams for resources and opportunities. Competition breeds secrecy of ideas and innovations; it breeds unfairness, it stifles collaboration, and limits cooperation. The responsibility for removing competition between teams lies with the leaders of each team and the leadership team. The lived reality of a disconnected, ununited leadership team is magnified throughout the organization. If the leadership team fails to have trusting relationships, fails to work collectively around their purpose as a leadership team, competes for resources and status, and is seen to be in competition with each other, then the rest of the organization will follow suit. There will be no trust between the parts of the organization, no relational connectivity, no sharing of knowledge and information, and no overall success.

Interpersonal Connectivity and Cooperation in Organizations

Trust across an organization both requires and creates interconnectedness, relationships, and collaboration between the teams or departments of the organization. Without this connectivity, individuals and teams become isolated from the bigger picture and thus the culture of the organization becomes progressively disunified. Without unity there is no trust throughout the organization, and without such trust, suspicion arises and competition between teams becomes a "them and us" norm. It leads to in-house fighting at all levels of the organization and a complete breakdown in the flow of information, resources, ideas, and energy between teams. When this happens the individual employee's trust in the organization is severely diminished and teams operate in increasing isolation from each other. One employee we interviewed during an organizational cultural review summed this up nicely as "work makes sense to me in my department, but outside of my department is like stepping into another world."

But this highly collaborative and productive interconnectedness does not happen automatically in teams or between teams—it needs to be deliberately orchestrated and modeled by more senior teams and supported by the organizational leader. This requires knowing more about how a team functions and how a leader can actively enhance this functioning without having to take full charge.

The greater the connectivity and cooperation within and between teams, the more likely they are able to reach optimum levels of effectiveness and achievement. Albrecht describes this as the realization of syntropy, which he defines as "the coming together of people, ideas, resources, systems, and leadership in such a way as to fully capitalize on the possibilities of each" (2003: 42). As described above, organizations including schools have not as yet been able to reach the reality of syntropy.

The first step on this journey to syntropy is to recognize the uniqueness, indeed the abnormality, of the organizational team. We suggest this is a result of the nature of both the employment contract and the role description outlining very individualistic work expectations. While that makes sense in employment law and human resource processes, it does absolutely nothing but impede collectivism, team commitment, and syntropy because each person has their own legal description of what they are to do. Rather than creating collectivist teams, it creates a team of individuals. Oddly, organizations cluster people with similar role descriptions and call them a team, and then wonder why they have a problem. This is a major issue through the corporate world. A quick online search on "Creating High Performing Teams" provided over one billion site options, which is indicative of the universal scale of the problem.

Why are teams such a problem? The answer—organizations have got this very wrong; they separate the individuals from the team by giving each of them their own purpose for which they are responsible for and monitored against, rather than giving the team the responsibility of achieving the team purpose. It's a no-brainer; no sporting club, for example, would tolerate a team of individuals. Rather, successful sports teams have a single aim to achieve, to be the best they can be. Thus, organizations must put an end to their focus on the individual contract and performance management, and shift to supporting the relational and creative mechanisms that ensure teams are successful.

Historically, humans are social beings. We are tribal (Lawton 2017); 90–95 percent of our evolutionary history has been in small groups/bands (Sapolsky 2017)—which has worked very well for the success and survival of homo sapiens essentially because the success of the individual is enhanced by belonging to a group, and the success of the group is enhanced by the success of its members. A group/band grappling with its environment for food, safety, and shelter is a better option than an individual going it alone. It is a win-win strategy for survival. Survival is serious business; it is not left to randomness but rather is controlled by the cultural norms of the group that are in place to guide decisions and actions around survival. In a contemporary context, humans are still doing what humans have always done. We seek belonging and socializing and being a member of desired groups. In contrast, isolation is often used as a punishment, a banishment from connecting with others with whom we have connections. Belonging to groups is as important now as it was fifty thousand years ago.

However, although we are genetically programmed to belong to groups, as noted in Chapter 2, organizations are abnormal gathering places in multiple ways. First, unlike other socio-relational groupings such as families, sports teams, and other community groups, most workplaces are populated by individuals each with their own motivations for being there and their own aspirations for staying. Reasons may range across a broad spectrum from career aspirations and financial gain to convenience and flexible working options.

In addition, the individualism of modern Western society is transferred to organizations. Rather than striving for the benefit of all, such as in a tribal situation or a sporting team, most organizations have "stayers," employees who are only interested in what is best for themselves. Often these people have worked in the same organization for many decades and consider they are holders of the rightful corporate/school/organizational knowledge. However, the reality is that they are often stuck in their outlook by a fixed mindset and possess a limited set of life-work experiences to challenge their narrow views and opinions. Hence, their best strategy is to stay put, undermine progress, and concentrate solely on doing what they have always done without needing any help or facing any hindrance from anyone else.

Also, as noted in Chapter 2, relationships are imposed on people in workplaces. This happens in at least two ways. First, people are employed based on judgments about their relevant workplace knowledge and skills. This is more about what the new employee can do and very little to do with who they are as a person and how well they might be able to get along with the existing employees. Essentially, this means that strangers are thrown together and expected to immediately connect and cooperate with the other. In life, generally, we do not assume that we can get on with everyone. We are each very selective about who we are willing to develop a relationship with. But often in a workplace, it is assumed that everyone can readily get along with everyone else. Secondly, it is most common that individuals are placed in workplace teams based upon the opinion of those in higher positions within the organizational hierarchy. Mostly, this decision is formed upon the nominated team member's workplace knowledge and skills or past experiences in previous teams being considered a necessary requirement in light of the team's prescribed tasks and responsibilities. But such a choice does not consider the interpersonal connective capability of the nominated person and whether or not they will be able to fully utilize their knowledge, skills, and past experiences in the team.

Another interpersonal connectivity abnormality, which can easily arise in organizational teams, is that people are very quick to form "*Us versus Them*" dichotomies when regularly having to associate with many and diverse others (Sapolsky 2017). We are so prone to form "Us and Them" perspectives that it can even form over something as trivial as the color of another person's shirt or the way they speak. But more serious examples can form from unconscious or conscious personal biases associated with diversity of ethnicities, ages, genders, religions, capabilities, life circumstances, and life experiences. In an organization, such disunity can manifest in a team as in-group and out-of-group cliques as well as inter-team disconnection and competition. These divisive dichotomies are commonly seen in organizations, particularly in large organizations that have multiple departments, branches, or faculties. However, smaller organizations can also see the formation of social cliques. An added complexity is diversity of peoples that work together and the tensions that our unconscious biases bring to the way we view the differences in others.

Also, the transactional nature of the contract that employees have with their employer, often embedded in employment law, tends to engender highly mechanistic management rather than relational leadership practices. It becomes far too easy for the employment contract to become the motivational mechanism. Perform according to your employment contract or you face dismissal. The employee becomes a resource to be managed. Thus, the go-to response by Human Resources personnel is mostly around performance management regimes, which adds to the problem because it is simply and clearly the wrong approach. According to Bauman (1992), individuals naturally desire to be self-determined and self-monitoring; therefore, enforced accountability procedures, such as performance management, are likely to undermine the natural and more powerful self-accountable, self-motivating practices. As Rock, Davis, and Jones put it, "if you want a high-performance organization, you have to reverse the destructive effects of conventional performance management" (2014: 1). Such simplistic practices work against collectivism as it fosters individualism, thereby effectively undermining interpersonal connectivity and the collaborative work of teams.

Thus, workplaces provide atypical relational environments for people to attempt to navigate, survive, cooperate, and flourish. Given that a team's or an organization's success should be greater than the sum of its parts, if these parts are not working well together then the collective potential of the team or organization is never reached. Hence, it behooves organizational leaders, regardless of their specific context, to not only acknowledge this truth but also to know how to overcome the presence of any relational uncertainty, tension, or division among employees, and within and across teams, and to confidently act so as to develop positive and constructive interpersonal connectivity within teams and throughout the organization.

Such confidence comes from first knowing more about the essential relational ingredient that is missing when dysfunctional connectivity is present either among employees or within teams. Then, it stems from knowing and enacting the pivotal leadership practices that are able to develop and support collegial collaboration in teams and throughout the organization. Any leader who ignores monitoring and influencing how well employees and workplace teams are cooperating together is inviting trouble. Having the capacity to be aware begins with acknowledging the importance of trust in successful organizational teams.

The Importance of Trust in Successful Organizational Teams

The previous chapters expanded upon the contemporary understanding of leadership by highlighting how its genesis is in mutually beneficial relationships and briefly raised awareness of the crucial role played by interpersonal trust within this relationship. However, this description largely assumed an individualistic perspective—how the individual employee is affected by the level of interpersonal trust they have in their leader. This section extends this discussion of interpersonal relational trust in the workplace beyond simply between the employee and the leader to that between co-employees and among the members of workplace teams.

According to Costa, Fulmer, and Anderson (2018), more than four decades of research has unequivocally shown that trust in teams is the essential relational ingredient for the effective functioning of all forms of workplace relationships. This research has illustrated how trust becomes especially relevant in any organizational environment where high interdependence, close cooperation, teamwork, and requirements for flexibility and creativity predominate (Salas, Sims, and Burke 2005). With the ever-expanding use of team-based work in our organizations, the study of trust in workplace teams has gained momentum, and considerable research has been accumulated, particularly at two specific levels of analysis—interpersonal trust between individual members at the individual level and group trust that is shared among members at the team level. Although a unified definition remains elusive, scholars researching trust in teams largely recognize trust as a psychological state that is influenced by the complex interrelations between personal and group expectations, intentions, and dispositions (Fulmer and Gelfand 2012).

Team trust involves a continuous social process of sensemaking, interpreting, signaling, and reciprocating, and develops and emerges over time. The dominant theoretical perspective informing insights into team trust is social exchange theory, which proposes that the socio-relational behavior is the result of an exchange process between persons whereby the purpose of the exchange is to maximize personal benefits and minimize costs. Where team trust is strong, there are high levels of reciprocity in the social exchange between team members along with reinforcing social exchange cycles where initial experiences of trust play a critical role in subsequent trust development. Trust can decrease when the assumed reciprocity is violated even though beliefs of imbalanced exchanges may be realistic or imagined.

However, another perspective is that of social informational processing theory, which suggests that an individual's perceptions and attitudes are influenced by the culture in which they are embedded. According to this theory, the team culture shapes trust among its members at the individual level and plays a role in facilitating the emergence of trust at the team level through team members sharing important information with one another and by reaching a consensus in their thinking. If the team culture is judged by each member as being inclusive, supportive, open, respectful, and purposeful then it is most likely that each member will trust that they can openly share their thoughts, opinions, beliefs, and experiences, which, in turn, reinforces the productivity of the team. In this way, the culture can be seen as having exerted a positive influence upon personal and team sensemaking by guiding the team members toward establishing a consensus about what to pay attention to, what is expected of each team member, and how the team will function best toward successfully fulfilling its purpose.

An additional understanding about trust within teams is provided by the two theories of trust propensity and social categorization. The trust propensity theory posits that the level of trust that a team member is willing to give is strongly influenced by their existing disposition to trust different types of people across different situations. People do not each share the same propensity to trust another person. A person's willingness to trust another person is strongly influenced by an array of idiosyncratic principles inclusive of, but not limited to, family upbringing, socio-emotional maturity, experiences of sociocultural diversity, and past experiences of outcomes resulting from trusting others, while social categorization theory argues that individuals group their self and others into social categories, such as by knowledge, skill, gender, perceived competency, or past experiences. This categorization can arise out of observations, interpretations, and differences in opinions with other team members. Each category incorporates identified similarities, which are then used as a means for defining their in-group—those team members who they will readily trust and collaborate with. The outcome to be learnt from these theories is the knowledge that trust develops more naturally and quickly in teams where members are promptly seen to have commonalities and so are comfortable interacting with each other. Hence, a key responsibility for the leader is to adopt strategies that hasten the recognition and promotion of team member commonalities and tolerability in order to accelerate interpersonal comfort and collaboration.

Meyerson, Weick, and Kramer (1996) have also developed the concept of "swift trust" to explain how problem-based teams can enjoy instantaneous high levels of trust, even in the absence of the other sources of rationalized trust as described above. This concept suggests that individuals can build trust initially by importing expectations of trust from role-based criteria with which they are familiar. In essence, swift trust emphasizes the strategically desirable specific knowledge and expertise that each member brings to the team, thereby de-emphasizing a dependency on the development of socio-relational components of trust. For example, where a team is tasked with solving a critically important organizational problem quickly, team trust can be formed based upon the team-wide recognition of each team member's strategically important knowledge and performance capabilities that are immediately identifiable as being essential in solving the assigned organizational problem. Importantly though, while swift trust can provide the necessary initial or early impetus to team interaction, this level of trust requires ongoing verification that the team is able to manage other more rudimentary interpersonal relational vulnerabilities and expectations. Swift trust can be maintained only so long as the team members communicate enthusiastically, each member lives up to expectations, and the team is achieving its assigned task.

While, on the one hand, each of these research-based theories provide a specific insight into what can be influencing an individual employee's or a team's trust willingness and capacity, on the other hand, the combined impact of these theories emphasizes the diversity and complexity associated with the concept of trust within an organizational context. Indeed, some might argue that this diversity and complexity renders it impossible for a leader to manage and control the levels and vagaries of trust in the organization. This might be so from a traditional leadership perspective, which tended to assign specific responses to each and every responsibility. However, when organizational leadership and culture are viewed from an ecological perspective, this is not so.

Leadership of Team and Organizational Trust

Clearly, organizational leaders who choose to ignore the powerfully influential roles of connectivity, trust, and relationships, both within the constructive functioning of teams and across teams, do so at great risk to the organization's core business. What must be realized by leaders also is that no organizationally mandated rule, policy, or process will ever achieve anywhere near the optimum level of connectivity, trust, and relationships. You can't manage the achievement of these outcomes. And micromanagement makes it even worse because this immediately suggests that the leader can't trust the employees; it is the antithesis of what is required. Leaders must first show trust in others in order to have trust in them returned and for interpersonal trust to become an integral characteristic throughout the organization.

How can the leader build team trust? Simply put, the leader must become a fully participating member of the team they lead, clarify the work of the team, grow the capability of the team, and connect the team to the organization through inter-team connectivity. As will now be described, this doesn't mean the leader has to take full control.

The organizational leader must engage in the team's activities to some degree in order to consolidate the development of the intra-team's connectivity, trust, and relationships. You will recall, from our argument in Chapter 1, that a leader is readily able to develop interpersonal trust between their self and each and every employee through the four steps of (1) being an integral member of the organization, (2) regularly affirming and championing individual and organizational performances, (3) growing both employee knowledge and skills and organizational learning, and (4) preparing employees and the organization for future demands. We now propose that these same four steps can be used to essentially guide the leader in understanding how best to develop team connectivity, relationships, and trust, thereby gaining the highest performance from their organizational teams.

First, being an integral member of the team doesn't mean that the leader leads the team but rather that they are involved in establishing the team. This includes ensuring the team understands its purpose, clarifying the roles required of team members, describing the relevant knowledge and skills brought to the team by each member, explaining the team's avenues of communication, explicating the resources available to the team, proposing a possible timeline, discussing likely milestone achievements, and responding to other questions raised by team members. Overall, this is about encouraging swift trust as much as possible. Also, all of these actions aid in the important development of sensemaking about the team's goals and functioning while also ensuring that there is far greater uniformity in how each team member interprets the team's roles and tasks and signaling how the team might go about completing its purpose. The worth of each of these outcomes was highlighted in the previous section as being crucial in the development of team connectivity, relationships, and trust.

Secondly, the leader must keep regularly meeting and communicating with the team in order to be able to affirm and champion team performances. This is not only to directly acknowledge team member and whole-of-team performances that are tangible steps toward achieving the team's purpose but also, by doing so in public arenas as well, to strongly enhance pride, satisfaction, motivation, and commitment within the team and make everyone in the organization along with its stakeholders fully aware of the team's valuable work and its contribution to the organization's core business. In addition, such actions consolidate the team's trust in their leader, which enhances intra-team trust too. It also significantly fosters the organization's integrity and reputation with its clients and stakeholders, which, in turn, increases organizational trust among all employees.

Also, by regularly meeting and communicating with the team, the leader is in a far more favorable position to be able to grow both each team member's knowledge and skills along with their capacity to work together as a united and high-performing team. This is about using empowerment-building and conflict-minimization aligned actions to ensure trust propensity, knowledge sharing, consensus reaching, and reciprocity are maximized. This allows the team to work more autonomously but without acting irrationally or irresponsibly. It is also about becoming aware of, and responding promptly to, a need to provide some essential professional learning or additional resources to team members and/or the team well before such deficiencies begin to undermine team connectivity, trust, relationships, and performance.

Finally, by maintaining a close and supportive relationship with the team by regularly meeting and communicating with them, the leader is in a prime position to aid the team in overcoming any perceived future demands. Through the ongoing mutually beneficial relationship between the leader and the team, the team's progress can help to clarify potential obstacles to the achievement of the team's initial purpose. Through the sharing of beliefs, perspectives, and existing knowledge by all team members with the leader, a meaningful and comprehensive dialogue can provide lucidity where initially there was only uncertainty.

Connectivity and Teamwork in Action

If you are the leader, who are your colleagues and where do you belong? Surprisingly, this question is not straightforward for many team leaders or organizational leaders. The answer to this question is as follows: you belong to, and have colleagues in, at least two teams: (1) the team you lead, and (2) your team of fellow team leaders throughout the organization. This might be the senior leadership team or a middle management team.

Confusion for leaders arises in those organizations that are disconnected and/or follow hierarchical managerialism. Although you might well be connected in the team you lead, you and your team can be isolated from other teams. You might be an active member of the team you are leading and be creating good connectivity in the team but, at the same time, fostering isolationism from other teams and the rest of the organization through the lack of connection you have with the leaders of other teams in the organization. In the latter situation of hierarchical managerialism, leaders can position themselves outside and above the team they lead and connect better with their fellow team leader group.

For example, during one of our consultancies we observed that this particular senior leader in a large organization was a member of two teams—a member of the senior leadership team and the leader of a large department within the organization. This leader was highly respected by those in his large department and by the team leaders within his department. He was technically capable and experienced, and relationally connected well to the staff in his department. He was very much part of the group and regularly worked with each team. However, he was often roadblocked and under-resourced due to the competitive culture in the senior leadership team. This team was divided and antagonistic toward each other, and so the whole organization suffered the consequences of this disunity. In many areas of the organization, staff were struggling with the constant competition between the various departments.

During our investigation of the problem in the senior leadership team it emerged that there was one member who was highly competitive and divisive—a powerful, controlling force in the team with an eye on promotion. Subsequent actions taken by the chief executive included uniting the senior team around a shared understanding of the purpose of the organization and the commitment by each team member on how to achieve it. This included a commitment to senior leadership team unity through finding ways to work better together as a team. Within a relatively short period of time, senior team members began to share positive comments about how much more meaningful and enjoyable their work had become due to their personal commitment to the unification of the team. Trust, between team members and in the strength and purposefulness of the team, began to form.

Indeed, plans were made to maximize collaboration and the sharing of resources across departments. This plan required staff members to interact with staff in other departments and other teams, who they had previously never connected with. Within three months increased connectivity was obvious in many places throughout the organization but some areas were lagging in this regard. Also, the general employee attitude improved—the culture had become much friendlier and collaborative. Resources were now being shared fairly, which meant that the staff felt that they could fully engage with their work and the resources were actually being better utilized overall. After a year, there were still signs of some lingering disconnection but only at an individual level—staff who simply could not move on to a relational way of doing their work.

Implications for Schools

One of the fascinating yet frustrating understandings that we often gain when working with schools and tertiary institutions is that their leaders do not apply relevant classroom knowledge to guide their leadership practice. A prime example of this speaks directly to the key message of this chapter. As advancements in pedagogical knowledge embraced a move away from a sole dependency on the individualized learning of students to include group and cooperative learning among the students, teachers soon learned that the students first needed to be taught how to structure group-based cooperative learning. The students needed to learn how to best work cooperatively together before the desired levels of learning could be achieved. In our drive to create an individualized world it seems we have forgotten how to maximize cooperation. We have to be taught how to cooperate and work jointly with others. For school leaders, this understanding has immense significance. On the one hand, it emphasizes the importance of organizational learning, of teachers working with teachers to improve pedagogical knowledge and practice but, on the other hand, it highlights the likelihood that the teachers, too, won't automatically know how best to work collaboratively with their colleagues. It is up to the school leader to make sure that each and every staff team is able to function effectively and productively.

Arguably, paying attention to the functional quality of the connectivity within and between teams is a greater imperative and challenge for leaders of schools than it is in other organizations. The reason for this claim is fourfold. First, unlike most organizations in which employees are required to work with others on a daily basis, the key function of a teacher is essentially individualistic. They teach by themselves. When performing their key daily function there is no need to be cooperating with other teachers. Certainly, in recent years there have been moves to modify this isolationistic professional environment, but this is more to do with professional learning about practice rather than the day-to-day life of a teacher. Simply put, if we want teachers to work better together, then their leaders need to help them know how this can happen and support them in putting this knowledge into practice.

The second reason that team synergy and functioning require explicit attention by school and educational leaders is the critical need to overcome the dominating influence of knowledge specificity within the profession. Indeed, it is incredibly common for teachers to develop the belief that their professional reputations are directly aligned to their professional knowledge. Hence, they are prone to being highly defensive and protective about their professional knowledge, be it a particular class or grade level in the junior years or subject or discipline knowledge in the senior and tertiary levels. Consequently, they are prone to bringing and applying their professional bias when called upon to be a member of a school team, department, or committee. This issue is made even more problematic in those teams or committees in which not only is their discipline-based defensiveness brought to the fore but also their subject-based elitism. For example, the effectiveness of curriculum committees can be thwarted when those members representing the Mathematics and/or English departments feel the need to completely undermine any discussion of a matter that might potentially detract from their subject's current time, resource, or staff allocations.

The third reason is the traditional dependency upon delegated managerialism. Teachers are expected to take on additional responsibilities as they progress through the ranks of the teaching profession. However, more often than not, appointments to middle and senior leadership positions are based more on the observed capacity to administer and manage than it is upon the capacity to relate to and collaborate with other teachers. Administering, managing, and monitoring curriculum implementation, standardized assessment procedures, allocated budget expenditure, resource maintenance and audits, and student-to-teacher interactions are deemed to be the most important responsibilities because that lightens the load of the school leader and their attempt to ensure that the school meets its externally imposed verifications and accountabilities. Too often schools are being consumed by chains of managerialism—the governing authorities (inclusive of government ministerial personnel where relevant) are managing the leader who is managing the middle leaders who are managing the teachers who are managing the students. In such an environment, no one is learning how to work synergistically with others. There are no accommodating interactions within and between teams and no cooperative teamwork.

The final reason why school and educational leaders need to specifically attend to the connectivity and unity of their organization is simply because people are time-poor. Cooperative teamwork takes time to develop and maintain. Team interaction among teachers during the school day is impossible because classes can't be interrupted to allow teachers to attend a team meeting. Thus, before or after the working day become the meeting times in schools but neither of these are ideal when it comes to seeking rich discussion, dialogue, and discernment because these are the times that teachers prepare, meet with parents, and participate in other school activities. As a result, these meetings are more often rushed with a focus on administrative or information-giving processes than collaborative, in-depth professional discussions. They are more like communication forums than professional meetings. When discussing their experience of these meetings, teachers regularly describe that teamwork is *diluted or nonexistent* because some *teachers do all the talking* and mostly the aim of the meeting *is for the principal and deputy to tell us what we need to do*. Others note that they have *lost their say about the broader issues*.

In short, schools and other educational organizations are often operating as a sum of their parts because there is no time for team membership, professional relationships, collaborations, support or sharing of information within or between teams or departments. The system is broken—it relies on the dedication of individuals to perform their best in a culture where belonging, collaborating, and interacting with colleagues is far from ideal. Operating in parts, rather than as a whole, diminishes the potential of the school, its staff, and its students.

Therefore, the challenge for the governing authorities, inclusive of ministerial personnel where relevant, and educational leaders is to see the situation for what it is and do something about it. Already, too much is being asked of the teachers. If we want quality education, then those with the power and authority to make a difference need to take responsibility for doing so. When those in the position of being an educational governing authority realize that they are actually members of the educational team, and not spectators judging the quality of the team's performance, then they must also accept responsibility to play their part for the team. Then, and only then, will we begin to see what our educational systems—our schools and educational institutions—can truly produce for the good of students.

Concluding Comments

As life in organizations has become far more complex, sophisticated, strategically structured, and susceptible to external pressures, we have come to realize that the way we currently approach organizational effort as a whole is either absent or simply not working. The connectivity and relationships are missing across organizations, across teams, and among the people. They may well be working at the team level but, even then, teams tend to be dominated by competitive behaviors and cliques. What must be realized within the complexity of the work in organizations today is that no one person has all the answers, especially not the leader. No one person has all the knowledge, all the skills, all the past experiences, all the wisdom, or all the intuition about future demands. Hence, it is now accepted that the best way forward for organizations is to combine together the diverse knowledge, skills, past experiences, wisdom, and intuition of many employees through the use of teams. This collective relational collaboration creates the energy that drives further collaborations, innovations, and possibilities for the organization. As such an organization becomes a "whole" and not the sum of its parts. It is a system, where the energy flows; this is the ecology of an organization. This chapter has comprehensively described what manifests collaborative and productive teamwork and what this requires of the leader.

However, the context for this essential relational-building work of the leader is a world of rapid, vast, and constant change. Therefore, creativity and innovation become cornerstones for the success of the organization. It is through a highly functional and relational organization that creativity can manifest as innovations. We argue that regular and methodically productive creativity can only be effectively supported by an organizational culture that fosters collaborative and productive teamwork. This important view is the focus of Chapter 5.

5

Creativity and Innovation

Principle of Organizational Ecology #5: Organizational Change Is Constant

Introduction

In today's highly competitive and uncertain world, leaders need to be fostering and harnessing the collective effort of their employees rather than trying to control individual and team engagement and performance. Today's organizations exist in constantly changing environmental, economic, technological, social, cultural, and political conditions. "Survival in such competitive and highly complex conditions requires alertness to the environment and a timely and appropriate response" (Khanghahi and Jafari 2013: 1). For example, the impact on people and society of the current pandemic situation around the world has left many organizations struggling at the point of survival. Those that continue to operate do so through innovation and ingenuity. Hence, creativity and thinking diversification are the factors now being promoted as essential for organizational productivity and survival. And these can only be accomplished by engaged employees whose curiosity and quest to grow, learn, and create new ways forward as an integral part of their work is supported by their leader. Old thinking reproduces old ways. New thinking depends on having an organizational culture that not only encourages new thinking but also supports it and profits from its enactment.

Hence this chapter argues that an organization's culture, which is productively interconnected throughout via trusting and collaborative relationships, not only readily promotes emergent innovative, creative, and divergent ideas but also enthusiastically recognizes, acknowledges, supports, and adopts them, irrespective of the mode of working. Moreover, such a culture produces a steady flow of curiosity, creativity, and innovation, which reenergizes the employees and the organization, and further strengthens trust. Within this chapter, literature from the fields of psychology, neuroscience, sociology, complexity theory, and business science are used to more clearly define and describe these essential organizational forces of curiosity, creativity, innovation, and divergent thinking, along with explanations for how these are best nurtured.

More specifically, this chapter first discusses organizations as quasi-dynamic systems that, like it or not, are constantly adapting to change. The chapter then illustrates how organizational change more readily develops from innovations that arise out of a creative idea and leads to a new and better way of doing things. Hence, the chapter proceeds to explore the nature of creativity and how it can be promoted and supported. Discussion then ensues with respect to the current acknowledged importance of creativity and innovation in both corporate and educational organizations. Here, it is acknowledged how the full benefits of creativity and innovation can only be realized within an authentically connected and relational culture as promoted in our ecosystem understanding of organizations. The chapter then describes the implications for leadership practice of this knowledge about how successful organizational change is explicitly dependent on the encouragement, support, and promotion of employee creativity and innovation. Some practical examples pertaining to this understanding, as gained from our research and consultative activities, conclude this chapter.

Organizational Life in a Changing World

For the most part, we accept that life does not stand still, that nothing stays the same. Many are dedicated followers of technology and fashion trends and so constantly monitor changes and, if personal finances permit, shop for the latest and greatest items with keen eagerness. Yet, despite accepting such changes as part and parcel of our daily life, we can see no rhyme nor reason why our workplace needs to change. This view has become even more concerning because we now find ourselves living in an era of, arguably, unprecedented social, economic, technological, and environmental change. Hence, as individuals and as employees we are experiencing disruptions in our normal ways of thinking, our decision-making processes, and our preferred ways of acting. As Isaac Asimov (1978) puts it:

> It is change, continuing change, inevitable change, that is the dominant factor in society today. No sensible decision can be made any longer without taking into account not only the world as it is, but the world as it will be. (n.p.)

This is particularly the case in our organizations where leaders and employees have come to accept that the *only constant is change*. But what exacerbates the impact of constant organizational change is that many organizations have grown inflexibly cumbersome due to their reliance upon rigidly linear structures, overtly mechanistic polices and processes, and ineffective hierarchal channels of communication—all of which are at odds with the very nature of an organization as an ecosystem.

Ecosystems are considered to remain in a state of dynamic equilibrium over time as they progress through stages of natural growth and succession despite experiencing continual change. Without any seriously disruptive disturbance, the lifespan of an ecosystem is considerably lengthy and unrestricted. Hence, they are considered to be in a state of dynamic equilibrium (Figure 5.1a). Organizations, on the other hand, are short-lived. Indeed, according to Mark Goodburn of the World Economic Forum (2015), the lifespan of contemporary multinational organizations is forty to fifty years. Unlike undisturbed ecosystems, organizations are in a constant state of modification and adjustment as they strive to remain competitive, economically viable, relevant, modern, and to move toward an uncertain future. Theoretically, this can be described as a state of dynamic quasi-equilibrium (Figure 5.1b) within which the day-to-day adjustments, anomalies, and innovations are absorbed by employees as the organization attempts to grow and improve according to the external influences.

However, sooner or later, the organization is disturbed by either an internal or external large-scale perturbation, which cannot be absorbed but instead creates a threshold to a new way of existing for the organization. The 2020 Covid-19 pandemic is an example of an extreme threshold situation where organizations suddenly had to accommodate the new social and market forces. In doing so, they had to adjust to a new order by absorbing and adjusting to daily social anomalies as they strove to resettle into a state of quasi-equilibrium. However,

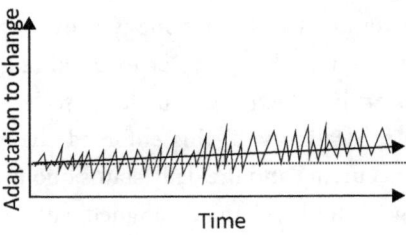

Figure 5.1a A graphic illustration of dynamic equilibrium.

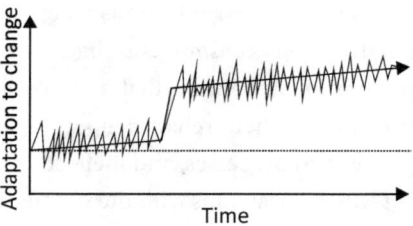

Figure 5.1b A graphic illustration of dynamic quasi-equilibrium.

internal disturbances can also alter the organization. These might include, for example, changes in its leadership either good or bad, in its market share, in its resource availability, in its skills requirements, in its level of competition, in its staff turnover, or in its technological necessities.

In a state of dynamic quasi-equilibrium, the organization is committed to being actively and continuously improving or growing in some way toward a visionary ideal. The achievement of this state provides all in the organization with the experience of continuous organic change, which engenders confidence in their capacity to cope with adapting to change. Organic change contrasts with periodic change. Organic change refers to the open acknowledgment and commitment throughout an organization that small but essential changes need to be adopted regularly if not daily. This engenders the ability of employees to be continually thinking about and analyzing what they are doing and to "adapt on the go" whenever necessary. For these employees, change is not something to be feared but rather it affords them an opportunity to review, learn, and grow. This confident attitude then places the employees in good stead to successfully overcome an unexpected large-scale perturbation event when it arises. In short, the day-to-day adaptations are important because in the long term the constant and steady adaptation may achieve far more than any periodic major change event.

However, most organizations are more accustomed with periodic change. These organizations assume there is only one type of change—a major internal (e.g., a restructure or a new technology) or external (e.g., a new competitor's product or a new government expectation) large-scale perturbation. Outside of the time assigned to dealing with this enforced change it is assumed that there are no changes occurring and the daily status quo practices are more than adequate. In these organizations, change is aligned with being a major upheaval and, thus, is often accompanied with feelings of uncertainty, anxiety, and a lack of confidence for many employees. It is not just the reluctance of the workers to change that is at fault; rather it is the management approach in dealing with change, which is to recover and normalize between intermittent bouts of large-scale change processes.

Given this propensity of organizations to choose the periodic change option, change initiatives are regularly far from ideal mainly due to the logical sequential change management program often adopted by organizations that assumes change is a shift from one steady state to another. McKinsey research shows that 70 percent of change initiatives fail (Ewenstein, Smith, and Sologar 2015). Yet the business and consultancy literatures are bulging at the seams with the latest and greatest ways to better manage change with catchy phrases, attractive designer graphics, digitally impressive this, that, and the next big thing, and a wide array of expensive professional development courses—all of which have one thing in common: managing and controlling the change. This means managing the employees—coercing the employees to make the change and obliging them to keep up with the change, all camouflaged under some harebrained notion of "creating a culture of change."

What this loudly and clearly indicates is that many leaders have a very poor understanding of how employees gather and engage in their work, and the cultural context to which they conform. Alas, all these new change management solutions remain controlling strategies which are not, and never will, achieve successful change because the problem is management itself. Management, as a discipline and as a practice, is navel-gazing on this matter. It keeps on promoting essentially the same strategies. It does not appear to have the ability to look outside of itself for better ways. Indeed, a Forbes (2017) article describes the single reason for the failure of most change management efforts as *change battle fatigue* (Gleeson 2017). Employees are sick and tired of essentially the same worn-out and ineffective change management programs. So, how do many employees deal with these change management programs? In short, they resist them—big time.

Large-scale disturbances impact the whole organization and, thus, this necessitates a whole-of-organization response. The answer is of course lying in the wisdom and capability of the leader to encourage organic change through creative thinking and ongoing improvements, and to capture and share any new ideas throughout the organization by connecting, resourcing, and encouraging further innovative thinking. This approach moves employees away from a fixed mindset thinking, *"this is the way we do things here,"* to an open mindset thinking, *'why are we doing things this way and how might it be done better."* Therefore, during times of larger-scaled perturbations, these employees

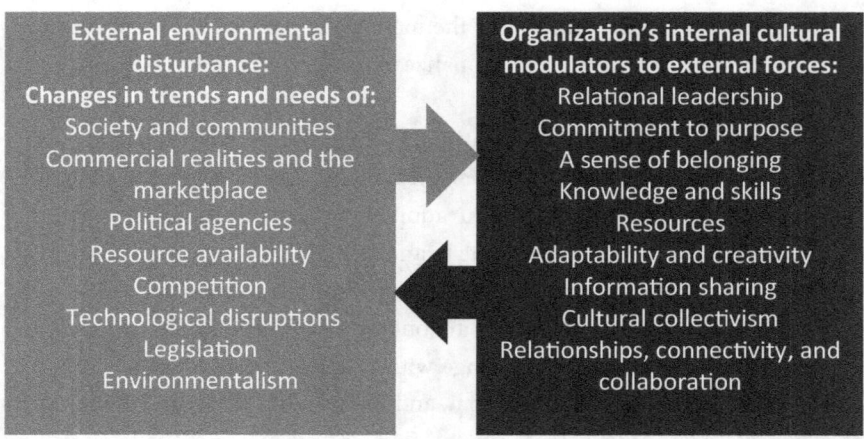

Figure 5.2 Disturbance and modulation in well-connected organizations and/or teams.

are already equipped with the skills to adapt and innovate. The organization is safeguarded through strengthening forces that are not only the drivers of connectivity, engagement, and productivity but are equally the modulators against cultural upheaval.

Figure 5.2 provides the summary of the interaction between external disturbance and the factors modulating that disturbance. By focusing on the work and opportunity to innovate, the leader essentially redirects primacy away from the hierarchies, structures, policies, and processes to that of the culture, which prioritizes flexibility and adaptability. Where there is an organizational culture that supports strategic intentions of the organization, employees are free to adapt and grow in their teams—which makes them resilient and able to adjust and modulate within the ever-changing nature of their work demands. Without such abilities to adapt and modulate, the individual and the team is fragile and vulnerable to the forces of change. In an ecological context, in conditions of environmental change, species have three choices: to move, to adapt, or to die out. To move means dispersing to locations where the environment is more suitable. There is abundant scientific literature showing that species move to ideal conditions in response to change so that they don't need to change (Marra 2013). To stay and adapt means that species need to change in some way to survive the new conditions. To stay and not adapt for some reason or another is to die out and become locally extinct (Marra 2013).

These options of move, adapt, or die out are the same for employees in organizations when faced with change. For example, people can choose to move, to find another job rather than adapting to the change. Alternatively, they can choose to stay and adapt to the change; or they can choose to stay and refuse to adapt. To stay and refuse to adapt essentially means the person is left behind, and/or becomes out-of-date whereby their knowledge and skills become superfluous to the needs of the organization. Unfortunately, the movers and the refusers are commonplace in organizations; they are manifestations of, first, the effect of a disconnected, often toxic, organizational culture and its impact on the commitment that employees have to their organization and, secondly, the inability of the organization to modulate and adapt to change.

Also, the capacity of an organization to adapt to externally imposed changes is greatly reduced when its internal relationships, connections, commitments, and engagement are significantly diminished or absent in some areas. For example, any competition between employees and/or teams diminishes an organization-wide collectivist approach when trying to adapt to a seriously significant external force for change.

Thus, the first step toward successfully leading organizational change is to recognize that change is constantly happening and to publicly acknowledge this and draw attention to how readily and confidently it is being handled. Then the next step for the leader is to ensure that the organization's culture is not only able to move forward through small organic changes but also through the less regular but far more demanding, unavoidable periodic changes. This demands that the leader knows what is the basic ingredient that is required when meeting such a demanding challenge and ensures that the culture fully nurtures these outcomes.

So, what is the basic ingredient for successfully accomplishing an organizational change, generally, but especially when embracing a demanding periodic change? Innovation—each and every organizational change, no matter how small or large, emerges from an innovation. If organizational change is endemic, then it behooves leaders to fully understand the concept of innovation.

How, When, and Why Does Innovation Emerge?

Innovation is generally regarded as essential to the growth and evolution of a human system and incorporates a number of cognitive processes including curiosity, questioning, seeking answers and truths, understanding the world more deeply, learning new ways, and developing beliefs. All of which can inspire intrinsic motivation. When people take an active interest in the world around them, they learn, they become eager and curious, they become intrinsically motivated. The concept of innovation has been defined in many different ways, such as:

- "Innovation is change that creates a new dimension of performance." (Drucker 1985)
- "Innovation is the creation of something that improves the way we live our lives." (Obama 2007)
- "Innovation is any idea that adds value." (Baxter Healthcare, Australia 2020)
- "Innovation is the creation, development and implementation of a new product, process or service, with the aim of improving efficiency, effectiveness or competitive advantage." (Government of New Zealand 2020)
- "Innovation is the successful implementation of creative ideas within an organization." (Amabile 1996: 1)

However, the commonality in these and other definitions is that innovation arises out of a creative idea and leads to a new and better way of doing things. The creative idea comes from a thought-provoking question, a curiosity about the way the world works, or from the need to solve a problem. Therefore, it is essential to understand the precursors and conditions that steer innovation—namely curiosity and creativity.

Although we might often associate creativity with a select group of people deemed to possess particular capabilities, research shows that creativity is a quality possessed by all humans. Right from the day a person is born, creativity has pervaded most areas of their daily lives. Babies depend on creativity to learn and successfully interact with their environment. From a biological perspective, the roots of creativity run deep and are associated with survival and the need to adapt (Zaidel 2014). For example, the archaeological remains of human history throughout the world record a history of creativity through the evolution of tools, materials, and other artifacts over time.

The vast amount of literature researching creativity generally defines creativity as being the person's capacity to produce work that is novel and meaningful, as opposed to unoriginal and trivial. From the psychological perspective, creativity is described as the brain's ability to put together two or more images in different combinations at the same time in space, which are then seen as new developments (Yaniv 2012). Simply stated, creativity is the ability to perceive the world in new ways, to find hidden patterns, to make connections between seemingly unrelated phenomena, and to generate original solutions.

This implies that the creative mind is a curious mind because it resides in thoughtful questioning and a desire to seek greater understanding of how and why things work, and what this knowledge might lead to. Curiosity, the intrinsic desire to know, is a basic element of our thinking that has long been recognized as an important motive that influences human behavior throughout our life (Gottlieb and Oudeyer 2018). Although curiosity has been found to be a characteristic of animals as they investigate their surroundings, humans, however, are not only curious but also question and arrive at solutions and ideas that lead to innovations, new learnings, and different experiences. For Leonardo da Vinci, curiosity was the fuel for his creativity and inventions. By his own account, he was driven by an intense curiosity, questioning everything in his pathway from which his many highly innovative inventions were created. Thus, throughout history, questioning why and what might be has driven the exploration of our world and the universe beyond our world. It has provided humans with the constant motivation to make things better. From the development of the wheel to the printing press and to space travel, humans have changed the course of their own history including the evolution of the digital world we now exist within. Throughout history, many curious minds have enabled leaps forward in thinking and innovation.

Defining curiosity has attracted many alternative views. Plato considered that curiosity involved seeking new experiences for the sake of knowledge that is inherently satisfying. More recently, it is understood that creativity comes from curiosity and the more curious you are the more you experience and learn, and the more you increase your ability to find innovative solutions to problems. According to Gupta and Banerjee (2016), curiosity requires a creative personality that includes not only a thirst for curiosity but also an attraction toward complex and abstract matters and a capability to think along nonconventional lines and in abstract dimensions. But, together, the collective understanding is that our human history is loaded with examples of discoveries that have arisen from curiosity-driven investigations manifested through the desire to question—which inspires creative ideas upon which our world has been, and will continue to be, built. Creativity provides the seeds and the soil for new endeavors to grow.

For humans, curiosity is crucial for two critical reasons. First, it stimulates the generation of new knowledge and learning, and has been linked with increased motivation, memory, and attention (Gottlieb and Oudeyer 2018). Curiosity inspires people; it motivates and energizes them to acquire knowledge and learning, which improves performance and decision-making by providing informative options and actions (Kidd and Hayden 2015). However, like any human capacity, some people are more inclined to question their experiences and be more curious than others and, therefore, be more inventive in their daily lives.

Secondly, curiosity is an essential element of well-being. Neuroscience data shows that high curiosity ratings are associated with increased midbrain reward structures, which is important in the development and persistence of well-being and personal growth. For example, people with higher levels of curiosity challenge their views and their world and thereby expand their information, knowledge, and skills from which they obtain greater meaning, purpose, and satisfaction in life (Kashdan and Steger 2007). Where there is curiosity and creativity there is meaning. Life becomes far more meaningful when we feel curious and creative in what we are doing. As described by Wheatley (2006: 133), "with meaning as our centering place, we can journey through the realms of chaos and make sense of the world. With meaning as an attractor, we can re-create ourselves to carry forward what we value most." What then does this mean for organizational life now and in the future?

The New Organizational Forces

It is essential to acknowledge that the organizations of 2020 and beyond, regardless of context, are knowledge-based and highly technical in a fast-paced world, and their success and survival depend on curiosity, creativity, discovery, innovation, and inventiveness. Therefore, organizations need to rapidly evolve in their commitment to creative innovation and insist on behaviors to meet these needs. These behaviors must include relationships within and between teams at all levels to foster the flow of ideas and innovations because no innovation can happen in isolation. And no innovation will truly succeed if its benefits are only available to a few individuals or teams within the organization. It is critical for people and teams to be connected, questioning, creative, and sharing ideas to discover options and develop innovations that can respond to the organization's global needs and, thereby, ensure its ongoing success.

Although, from an organizational perspective, curiosity is a vital cultural outcome that needs valuing, growing, and appreciating because of the benefits it brings to both the individual and their organization, to date, most leaders stifle questioning and curiosity for fear of causing an interruption or disruption to the existing familiar daily routines or because they are not open to the critique of their own decision-making. Our leadership research shows that most leaders feel far more at ease with focusing on trying to maintain the status quo, and not on questioning the rights and wrongs of what is happening and developing new creative ideas for improving performance and output. This observation is supported by the research of Gino (2018), as published in the *Harvard Business Review*, involving three thousand employees from a wide range of businesses and industries, which found that only about 24 percent of employees said they felt curious in their jobs on a regular basis and approximately 70 percent of employees said they faced barriers to asking questions about their work. Fortunately, this is not the case in some organizations that clearly value employee curiosity and innovation. For example, the Japanese car manufacturing company, Toyota, expects its employees to provide up to one hundred innovative suggestions each year. Similarly, Google employees have 20 percent of their work time dedicated to work-related curiosity and innovation activities.

Furthermore, according to Gino (2018) cultivating employee curiosity at all levels within an organization is a factor in lifting performance because it helps the employees to adapt to external pressures through creative solutions and improvements in how they perform their work. Where creativity and innovation coexist in an organization, there is greater communication and teamwork and less conflict. In a workplace setting, the employees need to work together toward achieving a common purpose. Ideally, they are working in well-functioning teams where each person is connected through positive professional relationships and collaborations, and where information and ideas flow readily. In such teams, diversity of ideas and life experiences enrich the team's thinking and enhance creativity and innovative ideas. It follows that creativity is more likely to be stimulated, encouraged, and developed in teams that are highly diverse and cohesive.

Fostering a Creativity-Led Organizational Culture

In organizations, the existence of cohesive and creative teams begins with having a culture in which the norms both promote questioning, learning, curiosity, creativity, and innovation as well as boosting relationships that allow these to flow freely. Importantly, this must also be inclusive of the encouragement of risk-taking. Innovation carries risk for individuals and the organization. It is far too idealistic to think that every innovation will be automatically successful. Some innovations might fail—but to avoid innovation for fear of failing is the greatest failure of all. Any innovation not achieving its desired success should be regarded as an opportunity to learn and not as an expensive mistake.

Another form of risk is that which could be felt by the potentially innovative employee. This employee needs to feel safe in sharing their creative ideas with others. The risks here are that they might fear being ridiculed, or that their innovative idea might be stolen by another employee for their own benefit and kudos, or that their idea might simply be ignored and lost—all of which can create despondency, suffocate any future creative activity, and could lead to decreased engagement. Organizational culture needs to be open and supportive of the risk factor associated with creativity, inventiveness, and innovation.

Also, the organizational culture must provide the following four critical features: (1) clarity about the purpose of the work of the organization and how each team and its members contribute to it, (2) mechanisms such as policies and processes designed to grasp and grow new opportunities and to channel the optimism of creativity, (3) top-tier and middle leadership capability that focuses on relationships, trust, connectivity, and collectivism, and (4) resources, time, and investment in employees' creativity and innovative ideas. Essentially, fostering creativity fosters engagement, which fosters high performance and quality organizational outcomes. Because, as noted above, creativity is part and parcel of being human; it provides the essential element to inspire and boost engagement. It may well be the panacea for the global epidemic of disengagement. The plethora of literature on disengagement in the workplace identifies that creativity is one of the factors that lifts engagement.

All this is well and good, except creative ideas need to go somewhere or people will become despondent and resistant to providing creative ideas. Currently, where do all the good ideas go in most organizations? Sadly, many creative ideas either do not get presented or they get ignored. The leader and culture must foster growth mindsets at all levels of the organization—the willingness to try something new and learn from its success or failure, and to grow the idea even further. But, unfortunately, there are many examples evident of fixed mindsets in organizations where the leader and other employees don't like having better ideas than their own being promoted or cannot abide any hint of failure from untried new ideas. Thus, these fixed-mindset people resist any change or innovation or only partially and half-heartedly attempt to introduce a proposed innovation, thereby guaranteeing it will fail. Common statements from fixed-mindset people include lacklustre statements such as the following:

- We tried that once, but it didn't work so let's not try that again.
- This is the way we have always done it.
- If it ain't broke, don't fix it.

Alternatively, the motivated growth-mindset responses would inspire the energy of growth and opportunity—for example, see below:

- Why didn't it work? What did we learn? What might work?
- If we all thought like that, we would still be in the Stone Age. There are probably better ways, more contemporary or efficient ways of doing things.
- If you wait for something to be broken it's too late to fix it.

The presence of negative or resistant attitudes stem from cultural artifacts, which do nothing to modulate adaptation to change. First, at the individual level, employees can be highly resistant to change and deliberately obstruct any creative idea. They are frightened of new ways of doing things because they are uncertain about their own capability. They are frozen in ordinariness and outdatedness; they do not have the energy to shake themselves into the excitement state of creativity and innovation. Therefore, they promote the status quo and will go so far as to sabotage innovation. These are the people who refuse to adapt. As such their commitment to the organization is limited at best; they are disengaged and blockers of the flow of energy in the organization. Typically, this is a consequence of managerialism and the absence of good leadership over a period of time, which manifests an organizational culture that is divided, competitive, and antagonistic. In effect, the organization does not have the wherewithal to modulate and adapt in the face of a disturbance.

Secondly, at the organizational level, change and innovation simply will not be successful if the organization is not connected and exists as parts—each their own entity mostly in competition with the other parts of the organization. As parts, there is no flow of innovative ideas through the organization, there is no commitment to possibility, there is no energy of excitement, no valuing of creativity and innovation, no celebration of the success of other parts/teams, no sharing of new ideas or information, and no commitment that fosters adaptation and modulation. Is it any wonder that 70 percent of change initiatives fail when, typically, organizations are a disconnected sum of their parts.

The solution to this untenable situation is cultural and not procedural. Creativity and innovation in an organization need to be highly valued as opportunities for renewal, growth, and a source of endless possibilities for the employees and the organization. In order for this to be so, the culture of the organization needs norms and values that promote curiosity, innovation, and possibility to ensure there is toleration for testing and learning and a sincere willingness to commit to trialing an innovation and investing resources toward its success. This means that the organization's culture must be underpinned by the values of honesty, fairness, justice, integrity, (mutual) respect, equality, and openness, relational trust, and the common good. It is upon these values that employees are willing to take risks, to try new and unusual approaches, to share different and critical opinions, to acknowledge personal weaknesses, and to challenge the status quo—all of which are essential ingredients for advancing creativity, inventiveness, and innovation.

Lastly, but certainly not least, for the organization's culture to not only encourage and support but also spread the benefits of an innovation it must also foster relationally based connectivity among all of the parts of the organization. Pervasive connectivity among the employees, among the teams, and between the leader and the employees maximizes the flow of information sharing about the innovation throughout the organization. It is the work of the teams, and the connectivity between them, that gives creative ideas life for, without such connectivity, good ideas go nowhere. Leaders must recognize and congratulate all the employees for their general commitment to learn and grow from innovation, in addition to acknowledging the importance of creativity within the individual. In this way, the organization's cultural norms in support of innovation and creativity become embedded in the organization, thereby encouraging others to be creative, and induces widespread confidence in the organization's capacity to assuredly cope with change. Thus, this flow of information significantly increases the energy throughout the organization.

In short, an abundance of research literature on this subject confirms there to be a direct relationship between organizational culture and innovation. A fertile culture enables creativity and innovation to flourish. This is a culture that fosters and supports all the precursors and activities of creativity and innovation. Positive creativity and innovation will not happen in an obstructive organizational culture. Here, negative or deleterious creativity is likely to happen. In an obstructive culture, the employees are prone to seeking ways to get back at the organization through counterproductive means. Under toxic management, employees can feel betrayed—the organization and its leadership cannot be trusted to abide by the expected psychological contract of a reciprocal beneficial interaction. As a result, they seek ways to "even the score" through counterproductive behaviors such as damaging the brand by publicly criticizing the organization away from work, by deliberately making errors, by slowing down their work rate so that it impacts on the capacity of others to complete their work, or through the theft of time (taking extended meal or toilet breaks), goods, or money.

Creativity and Innovation in Education

Schools are places of learning and growing. However, the challenge of creativity and innovation is twofold in an educational context—student learning centered, and teacher professional learning centered. There is little doubt that the learning experience for today's students must encourage problem-solving rather than simply the gaining of knowledge. Teachers are now aware of the need to present cognitive challenges that have the effect of disrupting or questioning the student's current knowledge so as to stimulate their curiosity and motivate them individually or with the help of some other students to innovatively resolve their knowledge dilemma. While this technique is applicable to all subject areas, it has gained significant prominence in the push to promote STEM learnings. As our world transitions toward Industry 4.0 with its emphasis on artificial intelligence and the internet-of-things, there is a perceived growing need to ensure that our current students are highly confident and capable in the STEM-related disciplines.

However, although the inclusion of curiosity and innovation in teacher professional learning is of similar necessity, its achievement is proving problematic but not entirely due to teacher resistance. Governments and educational systems authorities—those who fund and administer educational institutions—have, on the one hand, voiced strong yearnings for such teacher professional learning but, on the other hand, have tended to ignore the logistical and resourcing implications that such a commitment demands, thereby stifling the spirit of creative thinking for innovative learning and growing.

A prime reason for the introduction of the professional learning community concept into the educational arena was the assumption that such a forum would not only encourage questioning of taken-for-granted teaching practices but also replace these with far more creative, innovative, and student-centered teaching methods. Indeed, innovation was promoted as a pivotal outcome. The traditional isolated and individualized teaching environment was viewed as being incapable of providing a teacher with either the motivation or the capacity to question their teaching preparation, methods, or strategies for evaluating student learning. As Bryk, Camburn, and Louis (1999) proposed during the very early development of professional learning communities, if this strategy "in fact fosters instructional change, it does so by creating an environment that supports learning through innovation and experimentation" (771).

Clearly, teaching practices have come a very long way since the introduction of professional learning communities but the degree to which these brought about the pedagogical improvements is highly debatable. Arguably, the significant length of time it took to gain appreciable changes in teacher practices suggests that these were more a result of other influences rather than school-based innovative thinking teamwork. Indeed, many of the current pedagogical changes occurring in schools are the result of external international expert advice from the likes of John Hattie, Michael Fullan, Lyn Sharratt, Alama Harris, and Pasi Sahlberg, to name but a few. Importantly though, the schools and educational systems that have benefitted the most from the advice provided by such experts are those that already have a culture that embraces critical reflection on teaching practices with the intention of improving the student learning experiences via relevant creatively innovative approaches to teaching. Here the school staff are working more as a highly motivated and united team rather than as a system of effective teams.

However, we argue that the seemingly ineffectiveness of the professional learning community concept in many schools is not entirely the concept's or the individual school's fault. Unlike a normal organizational environment, a teacher is directly in face-to-face contact with key stakeholders (their students) for much of their working day. Given the teacher's duty of care and legal responsibility, they must remain in the classroom with their students throughout the lesson. This means that they can't set the students to work at the beginning of a lesson and then leave the classroom to attend a professional learning community team meeting. In other words, any such team meetings must occur outside of classroom teaching time. Since a teacher is in a classroom for much of the day, and has nonteaching/preparation-time at the same time as only a few, if any, other teachers, any team-type meeting can only occur outside of the school day either before teaching begins or after teaching has finished. Also fitted into these "meeting times" before or after school are the usual staff structural/ discipline meetings, which deal with the day-to-day administration, logistical, and curricula matters. Simply put, often professional learning community team meetings are slotted into an already crowded meeting schedule, thereby diminishing and confusing its relevance, importance, and purpose. Until governments and educational systems are willing to increase staffing resources in order to create more opportunity for team-based professional learning to occur during the normal school day, schools will continue to struggle to maximize the benefits to be gained from such a concept. Meanwhile, the adoption of pedagogical innovations will continue but ever so slowly and will be aligned more with global initiatives rather than with what is specifically needed given the learning support required by the school's unique student population.

The Role of Leadership

Based upon all of the discussion provided above, we maintain that only relationally attuned leaders understand the indispensable connections between individuals and teams that manifest initiative, creativity, and innovation. Creativity and imagination are suppressed in a culture overseen by managerialism's command-and-control protocols. Today's leaders must view their employees as sophisticated, independent-minded, and highly trained employees who require the freedom to maximize their initiative and imagination via collegiality and collaboration so that creativity and imagination can blossom to the best advantage of individuals and the organization. The role of the leader is not only to provide and model the vision that instills a commitment to collegiality and collaboration, but also to build connectivity across the organization by bringing together the right people with the necessary knowledge, skills, and disposition to solve a problem or to create new knowledge and practices, regardless of their relative levels or areas of employment in the organization.

A leader who readily promotes and supports employee curiosity and creativity engenders an organizational culture in which experimentation is democratized, allowing employees to make decisions and create improvements in their work (Thomke 2020). In order to do this, leaders need to not only role-model experimentation but also ensure that supportive systems and resources are provided, and employees are encouraged to embrace experimentation and value work-related surprises from which curiosity will prevail throughout the organization.

Furthermore, leaders who are attuned to the pivotal relational dimension underpinning their leadership are able to embrace multiple futures and are open in terms of what these might be. Rather than controlling and directing the organization's future, they concentrate on cultivating the conditions where others can produce innovations that lead to somewhat unpredictable yet largely productive future states. This influence derives from the leader's ability to allow rather than to direct and is grounded in people in the organization remaining engaged and connected. Through recognizing the importance of connectivity and interactions as the ideal source of employee engagement, high performance, creativity, and innovation, these leaders build correlation—the emergence of a common or shared organizational vision and united interdependent behaviors.

Ogbeibu, Senadjki, and Gaskin (2018) add that in order to engender employee creativity and innovation, leaders should consider the role of organizational benevolence—the extent to which individuals and teams model good intentions toward other individuals and other teams. Essentially, this is about creating the sense of belonging that people need. A more benevolent organizational culture has been shown to build stronger resilience and optimism in an ever-changing workplace environment. The greater the sense of belonging the more committed people are to do their very best work, in their team and for their organization. This requires the leader to have strong relational characteristics that reflect goodwill, compassion, care, altruism, and kindness toward each and every employee. Basically, this form of leadership demonstrates genuine and kind behaviors that have positive impacts on their employees and thereby ensures that each employee feels a sense of belonging and of being valued. Ogbeibu and colleagues further posit that such leadership characteristics engender an organizational culture considered by the employees as humane, supportive, comfortable, trusting, and respectful. Demonstrating benevolence within an organization requires the leader to exhibit emotional ties and concerns for employees' career growth and general well-being. Being benevolent may also mean becoming mentors or coaches to employees, and the creation of opportunities for correcting mistakes, and understanding why employees might act in ways that undermine creativity and innovation. This in turn instills a sense of care and reciprocity in employees who may consequently feel more inclined to exhibit positive behaviors and attitudes toward the creative initiatives of other employees.

A prime example of this way of leading within an educational context came to our attention during the Covid-19 pandemic. The Covid-19 pandemic imposed extreme pressure on all organizations, including schools, for one reason or another. One common pressure resulted from the strict lockdown rules which, for many students and staff, translated into having to study or work at home. Instantly four major issues arose for the staff: (1) resources for working at home became a number one priority, (2) the needs of the staff had changed, (3) the staff's technological capability and capacity were stretched, and (4) the importance of maintaining organizational connectivity gained prominence but also bafflement. The following description provides an example of how one school leader attended to these four issues.

Work had changed for the staff of this school. The focus of their work shifted from face-to-face education to supporting their students through technology. While the leader focused on his staff, their resources, and the new demand they faced, the staff focused on setting up an adequate working-from-home environment and on personal upskilling according to any new knowledge or skills that this unique home-based workplace environment now required. Different talents and experiences were now being called upon and those staff with these skills shone out like bright stars and became the go-to people. But, in the beginning, this was not a straightforward outcome. It required flexible and creative thinking to accept the need for new practices and a commitment toward filling gaps in hardware, software, digital networks, and user capability. Fortunately, due to the leader's reputation as always being positive, friendly, encouraging, available, and supportive, the staff approached these new challenges confidently and collaboratively and, despite the physical dislocation and isolation, they remained united in purpose and practice. Hence, constructive suggestions, success stories, new ideas, and generosity of spirit flowed freely throughout the now largely digital workplace and, eventually, the staff settled into providing their students with the service and learning experiences that now suited their new needs.

The key things that worked for this educational organization, and therefore the students, were: (1) the leader and the staff continued to work closely as a team around an externally imposed problem, which they believed they could not only learn how to overcome but also be able to pass on this new learning to create a benefit for their students, (2) the leader digitally connected with them as a group at the end of every day to ensure all staff were well and had all the resources they needed for what they were seeking to do with their students in future, and (3) the leader digitally connected with them individually each week to talk through any personal problems they were having.

Concluding Comments

The overriding message of this chapter is that an organization is far from being a static, enduring, collective mass of employees. Rather, regardless of whether it is recognized or not, an organization is an evolving entity. Life in an organization is always changing because the organization is, by necessity, having to change. This means that the employees are constantly facing, to varying degrees, the need to grow, learn, and adapt because the employees are the organization—not the buildings or the administrative structures. However, people will not automatically adapt to a new order. Instead, the leader must create the cultural context for them to feel a deep sense of belonging and therefore a willingness to acknowledge the need to change, for them to want to adapt, to embrace innovation and new ways of being, and to be creative—not just as individual employees but in conjunction with other employees because it is the combined work of all that produces the organization's end product. Therefore, the achieving of successful change requires that the organization has the capacity to modulate and adapt in response to change through its antecedent cultural conditions that ensure commitment to the success of the organization. This ensures that the organization works as a system in which the interconnectivity among employees, and in the work produced, assumes primacy.

Central in this acknowledgment is the inescapable need for the leadership practice and the organizational culture to both encourage and support the development, implementation, and celebration of innovative ideas because it is only in this way that successful change can be regularly achieved. This implies that the leadership and culture breed belonging, curiosity, creativity, initiative, and collegiality. New ideas and their benefits are openly shared, actively supported, publicly acknowledged, and widely distributed.

However, in saying this it must also be accepted that ongoing organizational change, in both its organic and periodic forms, raises the matter of organizational complexity. Although the current organizational theory has sought to address this need through the development of the Complex Adaptive System theory, this has proven to have had little, if any, impact on organizational life. It has remained an ideal rather than a reality. We contend that our Theory of Organizational Ecology readily overcomes this anomaly because it unproblematically achieves that which the Complex Adaptive Systems theory has failed to achieve. Chapter 6 comprehensively describes why this is so.

6

Simplifying Complexity

Principle of Organizational Ecology #6: Each Person Counts

Introduction

This final organizational ecology principle, which states that "each person counts," emphasizes that each employee is an invaluable contributor to the success of the organization and not just a resource to command, control, and manage. In a natural ecosystem it is universally accepted that the entire system absolutely depends on the active involvement of each and every organism in the ecosystem. There is no hierarchical distinction in terms of the organism's role importance or limitation on how much it can influence the ongoing sustainability and growth of the ecosystem. Thus, applying essentially the same understanding to an organizational context means that the role of each employee is vitally significant, and each employee must have the freedom, encouragement, and support to be able to provide their own unique input into the ongoing productivity and growth of the organization. This is a view that is very much in keeping with our current complexity-based organizational theory in which an organization is viewed as a Complex Adaptive System. This being so, it is essential to further explore the implications and applications of this seemingly common principle in order to distinguish the natural primacy of the Theory of Organizational Ecology (TOE) from that of the Complex Adaptive Systems (CAS) theory.

According to Zhao and Zhang (2013), organizational theory can be understood as the study of structure, function, and design of organizations. It aims to solve practical problems, maximize production efficiency, and make organizations better function and develop more effectively. More specifically, *organizational theory* is said to incorporate the set of interrelated concepts and definitions that explain the behavior of individuals or teams or departments that interact with each other to perform the activities intended toward the accomplishment of the organization's core purpose. It is clear from all that has been previously described in this book that TOE comprehensively meets these requirements of being an organization theory. However, as will be illustrated in this chapter, the same cannot be said of CAS since organizational leaders struggle to implement its theoretical principles.

Thus, although there may well appear to be a degree of similarity between TOE and CAS, we argue that a more in-depth examination, as provided in this chapter, affords a far different and more positively constructive insight. Basically, this chapter argues that a discord, an incoherence, exists between our current CAS organization theory and our contemporary leadership and culture theories. This means that, at present, there are serious theoretical inconsistencies in how we understand organizational culture, leadership, and CAS. Therefore, those working at the coalface, our organizational leaders, are faced with considerable practical ambiguity, confusion, and uncertainty. For many leaders, the thought that their organization needs to become a CAS is meaningless and carries little, if any, import.

Thus, the aim of this chapter is to describe how the application of the TOE, especially with its emphasis on the important contribution afforded by each employee, is able to achieve theoretical and practical organizational coherence—the harmony and synchronicity among leadership, culture, and organizational theory. Here, the achievement of harmony implies that all three theories are based on the same principles while the achievement of synchronicity means that all three are mutually supportive. This will be achieved by describing the developments in organizational theorizing during the past one hundred years, which has led to the current complexity-based theory and its CAS concept. This discussion will highlight, also, the perceived inherent ambiguities and inconsistencies in this current organizational theory which cause confusion, uncertainty, and indifference among leaders. Consequently, the chapter concludes with a description of how our TOE is readily able to redress these ambiguities and uncertainties so as to again achieve organizational harmony and synchronicity in our twenty-first-century context. Essentially, this chapter applies organizational ecology understandings, as presented and described in the previous chapters, to clarify and describe how a leader can easily develop the organizational culture and leadership practices that automatically manifest as a CAS while also achieving much more. Simply put, the outcomes automatically generated by TOE incorporates, integrates but, importantly, transcends those offered solely by CAS theory.

The Development of Organizational Theories

The first half of the twentieth century was the first period during which time there was a high degree of consistency among the basic tenets of organizational culture and leadership theories. This was the boom era of the Industrial Revolution with respect to the establishment of new corporations and organizations. Led by the economic growth and development in America, this period saw the widespread transition from small family businesses to large companies and factories. Employees were no longer just family members united by family values and traditions. Most were strangers seeking regular and secure wages. Furthermore, particularly during the early part of this era, they were often unfamiliar with the exact skills being asked of them in their new organizational employment.

Arguably, the most significant first occurrence of organizational theory formed during this time. Often termed the Classical Theory, it surrounded the work of Frederick Winslow Taylor following the 1911 publication of his book, *The Principles of Scientific Management*, where he argued that organizational productivity would be greatly improved if employee performance was optimized and simplified. In keeping with his mechanical engineering beliefs and principles, Taylor's view of an organization was akin to that of a machine with the employees being the cogs producing the required output. Just as a machine works best when it is built with a specific purpose in mind and, therefore, with the right-sized cogs that are kept well lubricated and regular monitoring of their proper functioning, Taylor argued that organizations can boost productivity if they

- Look at each job or task scientifically to determine the "one best way" to perform the job;
- Hire the right workers for each job, and train them to work at maximum efficiency;
- Monitor worker performance and provide instruction and training when needed; and
- Divide the work between management and labor so that management can plan and train, and workers can execute the task efficiently.

The implication of Taylor's model upon the Classical Theory meant that it regarded organizations as closed systems whereby their functioning is considered to be relatively independent from its environment. Thus, attention was focused internally with an emphasis that included the consolidation of a bureaucracy structure, rigidly hierarchical roles, centralized control, standardization of performance, extensive planning by the leadership group, and minimal consideration of the environmental conditions outside the organization. Essentially, organizations were viewed from a reductionist perspective in which they could best be understood by analyzing the individual parts and determining the linear relationships between inputs and outputs. The aim was to apply controlling mechanisms in order to minimize input demands (e.g., employee performance time, resources, and the range of employee responsibilities) while maximizing outputs (e.g., employee performance and profits). The organizational leader had total control while the employees were just considered as a means of production.

Arguably, Burns (1978, 2010) provides the ideal overview of the prevailing leadership theory that complemented this Classical organizational perspective, which he termed *transactional leadership*. For Burns, transactional leadership implies that leadership is about the action of the leader to get those being led to do what the leader requires. The leader controls and directs employees usually through physical or psychological, formal or informal, reward or coercive means. Rightly or wrongly, this type of leadership has often been aligned with what is understood as management—"getting others to do what is considered to be right." Transactional leaders are firm in their opinion that it is solely their responsibility to control and direct employee performance and thereby produce the desired quality of the organization's output. They believed they largely knew what was best for the organization and so instituted a predominantly exclusive, top-down, controlled, and inflexible working environment. Those they led saw them as being very managerial, authoritative, and single-minded. Only a select few, if any, other than the leader got to influence the important decisions that were made or to influence how such decisions were to be enacted. Hence the organizational structure was very hierarchical, which distanced the leader both physically and socially from most in the organization.

In order to reinforce this very aloof and impersonal environment, the transactional leader largely depended on coercive measures to try and achieve employee compliance to their directives, which were most often couched in terms of policies and expected processes. Such measures varied along a coercion continuum from the lesser end of annual goal-setting processes around meeting performance standards to the more coercive contractualization of employment and to the extreme measure of position disestablishment. The belief was that employees were motivated to comply and perform out of fear of losing their position or being overlooked for career advancement opportunities.

Accountability was the key feature used to determine the worth of the employee, with a skill-based focus and assessments addressing how well the employee's skills were producing what was required. Determining how to maintain the sustainability of the organization was a technical–rational decision, which regularly implied improving what was already happening. Similarly, where it was thought necessary to form a team of employees to produce a desired output, those who formed the team were chosen by the leader based upon the leader's opinion of who was best suited to be a team member. Often when such teams were formed they endured because the leader had a high opinion of the team members and so kept giving the team more tasks to complete even when the required skills, knowledge, and experience to complete a particular task did not sufficiently reside in any of the team members.

With a total emphasis on employee performance rather than on the suitability of the workplace environment, there was little need to be concerned about the culture of the organization. But, of course, given that these were still regular and consistent human gatherings, an organizational culture would have existed. Thus, the nature of organizational culture can be determined according to the views of key literary sources. For example, Schein (2010) posits that the culture of a new organization has its origins in the beliefs, values, and assumptions of its founding leaders. This opinion is echoed by Gao (2017) when describing how the initial formation of organizational culture is driven by "its leaders' individual and collective values, whether those values are consciously understood or unconsciously influential, spoken or unspoken, written or unrecorded" (52). This is especially pertinent because, as mentioned above, this particular era witnessed an unprecedented growth in the establishment of new organizations in which the culture was most likely to have reflected the values, beliefs, opinions, expectations, and behaviors of the founding leaders. Hence, the culture of most organizations during this era would have been overtly hierarchical, authoritarian, controlling, autocratic, and undemocratic. Despite such a culture being potentially oppressive for the employee, the benefit of receiving a regular and acceptable wage outweighed these strict and demanding conditions. But not forever.

Despite many of the values, beliefs, and practices still being widely applied in organizations today, the shortcomings of this mechanistic organizational perspective inherent within the Classical Theory had become apparent by the middle of the twentieth century. Research had clearly shown that money (wages) was not the sole employee motivator and that there was growing workplace discontent with the harshness of the culture. As more employment opportunities arose, employees were willing to seek employment in those organizations thought to provide a more humane culture or where their knowledge and skills were more appreciated. Thus, a new era in organization theory emerged. Rather than being viewed as a machine, organizations were now viewed from a more biological or organic perspective in what became known as "systems theory."

Under systems theory, organizations were considered to be open and dynamic systems containing interconnected elements that regularly interact with each other and the environment in order to function, adapt, and evolve. Arguably, the most commonly accepted organizational form was that of the General Systems Theory (GST), which understood "the behavior of systems as being the outcome of interactions among the components and relationships" (Kaine and Cowan 2011: 232). The emphasis in GST is on understanding the behavior of the system as a whole rather than on understanding the behavior of individual components or relationships. The effectiveness of the system is determined by how beneficially its components are arranged and how well they are interacting rather than solely the quantity of production. When applied to an organizational context, this GST understanding implies that attention must be directed toward employee well-being rather than just their performance.

However, being an open and dynamic system implies that the GST perspective includes the understanding that the organization is influenced by its environment. Simply put, the ongoing success of the organization depends on the state of the environment, as changes in the state of the environment will change the demands upon the organization. This means that the operation of the organization as an open system through time, its characteristic activity toward achieving its core business, can only be understood in relation to the changes occurring in the environment with which it interacts. If such environmental changes are minor or within expected limits, then the organization is considered to be stable because these environmental changes can be easily overcome within the ongoing functioning of the organization. However, should the environmental changes go beyond these limits, then the GST advocates that the structure of the organization must change in order to return it to a stable state. In other words, within the GST perspective, organizational stability and structure are related and thus stability can only be defined with respect to a given organizational structure (Kaine Cowan 2011). When structural change in the organization is required to retain stability, this is called "adaptation" in GST—provided the core purpose of the organization is preserved.

Naturally, this significantly different view of an organization necessitated a different understanding of leadership. It was no longer possible for the organizational leader to assume total control over their employees and to ignore the changing environmental demands upon their organization. In response, Burns (1978, 2010) advocated for *transformational leadership* to replace its outdated and largely ineffectual predecessor of transactional leadership. Transformational leadership is associated with employees becoming better at what they do—being "transformed"—due to the particular leadership actions of their leader. Ideally, the attention of the transformational leader is on looking after the needs and interests of the employee, whereas the attention of the transactional leader was on looking after the quality of the work that was produced. A leader with a far more transformational approach is described as possessing a sincere commitment to "forming" those they are leading and being willing to share or distribute leadership by providing opportunities, where possible and practical, for others to assume some leadership responsibilities. In this way, the organizational structure is more system-like as various individuals form part of the leadership structure for particular reasons at different times.

Hence such transformational leadership practice is founded upon a more inclusive, people-centered, and flexible approach to decision-making and workplace performance. The leader seeks to influence processes and outputs by being willing to involve others in defining, analyzing, and solving organizational problems and thereby creating a meaningful workplace culture. Essentially, the transformational leader allows for a "bottom-up" influence upon their personal organizational thoughts and actions in order to boost employee responsibility toward the organization.

Also, the transformational leader is alert to the changing demands of their organization's environment and so seeks, when deemed necessary, to help the employee to develop their skills, knowledge, and capacity in order to meet any new environmental requirements. The presumed benefit is a far more adaptable employee and, thereby, organization. As each employee adapts to sustain their desired workplace capacity, so the organization maintains its overall capacity and sustainability. Moreover, organizational success and sustainability is enhanced through a commitment to organizational learning and task-defined teamwork. This is a workplace environment in which individuals and teams explore ways to better understand the fundamental components of their workplace practices in order to create new ways of improving them and solving any new organizational problems.

This era of temporary organizational harmony and synchronicity naturally saw the rise in importance of knowing more about organizational culture. As previously described, a system perspective is not only about what organisms do individually but it is also about how they interact and relate to each other. Hence, the GST organizational perspective sought to understand and influence how employees interacted and related to each other, thereby raising the need to understand organizational culture.

Consequently, this era witnessed significant advances in theoretical descriptions of organizational culture. Though these have been more comprehensively described in Chapter 2, it is necessary to provide a brief review of this theoretical development here in order to offer insight into how the dominant view provided support and coherence to this GST perspective. It may be recalled that there are two main theoretical interpretations of organizational culture—the sociological foundation considers that organizations have a culture while the anthropological foundation considers that organizations are cultures. On the one hand, the sociological foundation invokes a functional approach to understanding organizational culture where it is believed to emerge out of the collective behavior of all within the organization and is something that can be manipulated and changed. On the other hand, the anthropological foundation invokes a semiotic approach to understanding organizational culture where it is believed to emerge out of the individual interpretations and cognitions of those within the organization. It was the sociological foundation that largely dominated organizational thinking during this GST era.

What is unique to the sociological foundation was its claim that it provided an analytical approach that was able to pinpoint objective elements of culture that can be measured in order to enable the leader to manage and control the culture. Hence, culture from this perspective can function as an agent of organizational control because it is believed to have the power to unconsciously determine and influence the attitudes and actions of employees. This is an important insight as it also highlights a general weakness in the GST perspective that, ultimately, led many to explore a new organizational theory.

Although the GST perspective grew out of dissatisfaction and discontent with Classical Theory's mechanistic and autocratic approach, it mostly failed to diminish the perceived central importance of the leader. It was still the leader's prerogative to decide how best to "transform" the employee and why there was a need for the transformation. Largely it remained the leader's role to monitor the organization's environment and determine whether or not it necessitated a commensurate organizational change. Also, given the presumed relationship between stability and structure, restructuring became an excessively common organizational occurrence throughout this era. It seemed that restructuring became the leader's panacea for most organizational ills.

Consequently, since the early 1980s restructuring became the go-to management tool for change used by senior leaders for various reasons, mostly in the guise of supposed efficiency and strategic direction. Another reason for restructuring has been to create a situation where the unacknowledged desired outcome by the leader is to reduce staffing through employee redundancies. Here, either the need to reduce expenditure means that certain employees are no longer valued—the narrative being, "unfortunately your job no longer exists." Also, another reason for restructuring is simply about a "new broom sweeping clean"—the arrival of a new leader who feels the need to mark out their territory by stamping their authority on the organization. The outcomes from restructuring typically include adding managerial positions at the expense of operational workers with the harebrained notion that more managers will ensure increased performance, higher productivity, and create efficiencies. It can also result in employees being shuffled around in new locations, role descriptions being revamped, new positions being created while others are removed, and team membership being swapped like the deck chairs on the *Titanic*. Regardless of the reason or outcomes, restructuring invariably had a negative impact on employees, teams, and the organization, which often led to further restructuring.

For example, one case known to us concerns a disillusioned employee who, in the past twenty years, has endured eleven restructuring events in the six jobs he has had during that period of time. His employment throughout this time has been as a technician and as the manager of technical teams, and these positions have been in both the corporate and government sectors. On two occasions, the restructuring resulted in him being made redundant. On another occasion, his employment contract changed from a continuing position to a fixed-term position and, on another occasion, part of the organization was subdivided and his role was redefined as a subcontractor to the organization. Many of these restructurings left him baffled by the logic, which ultimately proved flawed by the ineffective and senseless outcomes produced. Battle-weary, he has come to dread restructuring and the devastation it brings upon an organization's culture. Thus, in recent years he has become proactive. Like Pavlov's dog, the very first mention of the word, restructuring, in his employment triggers an immediate response— he leaves. Rather than staying where the organization's culture is going from bad to worse through restructuring, he prefers to work elsewhere in the hope that some leader, somewhere, "has some sense." He is currently interviewing for a new job. He takes with him a huge amount of digital technology capability and team leadership quality.

We are also familiar with a female employee who has a very similar poor view of the benefits of restructuring upon organizational efficiency and productivity. This woman has very specialized knowledge and skills associated with the training of new employees for a highly technical role in a factory setting. Be that as it may, during her time working for this factory, she has been involved in three expansive restructuring episodes which, on each occasion, led to her being made redundant only to be reemployed to essentially do the same work some months later. Her view is that the factory leaders have no idea what to do or how their decisions explicitly impact the "factory floor." What might look good in a budget spreadsheet doesn't necessarily work well in practice.

This GST-influenced period also witnessed the spread in the development and promulgation of organizational values. The simplistic but misguided belief was that an imposed set of values could dictate an organization's culture; the leader could control the culture by mandating the values employees would enact. As globalization, technological advancement, and intensified competition significantly complicated organizational life throughout the 1980s, the implications of these GST limitations became far more pronounced.

Hence by the last decade of the twentieth century confidence in the GST perspective was waning. Not only were there growing misgivings about the holistic benefits of transformational leadership theories and the incapacity of the sociological understandings of organizational culture to provide any real insight and benefit to leaders but also there remained serious ambiguities about what a "system" actually implied for an organization. Moreover, although the GST concept was founded on having to acknowledge the essential role of employee interaction and relationships, it did not provide sufficient knowledge regarding the nature of this interaction and relationships, and how these should be supported best by a leader in order to achieve the desired organizational outcomes. These perceived GST shortcomings led to an unfolding interest in applying the concept of complexity to how we understand organizations.

However, although viewing organizations through the lens of complexity has much appeal, there are, at present, significant limitations. Namely, within the context of achieving organizational harmony and synchronicity, the organizational literature surrounding complexity theory lacks a complimentary leadership and culture perspective. The remainder of this chapter will rectify these omissions by, first, describing the current application of complexity theory to how we are meant to better understand organizations. Then, secondly, it describes how our ecological understanding of organizational culture blends seamlessly with this complexity view. Lastly, the chapter then applies previously described organizational ecosystem understandings in order to overcome the existing terminological ambiguities, misgivings, and indifferences that limit or undermine the widespread application of our current complexity-based organizational theory. In this way, this chapter provides what no other literature has been able to do—the reunification of leadership, culture, and organization theories— all due to the application of our ecological perspective.

Organizational Complexity

Given that the Classical Theory had its foundations in Newtonian physics and the GST had its foundations in biology, it is unsurprising to note that science's complexity theory is now being applied toward expanding our understanding of organizations. In simple terms, complexity theory holds that a system is constituted by ongoing disorder and instability that, ultimately, results in the emergence of different actions and structures as the system evolves and organizes itself into something new. Moreover, this emergence of different actions and structures is not imposed upon the system by a controlling individual organism but, rather, occurs as a result of interrelationships, interactions, and interconnectivity among all constituent organisms within and between the particular system and its environment. It is argued that the interrelationships, interactions, and interconnectivity within a complex system produce largely unpredictable outcomes or emergent behaviors. Hence, a complex system is one whose elements interact with sufficient intricacy that they cannot be predicted by standard actions, measures, or expectations. There are so many variable interactions at work in the system that its overall behavior can only be understood as an emergent consequence of the holistic sum of the myriad behaviors occurring within it.

Where GST supported the view of interconnected organisms within a particular system engaging in linear exchanges of resources with each other and with the environment, complex systems theory recognizes a much larger number of organisms that have many nonlinear interactions inside and outside of the system. Changing just one organism in a complex system even a small amount can dramatically impact the nature and behavior of the entire system, as the whole can be very different from the sum of the parts. In simple terms, within a complex system, each organism counts. Complex systems also behave in a nonlinear manner because their organisms interact by means of a network of informational feedback loops.

Complexity theory, the study of complex, nonlinear dynamic systems, is essentially an umbrella concept that encompasses both chaos theory and network theory. Chaos theory proposes that the dynamics of natural interactions leads to random fluctuations, generating a large variety of unpredictable states, situations, and behaviors. An example commonly provided is that which is called the "butterfly effect" where it is described how the fluttering of a butterfly's wings in the Amazon might cause compounding turbulences in the air, which might ultimately cause a hurricane in Florida. It is in this way that chaos theory allows us to understand how successive branching actions, continuously amplified, can quickly lead to not only the emergence of new forms very different from the initial cause but also to the self-organization of complex structures. Network theory focuses on collections of organisms in a system in which the status of each one is determined by its connection to the others. Furthermore, network theory argues that multiple organisms, which can reproduce and maintain their structures and functions, form a population in coevolution within their environment. Their dynamic and unpredictable interactions, which are carried out through an intricate interconnected network, can readily lead to a large variety of unanticipated but substantially beneficial new structures, situations, and behaviors.

Thus, from the perspective of science's complexity theory, an organization is described as a complex, dynamic, nonlinear, evolving, quasi-equilibrium system in which chaos and order (change and stability as described in Chapter 5) appear to coexist. An organization as a complex system is said to consist of a network of interacting individuals, teams, and departments, which together produce complex, adaptive, emergent behaviors. This implies that the overall functioning of the organization cannot be lowered down to the outcome of the individual performance of each employee, since the combined emergent activity often exhibits unique collective properties and features that are of far more benefit to the organization. The organic, nonlinear, and multifaceted human interaction throughout the organization, and the changing conditions in which these operate, is characterized by uncertainty and unpredictability (constant organic change) but results in dynamic evolution for the organization as a whole over time.

More specifically, the aspect of complexity theory that has been applied most to the understanding of organizational dynamics to date is that of a *complex adaptive system* (CAS). Given its complexity foundation, a CAS is considered to be a diverse, interconnected organizational system that exhibits self-organization (purposeful internal change), hierarchy (certainty created through flexible structures that maintain a sense of order and meaning), emergence (a coherent and integrated dynamic of creativity and innovation), and learning (planned application of new innovative ideas formed through curiosity about experiences) based on internal and environmental feedback in response to new and unfamiliar demands or problems. According to this CAS perspective of an organization operating in a turbulent (constantly changing) environment, organizational change or "emergence" occurs as a result of a series of interactions, strategic conversations, and inputs among employees, which coevolve as a result of information and knowledge sharing in regard to internal and external requirements and concerns that results in the formation of new behaviors, objectives, and goals for the organization not originally considered.

Thus, the belief is that gaining an understanding of the characteristics of a CAS will provide insight into the nature and fundamental processes of organizations. This is significant because organizations trying to survive and prosper in fast-changing, turbulent environments need to be able to generate ongoing innovations, as described in Chapter 5, while continuously evolving and adapting to varying internal and external changes. It is argued that organizational leaders will be better able to cope with these changes if they view their organization as a CAS, understand the components and processes of such a system, and lead in accordance with the principles of such a system.

To this end, it is posited that the employees in an organizational CAS act in ways that are often not predictable based on previous events or current circumstances because their actions are interconnected, and one employee's behavior alters the context for others in the system. The individual capacities of the employees in an organizational CAS are diverse, and the organization derives its complexity from the level of interaction between each of these employees as well as the collective impact that the various employees have on each other and the whole organization. The employees in an organizational CAS use personal knowledge and skills, as well as their mental models of how best to perform their work developed from observations, learning, and knowledge sharing to help them understand their local and external environment and decide what actions are best to take. These models change over time as a result of experience and changing environmental conditions, and adaptation occurs at various levels in response to the perceived behaviors of other employees in the organization and the environment.

Importantly, it is claimed that there is no central control element in a CAS, making it difficult to attribute the behavior of the whole system to any one person. This has a critically important implication for an organizational CAS because of the traditional pivotal role played by the leader. From a CAS perspective, the leader is no longer the all-knowing, all-powerful, all-controlling, solution-giving figure within the organization. Instead, over time, the functioning and development of the organization is determined by the interaction of the employees as they connect with each other and the organization's environment. Each individual employee can make an important contribution to the direction of the ongoing development of the organization. Each employee counts!

Organizational learning occurs from these interactions and the organization reconfigures itself in an effort to successfully adapt to the changing environment. Internal and external forces that maintain order in the CAS coexist with counterforces pushing the organization toward change, disorder, or chaos. In organizations in which these forces are optimally in balance, increased adaptability and flexibility are achieved. This will ideally result in conditions that optimize creativity and generate innovations that enhance the organization's performance and sustainability as described in detail in Chapter 5.

However, the serious limitation of the CAS organizational theory is its seemingly jargonistic tenets that do not readily relate to everyday practice. While the central theoretical understandings make sense, the interpretation and application of its nominated fundamental practices inclusive of concepts such as strange attractor, network manager, tag creator, and storyteller are not easily discernible. Hence, the theory and its organizational leadership and culture implications have remained more a curiosity rather than a meaningful guide for practice. Consequently, the continued application of both Classical Theory and GST principles and practices predominate despite their worrying deficiencies and ineptness. For example, the use of restructuring to overcome perceived cultural deficiencies remains a frequent leadership action.

The following section will rectify this untenable situation by showing how previously described TOE perspectives straightforwardly incorporate the CAS principles. Furthermore, through the application of previously described organizational ecology guided leadership and culture understandings, the following section provides readily achievable ways for leaders to maintain their organization with all the desired outcomes promulgated as those of a CAS along with many additional beneficial outcomes.

The Theory of Organizational Ecology and Its Complex Adaptive System Outcomes

It is foolhardy to presume that past organizational leadership and culture theories remain applicable to a CAS. To do so is potentially disastrous for the organization. This became evident when CAS was first applied to organizations.

Although the principle of emergence—the development of new knowledge and skills from within the ranks of the employees rather than being designed and imposed by the leader—gained acceptance, the implication of this leading to the perception of a diminished prominent controlling role for the leader was not countenanced. Hence, the misguided belief was that the leader's new prominent controlling role was to push the employees to "the edge of chaos"—to deliberately disrupt their working environment in order to force them to apply their creative capabilities toward being innovative. Needless to say, this strategy only created further division between leaders and the employees and led to employee disengagement resulting from a deep sense of being overwhelmed by constant and seemingly meaningless imposed change demands. Hence, slowly but surely, the commitment by leaders toward trying to develop a CAS waned along with interest in its credibility and significance. The old ways seemed far more understandable even if often ineffective.

So, what essential TOE role does the leader play that simultaneously achieves the very same outcomes as those of a CAS? We argue that the role of the leader is that of a transrelational leader, as defined and described in Chapter 1, simply because one of the key roles for the leader within an organizational CAS is that of a relationship builder. But without a thoroughly comprehensive description of what constitutes a relationship builder, the CAS proposal has fallen on deaf ears. In contrast, the emphasis on relationships described throughout this book redresses this void. Simply put, understanding an organization as an ecosystem achieves what the CAS literature has not been able to do—comprehensively describing leadership as essentially a relational phenomenon.

In our previous publication (Branson et al. 2018), we argue that "leadership is best understood as a transrelational phenomenon as its essence is to move others, the organization and the leader to another level of functioning by means of relationships" (49). To be transrelational, the leader must be seen to be an integral member of the organization, whereby they appear relaxed and at ease as they wander and mix with others throughout the organization. They identify themselves completely with the organization and, therefore, are able to show ongoing interest and enthusiasm about what is happening in the organization and are able to readily and openly talk with all and show that they have the best interests of the employees and the organization continually in mind. Each employee is important in the mind of the transrelational leader. Thus, trust is at the heart of all relationships and trust is built upon predictability, consistency, and authenticity. Being trustworthy is about the leader willingly acting openly, honestly, and consistently. It is more than simply telling the truth. Trustworthiness in a leader means that they consistently display total congruence between who they say they are and what they do. In other words, how a leader is able to influence their employees must support and not undermine the relationship that binds them together.

Moreover, transrelational leadership is about influencing others above routine compliance. But it is most often non-reliant upon formal authority structures. Indeed, this form of leadership is often independent of, even contrary to, the traditional authoritative form as this would have a detrimental influence upon the process of emergence and self-organization as discussed in Chapter 5. Moreover, as described in far more detail elsewhere (see Branson et al. 2018), the leader's most effective source of influence upon those they are leading, their "power" to unite all in the achievement of a common purpose, is the relationships that the leader creates with each and every person they are leading. Their source of power or influence is more aligned with persuasion than compulsion. It is formed out of a search for truth in which all, including the leader, have the opportunity to describe the organizational reality and to present divergent, imaginative, and creative ways toward producing a successful and sustainable future. Through the sharing of divergent views, truth is discovered and new ideas for the organization's growth are revealed. In this way, all employees can feel more purposeful because they are able to contribute to the building of a far more secure future for the organization. Moreover, what is being encouraged is a holistic understanding of the organization in which all are committed to learning not only about how the organization functions and how this can be improved, but also about how they are contributing to the organization and how they can do so even more in the future. This is about providing a means by which each employee can come to know their strengths and can build upon them in imaginative and creative ways.

This understanding of the transrelational approach to leadership, in which the primary role of the leader is as a relationship builder, recognizes that truly beneficial organizational learning is situated across the interconnections among employees. It is about maximizing the flow of information and knowledge throughout the organization. The acquisition of knowledge by employees actively and directly working in collaboration is enhanced because the information received is typically better than what could be gathered independently. As illustrated in Chapter 3, information is considered to be a primary resource to be exchanged as widely and as readily as possible among all employees. This generates sensemaking and meaning-making, and thereby expands the learning effects desired within the organization. Through relationship building, the leader generates knowledge sharing—which aids in surfacing not only the individual employee's own thoughts and assumptions but also those of other employees they are able to interact with. This significantly helps to create new ideas, and to initiate new collective actions. Because the leader is central in the development of the organizational networks and the tagging processes, they have a strong influence on the exchange and interpretation of the information and the advice flowing throughout the organization. The giving and receiving of such information and advice from the organization's network of departments, teams, and cooperative groupings force each employee to think about the issues they are facing in ways that they would not if the information and advice were not offered.

Essentially, the leader's relational role is the foundation upon which they are able to effectively fulfill the other four nominated key CAS roles of being a network manager, a strange attractor, a tag creator, and a storyteller. Here, again, due to the unfamiliar, perplexing, and jargonistic nature of the names given to these roles they have had little influence on leadership practice, to date. But, when each of these roles is redefined, and described in far more plain detail using TOE understandings, they not only become more understandable but also more achievable. These roles are made more transparent and, thereby, more accessible and implementable for a leader, when they are translated into organizational ecosystem understandings described previously throughout this text.

The first of these unfamiliar and perplexing CAS components, which contributes to its general disregard by leaders, is the concept of a "network manager," which has been more simply described (see Chapter 4) as the essential role of the leader to take responsibility for intentionally intervening in the formation and support of the workgroups, teams, and departments. This is about being a connectivity leader rather than being a network manager. Employees need to be led and not managed! When employee connectivity is led appropriately, the organization gains the highest benefits that are generated by positive and collaborative employee interactions and relationships. This important responsibility acknowledges that a particular employee's knowledge and skills are always being influenced by the other employees with whom they mix and, therefore, there are incredible benefits to be gained from highly collaborative and inclusive employee interaction. Thus, the leader needs to be fundamentally involved in maximizing the cooperation and interdependencies among employees for the purpose of amplifying workplace learning and, thereby, generating innovative organizational development. Employee cooperation is more easily accomplished when their interactions are complementary, resulting in far less task duplication among employees while, at the same time, encouraging both employee task specialization around key personal strengths and the application of this to the benefit of other co-employees and to the achievement of the organization's core purpose.

The second of these unfamiliar, perplexing, and, thus, discouraging CAS components is that of a strange attractor. What this simply means is that the leader must be able to create a balance between order and disorder within an organization. Rather than applying this vague name, it is clear that this leadership role directly aligns with those responsibilities comprehensively presented in the organizational change discussion in Chapter 5. When understood from the TOE perspective, this particular CAS role is fulfilled when the leader both facilitates and contributes to the building and maintaining of the relational connectivity and interactions so as to maximize the flow of energy throughout the organization. This drives the capacity of the employees and teams within the organization to initiate and promulgate new forms of performance and productivity so that the organization is able to be slowly transformed and grow. Here, the role of the leader is not about constraining or directing the change but rather about encouraging, guiding, supporting, and championing the creative and innovative capabilities throughout the organization. This leader is helping all within the organization to acknowledge and embrace the fact that change is a constant feature of their work but through the unified, connected, and creative activities of all the organization will remain successful and sustainable. In this way the organization's connectivity system is, in turn, created, fostered, and maintained. The transrelational leader ensures that every person counts because every person plays a part and thereby the system is healthy and whole.

Rather than seemingly imposing another role expectation upon a leader, such as that of a tag creator, in order to fulfill a CAS need, we argue that this role is already a natural part of being a transrelational leader. When the leader automatically acknowledges and enacts a transrelational approach they invariably model, promote, and actively support collaborative relationships among all employees, which, according to the CAS literature, are the responsibilities of a tag creator. It is not necessary to include yet another ambiguous term. This role is already an integral aspect of leadership as understood through the TOE lens where it is about maintaining the desired levels of interpersonal trust and respect throughout the organization, thereby ensuring that all employees can fully and confidently contribute to, rather than diminish, the attainment of the organization's core purpose. Furthermore, the TOE understanding of an organization routinely includes the CAS requirement for the leader to be explicitly influencing the nature and types of employee actions and interactions to ensure that these support rather than undermine employee performance and engagement. Furthermore, from a TOE perspective, as it is for a CAS, it is essential that the leader also serves to coordinate the activities of different teams and departments by making sure that all within the organization are aware of what these teams and departments are doing and why their work is essential. As such, the leader defines and describes for all the role and outcome expectations of any differentiated organization groups or teams, and fully supports and affirms both independent behaviors within groups or teams as well as coordinated actions across groups or teams.

Arguable, very few, if any, leaders would picture themselves as a storyteller, the fourth proposed key component of a CAS leader yet most, if not all, would see the need for them to have a vision. It has long been accepted that every leader requires the capacity to describe a compelling vision; their role as an essential storyteller includes this responsibility but adds much more to it. Through publicly and privately acknowledging, affirming, and championing the work of individuals, groups, and teams, as previously emphasized as key leadership responsibilities within the TOE, the leader is in a far better position to be able to shape employee interactions and construct the shared meanings and purpose. Communication as storytelling enables the leader to provide a richly informative rationale by which the past, the present, and the future of the organization can be understood to be coalescing. Through such storytelling the leader is able to direct employee familiarity and knowledge about the organization's identity and vision, about the challenges it is currently facing, and how the future might influence current practices. Storytelling ensures that everyone understands the problems and threats facing the organization, as well as the opportunities and future direction of the organization. Rather than simply telling employees and key stakeholders what problems the future might bring and how these will need to be overcome, information giving in the form of storytelling offers a detailed description of the future and invites others to offer insight into what this might mean for the organization and its employees. Stories can help employees see continuity in the face of change and make the unanticipated seem far more doable.

Storytelling is far richer and captivating than general communication and information giving. It gives life to the knowledge being generated and shared among employees. Stories provide opportunities for all to share hard-won experience that can then serve as a point of interaction among other employees. It affords employees the chance to make sense of events by elaborating on past experiences in order to construct a positive future. By virtue of their unique structure, stories tend to sort information into coherent patterns, such as the appropriate sequence of events or the causal order of organizational phenomena. Stories make history available and help employees learn from their past and understand the implications of their possible future. Stories capture culture and informal learning and, as such, are the soft repositories of knowledge and wisdom.

Also, a powerful way of making new employees feel welcome and imparting tacit knowledge or its emotional component is through the leader telling stories about the organization. By understanding the stories of the organization, the new employee can begin to understand the reasons behind visible activity. Storytelling, rather than merely describing policies and processes, allows new employees to develop a more explicit understanding of the culture through which they can become more an integral member of the organization more quickly. Policies and procedures capture only a limited part of explicit knowledge. They do not capture the past and the historical journey of an organization. They don't capture tacit knowledge or the emotional component of knowledge. It is in the telling of stories by the leader that the cognitive processes of perspective making, perspective taking, and perspective shaping about why it is important for all in the organization to act in a certain way become more apparent.

Essentially, this is about the leader modeling the type of culture that is not only in keeping with seeing the organization as an ecosystem but also spontaneously builds the organization as a CAS. When the organizational leadership and culture are understood from an ecosystem perspective then it will be inclusive of it being a CAS. The next section illustrates why and how this is so.

An Organizational Ecosystem Culture and Complex Adaptive System

As is the case in the TOE, the fundamental principle of an organizational CAS is that every employee counts. However, in the CAS context, this perspective is narrowed to that which describes how organizational change, or adaptation, can be influenced by any individual employee anywhere in the organization. Thus, the CAS organizational theory argues that the culture of the organization must afford each employee with the freedom and support required for them to be creative and to think differently from others in order to be innovative and to do things uniquely. The leader must let go of any belief that they need to be in control, that they need to determine how the organization is to change, or they need to pick the employees who will decide how the organization is to change. In a CAS, it is assumed that beneficial organizational change can begin anywhere in the organization and be initiated by any employee. The role of the leader, then, is to ensure this can happen, to support it when it does happen, and to promote and spread the benefits from the change throughout the organization.

The problem so far for this theory is that these expectations and outcomes have not been supported by our organizational leadership and culture theories. With respect to our organizational culture theory it has mostly been aligned with the sociological perspective (as described in Chapter 2). Our traditional understanding of culture is one that is not inclusive of the belief that every employee counts. It does not embrace an individualistic influence upon culture but, rather, posits an understanding that the culture controls the individual. Hence, it tends to eliminate the possibility that an individual employee has the capacity to change the culture no matter their role. But this is not so with how organizational culture is understood from the TOE perspective as depicted in Chapter 2. Based upon an anthropological foundation, the TOE view of organizational culture innately includes the understanding that it emerges out of the everyday individual and personal aspirations, interpretations, and cognitions of those within the organization. It is precisely because of this unique explanation for how organizational culture forms that we argue that the TOE perspective, unlike any other organizational leadership or culture theory, is able to provide the theoretical and practical implications that support the CAS ideal.

This conviction is further confirmed when the practical components of the CAS ideal are listed against the relevant chapters in this book thus providing unprecedented, detailed elaboration of each component:

- Acknowledgment, promotion, and support of employee interaction and networking—as described in the Introduction;
- An environment that increases cooperation, collaboration, and teamwork—as described in Chapter 4;
- A leadership hierarchy that is interested, involved, meaningful, and supportive—as described in Chapter 1;
- Networks and teams that are relevant, inclusive, flexible, and adaptable—as described in Chapter 4;
- An environment that endorses risk-taking in order to encourage the emergence of creative and innovative new work practices and products—as described in Chapter 5;

- An environment that stimulates open and transparent sharing of information and knowledge—as described in Chapter 3;
- The collectivist cultural artifacts of connectivity, relationships, belonging, and commitment modulate the impacts of change and adaptation—as described in Chapter 5;
- An environment that fosters individual, group, and organizational learning that leads to change and growth—as described in Chapter 5.

Without doubt, the critical components of the TOE comprehensively and completely include each CAS requirement. Rather than being an add-on, our ecological understanding of an organization automatically incorporates CAS along with much, much more.

Three Case Accounts

On the one hand, this chapter to date has described an overview of the evolution of organizational theory but, on the other hand, it has indicated that there has been limited engagement with the concept of a CAS resulting in ongoing ineffectual leadership practices more affiliated with either the Classical Theory or the GST. The following three case stories from recent consultative work illustrate this opinion.

Case#1—The Leader Knows Best: Classical Theory

In one large hierarchical organization with a high customer service obligation, a decision was made by the leadership to change the client interaction process. This decision was made without consulting those operators who were in contact with the clients. Previously, each operator in the call center was required to meet the end-to-end needs of the client. They provided the advice in support of the client's needs from the first to the last call. It meant that the operator was able to speak directly to the client, email them with additional advice and information, and return calls to them whenever necessary. As a result, the operators gained work satisfaction from solving the issue with each client.

However, the new process disbanded this one-on-one support on the misguided view that it was too inefficient. Instead, the new process meant that

> each time a particular client contacted the call center their request went onto a list of awaiting matters to be resolved. This new process effectively queued the client in order of the time of their call. Furthermore, which operator responded to their call was determined by their availability when the client's call reached the top of the list. Thus, it was highly unlikely that the client would ever speak to the same operator. Also, if the client had more than one aspect of their issue then they would be directed to another operator, who may or may not have been available, because operators were now being differentiated by expertise and were required to only provide advice on specific issues. Thus, if the client's reason for calling had multiple issues, they were then re-queued for each issue—and often had to wait a week or more in queue to be contacted.
>
> The net results were as follows:
>
> 1. High-level client dissatisfaction for obvious reasons; and
> 2. Productivity dropped considerably because the operators lost the connection with the client.

This was a leadership decision that prioritized presumed efficiency over productivity. It was a top-down decision that ignored the actual reality of the work. Even though the interaction between the operator and a client was over a short period of time, the relational approach of the operators worked to assist the client through serious difficulty, and this provided satisfaction to both the operator and the client. It might have appeared inefficient to a distant observer but for those actively involved it was highly effective. The complexity of connectivity in larger organizations can be exacerbated through poor managerial decision-making regarding imposed changes to increase productivity. Classical Theory has had its day, yet some inept leaders still apply its practices.

> ## Case#2—When in Doubt, Restructure: General Systems Theory
>
> In one particular organization, the new CEO unexpectedly restructured the IT and Communications departments whereby they were reshuffled into several groups, each with various combinations. In one group, the employees became despondent— no one spoke to others and so a deathly silence characterized their office. Their breakout areas were unused. In another group, division and

> eventually verbal infighting broke out as the cultural mismatch of employees reached breaking point over any small issue.
>
> Net result was as follows:
>
> 1. Productively dropped; and
> 2. People left the organization.

Restructuring is a problem because it inexplicably moves employees from familiar physical environments, rearranges the workplace relationships, and shuffles where people are and who they are meant to work with, all without actually solving an identifiable problem. Rather than solving a problem, restructuring often creates multiple problems. It not only disconnects people and relationships, but it merges together employees from different parts of the organization where each part had its own unique culture. This means that each employee will expect that their new group will have the same culture as that which they have just left. Thus, restructuring mostly creates dysfunctional group culture.

While it was touted as the go-to leadership choice promoted in the GST, it is now accepted that restructuring is the curse of organizations. However, it often remains as the favored response for a new leader—a new broom sweeping clean the old ways of doing to make way for the new—or for the more experienced leader who has run out of ideas based upon the limitations of their past experiences. Essentially, restructuring is the response when managers do not know what to do.

> ## Case #3—Together We Achieve More: Theory of Organizational Ecology in Action
>
> Our work with a law firm toward developing organizational cultural alignment provides the third brief case study. Here the two owners of the firm were highly connected with their staff. They had moved the firm from a very traditional office arrangement, in which most of the staff were in personal office spaces, to a modern open-office space. Here, the two owners shared a workspace in the open office along with the rest of the staff. The move to an open office was a strategy designed to have everyone connected and working together. This outcome was considered essential because this firm had formed following the amalgamation of two small firms.

Although the owners' focus was for everyone to work as an interconnected system with the stated aim of, "Together We Achieve More," lingering undercurrents of "them and us" remained problematic. The owners were deeply concerned that there was strong cultural resistance to the move to a shared open-office space and professional resistance by many to working with certain colleagues. Thus, in consultation with the owners and directors, we were engaged to conduct a cultural alignment process. This involved offering a

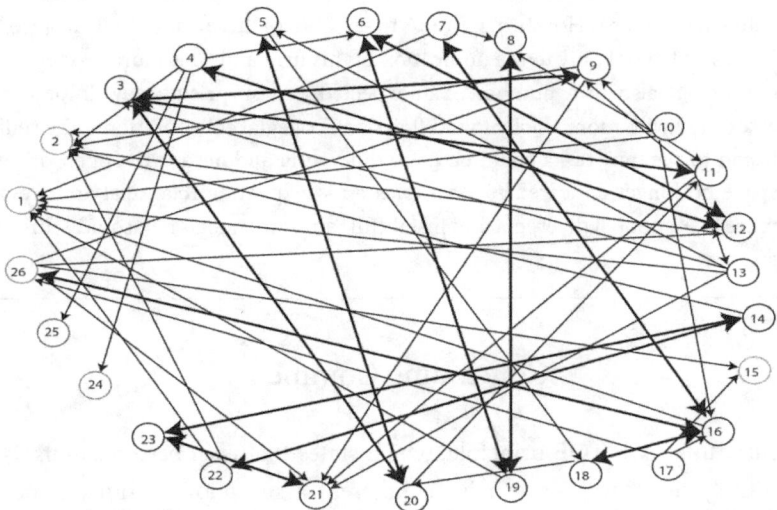

Figure 6.1 A sociogram illustrating the personal professional connects across the law firm.
Note:
Sociogram key: 1–2: Directors; 3–23: Lawyers, legal assistants, and secretaries; 4–25: External employees; 26: Nonemployee.

process that not only surfaced the existing cultural elements but also provided an explicit way forward to recreate a culture that actively supported the firm being "one team in a high-paced, high-impact workplace."

In keeping with our ecologically informed understanding of organizational culture, where the chief concern is in understanding the culture from the views and justifications provided by those who work in it, each and every staff member was individually interviewed about their personal values and beliefs associated with the move to a shared open-office space, how they understood and enacted their role within the firm, and who they worked with and why this was so. As a result, the following sociogram (Figure 6.1) was developed

> in order to indicate the existing connectivity, shared information, and work-related cooperatives across the firm. This provided the data from which specific remedial actions were implemented that redressed unacknowledged and unhelpful residual personal beliefs and attitudes in relation to workflow, conflict resolution, and workload collaboration.
>
> With respect to the provision of an explicit way forward to recreate a culture that actively supported the firm being one team in a high-paced, high-impact workplace, we conducted a cultural alignment process (Branson 2008), which is now widely used nationally and internationally. This process is described in detail in Chapter 7. However, needless to say, both of these ecologically inspired processes led not only to the unification of this firm and a far more productive output but also to a number of unexpected and surprising new initiatives associated with more efficient workflows and collegial collaborations. The staff began to see how tasks could be done differently and better. The open-office space no longer appeared as a complex and disquieting relational arena but more like a pool of divergent and insightful minds that, together, could achieve far more.

Concluding Comments

In truth, this sixth TOE principle, which states that *each person counts*, is not an entirely new ideal since it is an inherent assumption within our current organizational theory. Here, CAS essentially argues that each and every employee must have the freedom and support to be able to change the organization for the better. Given the opportunity, each employee can be the source of important new knowledge and skills that can benefit their co-employees and the organization. But the problem has been that our leadership and culture theories weren't able to support such an ideal until now. As shown in this chapter, through the lens of the TOE's understanding of an organization, this ideal becomes a reality without the need for any additional theoretical constructions or practical responsibilities. When leaders adopt an ecological understanding of their organization, along with its leadership and cultural implications, then they will have naturally created a CAS without having to consider any further notion or action. More simply stated, our ecological understanding of an organization seamlessly and coherently weaves together each of our contemporary leadership, culture, and organizational theories.

However, we acknowledge that there is much more to the successful adoption of the TOE than simply the leader knowing its principles and practices. Knowledge in and of itself is insufficient. Everyone knows that smoking can cause serious health issues, yet people smoke. Moreover, for far too long our leadership literature has been only feeding our leaders with knowledge-based practices. This literature has been largely telling our leaders what they should be doing. We argue that it is time for our leaders to be guided by wisdom. It is time for wise leaders. Indeed, it is time for the application of the TOE. But what is wisdom? What is a wise leader? Wisdom, and leadership wisdom in particular, is the topic of Chapter 7.

7

Leadership Wisdom

Leadership in an Organizational Ecosystem—Where Wisdom Surpasses Rational Knowledge

Introduction

Creating a connected, adaptable, engaged, and innovative organization simply will never happen by mandate, no matter how many policies, processes, or managers are in place to achieve such a desirable state. The essential ingredient for an organization to grow and flourish as an ecosystem is a leader with wisdom, for it is the leader that understands, values, and nurtures the employees and the relationships among them. Without the wisdom of the leader, the organization remains static, disconnected, and the sum of its parts with its employees disengaged and unfulfilled. Wisdom not only frees leaders from the constraints of our current mechanistic approaches to leadership that are essentially managerialism driven but also sets the employees free to feel they more fully belong in their teams and their organization.

Would you prefer to be led by a wise or an unwise leader? A ridiculous question you may say, for who would ever choose to be led by an unwise leader. But we argue that this is a critically important question that needs to be faced by today's organizations. Certainly, as organizational life, regardless of country or context, seems to be growing ever more uncertain and unfamiliar the need for wise leaders becomes a dire imperative. However, we stridently argue that our current array of corporate and educational leadership literature is more about producing unwise leaders. It essentially focuses on telling the person what they need to do to lead rather than providing insight and learning about the holistic nature of leadership practice. This is the crux of the worldwide problem in organizations for it is only through a holistic approach underpinned by wisdom that leaders can create the most appropriate form of leadership for their context, for those they are to lead, and for themselves as the designated leader.

However, this is not the case in the current literature. Here attractive-looking publications are being pumped out on a weekly basis enticing would-be leaders into adopting catchy-written action lists or recipes for leadership practice. When stripped of their gloss and glamor, these leadership action recipes are nothing more than managerial programs being mass produced in order to maintain an income and market share in a highly lucrative but also competitive leadership professional learning arena. Inevitably, of course, these recipes ultimately produce unwise leaders because each in their own way, despite its comprehensiveness, only concentrate on delineating and describing the practical elements thought to be essential leadership actions of the day. There is far much more to leadership than just the practical elements.

Clearly, this literature is providing objective knowledge mostly based upon quantitative research data often gained from impressively large participant populations. While this might sound reasonable, the gaping shortcoming with this approach and thinking is the inherent assumption that the leader, once they have accessed and internalized this objective knowledge, can rationally apply this knowledge to their leadership behavior and will continually be critiquing this behavior to maximize and perfect their application of this knowledge.

According to Aristotle's descriptions of knowledge, what the current leadership literature is mostly offering is *episteme* knowledge—the kind of knowledge that can be gained from extensive measurements, observations, and recordings that lead to somewhat generically applicable propositions, rules, or norms. This form of knowledge can be provided to a person but is independent of the person's own input. Because it sounds logical, it must be right. Importantly, this form of knowledge currently swamping the leadership literature would not have been considered by Aristotle to be wisdom. From an Aristotelian perspective, it is merely only one source of possibly important knowledge. In the absence of a clear understanding of what constitutes a wise, relationally astute leader such rational options appear as life rafts for resolving the major organizational issues concerning employee engagement and organizational change. Thus, if we want our organizations to be led by wise leaders then we need to know what constitutes wisdom and how it can, if possible, be nurtured and applied to leadership practice. More specifically, we need to change the focus of our leadership literature to ensure it truly develops wise leaders in practice.

To this quintessential end, this chapter will show how the leadership understandings and practices promoted by the Theory of Organizational

Ecology invariably foster wise leaders. Support for this understanding begins by drawing on current literature to describe what constitutes wisdom. Here it is vital to note that, currently, there is little literature from any context that details how leadership wisdom can be readily developed. Although the gaining of wisdom is desired, how this can happen remains a mystery. But if we want our leaders to have wisdom, then this situation cannot remain. Thus, the next section of this chapter synthesizes relevant literature in order to construct a model, a conceptual framework of leadership wisdom that can be used to not only more holistically illustrate the concept of leadership wisdom but also to guide its development. The chapter then concludes by describing and illustrating how the application of the Theory of Organizational Ecology to practical understandings associated with organizational leadership and culture inherently fosters and necessitates leadership wisdom both in organizations, generally, and in educational contexts, in particular.

What Is Wisdom?

Although the possession of wisdom is a universally admired and highly desired human quality, attempts to describe its origin have proven to be a far more varied and yearned-for outcome. Generally, our understanding of what constitutes wisdom is more often associated with how it can be experienced rather than in knowing how it is created. We mostly judge a person's level of wisdom based upon what we see them doing—their behavioral attributes such as heightened capacities in complex reasoning, openness and inclusivity, relational depth and breadth, insight and discernment, flexibility and adaptability, and cognitive integration and communication. Importantly within this perception there is also an assumption that not every person is wise or has the same levels of wisdom. A person can lack all such attributes and therefore be considered as not being wise—as not up for the job and not able to be trusted in their decision-making—while others can have some or all such attributes but to differing levels of development and so can display varying degrees of wisdom. What is also a commonly accepted understanding about wisdom is that it can increase with age. In many cultures, those deemed to be the wisest are the aged. Hence the term "elder" being indicative of those considered wise in certain cultures.

However, what this brief summary of the current literature on wisdom clearly illustrates is that it is not, necessarily, an innate human phenomenon. One is not born wise. Although some personalities might be more conducive to the development of wisdom, essentially it is a learned rather than a genetic human characteristic. This being so, especially given the urgency for wise leaders, more needs to be known about the constituency of wisdom. To this end, this discussion turns to reviewing how it has been defined and described based upon research data.

Although the task of defining the tangible elements of wisdom has occupied philosophers since the time of Plato, still there is lingering uncertainty about what constitutes wisdom. This is reflected in the varied focus and complexity divergence portrayed in how it has been defined in more recent times. Some authors have concentrated on describing a predominately singular characteristic such as a behavioral or personality focus. For example, Sternberg (2002) proposed that wisdom can be defined as the capacity of a person to take the right action at the right time. Similarly, but in a more detailed way, Jones (2005) posits that wisdom is a mental faculty that brings an awareness of the proper means and ends, which enables leaders to approach dynamic organizational environments with cautious confidence and the willingness to improvise in response to situational factors. In addition, Bierly, Kessler, and Christensen (2000) contend that wisdom relates to the ability to effectively choose and apply appropriate knowledge in a given situation and define wisdom as the ability to best use knowledge to establish and achieve desired goals. Other authors have adopted a far more personality-orientated focus when defining wisdom. Here, Ardelt (2004) defined wisdom as a personality that integrates cognitive, reflective, and affective personality traits while Clayton (1982) defined wisdom as the personal ability that enables the individual to better understand and work with others.

However, still there is significant divergence in viewpoints even where the authors have adopted a more complex definition of wisdom. Some of these authors offer such a view by incorporating a number of different, but largely undefined, elements while others add further clarity and/or breadth. For example, Small (2004) proposes that wisdom is having the power to apply experience and knowledge critically, ethically, and practically. Similarly, Srivastava and Cooperrider (1998) define wisdom as a dynamic process of constantly readjusting, restructuring, and rebuilding one's subtle way of judging and knowing. This somewhat unpretentious definition suggests a link between life experiences and the gaining of wisdom—the more that life is experienced the more one's capacity to know and judge is enhanced and, thereby, the wiser one becomes. A similar but more sophisticated view is proffered by Bellinger, Castro, and Mills (2000) where they suggest that human cognitive complexity goes from processing and producing data, information, and knowledge until it finally reaches wisdom, the highest level of cognitive processing and complexity. Holliday and Chandler (1986) assert that wisdom is a complex set of competencies cutting across the limitations of particular arenas of knowledge and is expressed as exceptional understanding, judgment, and communication skills, general competencies, interpersonal skills, and social unobtrusiveness. This understanding is closely shared by that of McKenna, Rooney, and Boal (2009) who propose that wisdom "is a process that brings together the rational and the transcendent, the prosaic and higher virtues, the short- and long-terms, the contingent and the absolute, and the self and the collective" (185). Labouvie-Vief (2000) elaborates further when arguing that the emergence of wisdom is based on relativistic and dialectical reasoning, which are advanced cognitive functions developed only in adulthood after diverse real-world experiences. Here, Labouvie-Vief introduces the relational aspect of wisdom through advancing the importance of dialectical reasoning, which is more specifically articulated by Sternberg (2007) who views wisdom as "the use of successful intelligence, creativity, and knowledge as mediated by values to (a) seek to reach a common good (b) by balancing intrapersonal (one's own), interpersonal (others'), and extrapersonal (organizational, institutional, and/or spiritual) interests (c) over the short and long term to (d) adapt to, shape, and select environments" (38).

Although necessarily succinct due to the structural limitations of this book, this review of wisdom literature still highlights that its nature is both diverse and complex, and therefore the difficulty in trying to capture in written form the fullness of its composition. Hence, the following section draws upon a wider array of wisdom literature in order to construct a far more comprehensive understanding by means of a conceptual framework for the phenomenon of wisdom.

A Conceptual Framework for Wisdom

The key elements of the framework are wisdom, intelligence, and knowledge, the distinctions between which are clarified as follows: Knowledgeable people know things. Intelligent people are able to interpret, analyze, and apply their knowledge. Wisdom then extends intelligence to a much greater scale. A wise person is able to assimilate multiple intelligences in order to discern diverse inferences and consequences beyond the immediate experience. Therefore, within this conceptual framework, knowledge is considered to be what a person practically or theoretically comes to know through some form of deliberate (e.g., educational) or unintended (e.g., social) experience whereas intelligence is taken to imply that the knowledge is not only known but more importantly understood and can be appropriately applied (Sternberg 2007). While a person can gain knowledge by learning facts or skills, this does not mean that they can immediately understand how to readily and capably apply this knowledge. Knowing numbers does not make a mathematician. Nor does knowing how to get the right answer by using a learned mathematical formula mean that the person can apply that knowledge correctly when presented with an unusual or unfamiliar context. Wisdom empowers intelligence to become more generative as it enables the person to see a wider array of possibilities, to be open to exploring new ways of doing things, and to be continuously focused on making things better for all (Disch 2009). Moreover, wisdom, given a key aspect of its genesis is in self-knowledge, sets the person free from their own limitations and promotes cooperative strategies among others with the intention of building new capabilities that address previously unknown opportunities (Whittington 2010).

Thus, informed by these distinctions between wisdom, intelligence, and knowledge, Figure 7.1 provides an illustration of our conceptual framework for the phenomenon of wisdom. However, before presenting Figure 7.1 it is essential to be reminded that wisdom is a learned phenomenon. One does not either have no wisdom or have perfect and comprehensive wisdom. It is universally accepted that wisdom can be slowly and progressively enhanced through ongoing learning by having a growth mindset, by learning more about one's self, by learning through relating more closely and collaboratively with others, by learning more about one's required work-related knowledge and skills, and by refining and improving one's rational, analytical, and judgmental capacities. The growing of wisdom requires a commitment to learning across all of these areas. But also, it is just as important to remember that all of this learning does not take place automatically or instantaneously. Not everyone has the propensity, the willingness, or the commitment toward growing their wisdom. Thus, the caveat associated with Figure 7.1 is to acknowledge that it represents the ideal— the big picture that those who are growing their wisdom are working toward. It is not, as such, the measurement of whether a person is wise or not. In other words, Figure 7.1 only aims to depict the integral elements of wisdom and is not meant to suggest that the person must be comprehensively adept in each and every element before they can be considered wise.

The unidirectional nature of the bracket parentheses in Figure 7.1 indicates the way in which wisdom forms overall as well as the antecedents of each

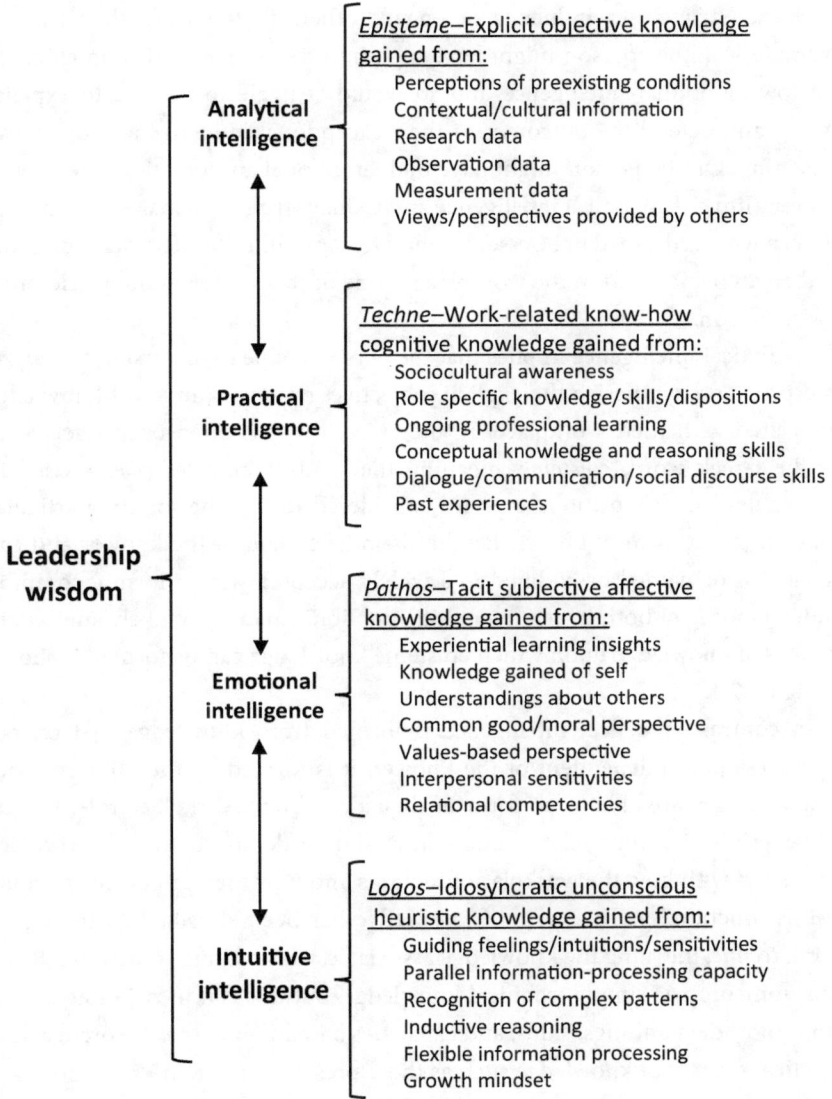

Figure 7.1 A conceptual framework for the phenomenon of wisdom.

level. Hence, we argue that, at its basic level, wisdom is the outcome generated through the seamless integration of analytical intelligence, practical intelligence, emotional intelligence, and intuitive intelligence. Importantly, elements of all four intelligences must be present in order to form wisdom. A person might have exceptional analytical and practical intelligence but little or no emotional intelligence such that they are socially inept, avoid mixing with others and, therefore, struggle to influence or engage others in the work they wish to promote. Another person might have high intuitive and analytical intelligence but low emotional intelligence and so would struggle to be able to explain, justify, and defend the outcomes of their exceptional inductive and deductive reasoning. Or, the person might have high emotional and practical intelligence but very limited analytical intelligence and so may struggle to make decisions, to discern what is deemed to be essential, and to communicate effectively about the challenges being faced in the workplace. None of these three examples describe a wise person.

Analytical intelligence implies that the person is able to understand, analyze, interpret, and synthesize the explicit, objective, rational sources of knowledge associated with their workplace. In literature, this has often been referred to by the Greek word, *episteme*, meaning the kind of knowledge expressed in facts, rules, or propositions that are considered to be true for the particular context. It is a form of knowledge that is independent of the knower and can be labeled or named or codified in a widely accepted way to form a common understanding of both its nature and its function. An array of likely antecedent sources of knowledge upon which episteme knowledge can be formed is shown in Figure 7.1.

In contrast, practical intelligence is formed from knowledge that cannot be represented independent of the knower. It is formed by the knower about how well they are able to perform in their designated workplace role. Hence, its genesis is in work-related know-how and in-depth cognitive knowledge associated with how the workplace functions and how they can best contribute to this functioning. This form of knowledge has been classified by the Greek word, *techne*, meaning the knowledge associated with making something. It can be summed up as simply technical knowledge, but this can incorporate a wide range of understandings, skills, and capacities based upon other theoretical and practical sources of knowledge such as those presented in Figure 7.1.

The third essential component of wisdom is that of emotional intelligence—a topic about which much has been previously written where the simple message is that emotional intelligence concerns knowing one's self in order to then be able to work better with others. Thus, emotional intelligence has its genesis in tacit, subjective, affective knowledge thereby naturally aligning it with the Greek word, *pathos*, meaning the knowledge associated with how people are influenced by subjectivity and emotions. Importantly, Aristotle argued that in order to maximize the desired outcomes of pathos the person must also incorporate a crucial moral component in order to establish credibility. Actions emanating from emotional intelligence must be seen to be deeply sincere and authentic. Such a stance is not based upon some externally imposed edict, obligation, commandment, or mandate but, rather, is personally formed through the awareness and synthesis of one's context, of human nature shaped from deeply knowing one's self, of the needs of others, and of the essential values and beliefs that will maximize the common good. These are delineated more clearly in Figure 7.1.

The final essential component of wisdom is that of intuitive intelligence. Leaders in today's organizational climate are constantly working within an environment that is changing, becoming more complex, and increasingly being filled with uncertainty. Under such unusual and trying conditions, the incorporation of intuition in a leader's decision-making process has become an imperative (Branson 2009; Kasanoff 2017). In times of ambiguity, intuitive intelligence enables leaders to size up a situation, to integrate and assimilate large amounts of data, and to successfully deal with incomplete information. Furthermore, this form of intuitive information-processing is shown to be effective for enhancing flexible thinking and inductive reasoning when endeavoring to find patterns or categories within large, complex, unfamiliar data sources. Within the literature, intuitive intelligence is described as the person's capacity to sense messages from their internal store of life experiences, of contextually informed feelings and sensitivities, and of awareness of their own bodily reactions to the task at hand. There is the element of instinct, a gut feeling that informs the person about what needs to be considered. Sometimes, despite all the evidence pointing to a particular action, it just doesn't feel right. Or, without all the supportive evidence, the intuitively intelligent person knows that a particular action is the right decision to make.

Thus, intuitive intelligence has been described as unconscious cognition (Isenman 2013) due to its formation often being initiated within the person's nonconscious mind. As Gigerenzer (2007) argues, those with intuitive intelligence can, without conscious awareness, both discover and then defend an analysis and interpretation of exceedingly large and complex data. They can see, describe, and justify patterns, or heuristics, in such data that is, initially, beyond the view of others. Neuroscience describes how intuitive intelligence is created by *parallel interactive* information-processing in which each neuron is able to interact simultaneously with many others, thereby enabling heightened pattern recognition because it automatically registers complex co-occurrences and interacting regularities. Such a capacity is aligned with the Greek word, *logos*, which means an opinion, view, judgment, or argument formed from personalized reasoning. Aristotle argued that logos enables a person to perceive and make clear to others through reasoned discourse that which is normally beyond the capacity of others to see or deduce. Figure 7.1 is inclusive of some of the antecedent sources of knowledge that can form intuitive intelligence.

This interpretation of what constitutes leadership wisdom does have some literary support. For example, leadership wisdom was characterized by Whittington (2010) as inclusive of intellectual capability, wholeness, expansiveness, inclusiveness, depth, and presence in the leader's engagement in their organization's life, while Stenberg (2002) proposed that leaders need wisdom because they need creative abilities to come up with ideas and analytical abilities to decide whether their ideas are good. He added that leaders need practical abilities to make their ideas functional and to convince others of the value of their ideas. They need wisdom to balance the effects of ideas on themselves, others, and institutions in both the short and the long run. Furthermore, he stated that for successful intelligence there is a need to combine practical intelligence, analytical intelligence, and emotional intelligence. Importantly, Stenberg also added that wisdom encompasses insight or insightful intuition, openness, inclusiveness, far-sightedness, wholeness, awareness, feelings, future visions, relevant stories, and care and consideration for others. Thus, we posit that our leadership wisdom conceptual framework includes all of these features described by Sternberg.

The unfortunate reality is that, to date, the leadership wisdom literature has had little practical impact upon leadership theory. Its possibility has captured the imagination, but it has not led to any behavioral benefits. It has remained only an auspicious ideal most likely because its development and practice remained a mystery. This is no longer the case. The next section clearly describes how the Theory of Organizational Ecology not only mandates the need for wise leaders, as described above, but also how leadership wisdom can be developed and practiced.

Organizational Ecology and Leadership Wisdom

This concept of leadership wisdom, with its integral binding together of the analytical and practical with the emotional and intuitive, is consistent with the turning of the tide away from our current dominating leadership theories. While we might all innately accept the rightful place of emotion and intuition in effective leadership, the current leadership theories have consistently avoided acknowledging this connection in a real tangible way. Throughout the past century, our leadership theories have directed our leaders to act in prescribed, rather than individualistic, ways. These theories have urged our leaders to act according to externally articulated customs that mostly attempted to circumvent their use of emotion or intuition. Current leadership theories have ensconced the view that effective leadership is about behavior rather than character and so overemphasized bureaucratic, psychological, and technical-rational authority. These leadership theories have concentrated more on telling the leader what they should be doing rather than on helping the leader to understand how they, themselves, could become a more effective leader. As such, our leadership theories have been more like a recipe than a guide as they have tended to ignore the issues of context and individuality and, in short, are simply not working for employees as seen by the unsustainable magnitude of disengaged workers.

Thus, it is crucial to recognize that an overdependence upon this source of knowledge by a leader has both created employee disengagement and underperformance while, at the same time, has posed as the solution. These have played the role of both the cause and the solution, both the poacher and the gamekeeper. Ultimately, the outcomes of these theories manifest as layer upon layer of line managers administering a profusion of policies attempting to target increasing employee performance and redressing perceived cultural glitches. However, as anthropologist James Suzman (see Hunt 2020) states, the problem of employee disengagement and cultural glitches is *a problem with the nature of work*, the responsibility for which lies at the core of managerialist leadership practices. Also, Hunt goes on to illustrate how the late anthropologist, David De Beers, described as "bullshit jobs" the proliferation of line-manager and administrator positions needed to oversee the overwhelming number of policies generated by such a managerialist approach—policies that achieve little more than creating work for work's sake and which seem to exist more to further enhance the good fortune of the few top performers than to help create a better working environment for all. Where is the wisdom in this leadership practice? Indeed, the form of limited knowledge upon which our current leadership theories are based would not have been considered by Aristotle to be wisdom.

In truth, all that is required by leaders wishing to improve employee engagement and organizational culture is to know how to treat their employees not as resources to be managed and controlled but as individual humans who need to feel a sense of belonging and connectedness and to be valued for their good ideas and efforts that they can bring to the organization. The successful solution involves the leader being able to create workplaces that provide for the basic needs of the employees—to belong, to be valued, to be supported, to be connected, to be creative, and to be working on something they believe in. This solution is not "rocket science"; rather, this solution is simple, but it requires leaders, not managers—leaders who have the knowledge, intelligence, and wisdom to create workplaces where people thrive.

The wise leader knows that the workplace is its people and not its administrative structures, policies, processes, or facilities. It is time to rehumanize workplaces, and to do that requires leaders who have the wisdom to establish organizational practices and systems that support and enhance the employees and to do away with the controls that constrain, monitor, and control them as if they are cattle. Hence, we argue that the right type of culture for today's and tomorrow's organization is an ecologically connected organization with its emphasis upon leadership that naturally creates connectivity through cooperative relationships and the free flow of knowledge and creative ideas.

The connections between leadership wisdom and the foundational understandings of the Theory of Organizational Ecology are illustrated in Figure 7.2. In this figure, there are two parts—acceptance and authentication—that are the enduring cornerstones of leadership. As argued in the earlier chapters, before one can be a leader of people, first the person needs to be accepted as the leader but then, secondly, they need their actions to be continually authenticated by those being led as being acceptable leadership practices. If the person's

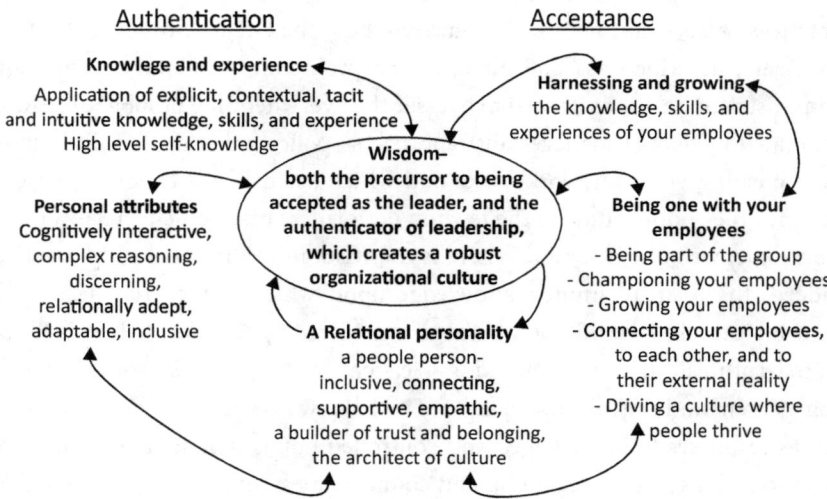

Figure 7.2 An illustration of how the interplay of leadership wisdom and the Theory of Organizational Ecology underscores appropriate contemporary leadership practice.

leadership actions become viewed as inappropriate leadership behaviors, they lose credibility and become unaccepted as the leader. As the Figure 7.2 illustrates, leadership wisdom not only helps the person to become accepted as the leader but also helps to ensure that the person is able to remain as the accepted leader. The ongoing development and application of leadership wisdom ensures that the person's leadership capacity is being continually authenticated in the minds of those being led.

Figure 7.2 not only shows the connection between the leader's authentication and acceptance, but also that the knowledge and wisdom is not solely held by the leader. Indeed, it is a foolish leader who thinks themselves to be the sole authority on all things and, thus, invariably always makes the right decision. This is neither wisdom nor leadership by any stretch of the imagination. Rather the wise leader recognizes, acknowledges, seeks, and grows the collective knowledge and wisdoms of their employees in all significant and unfamiliar decision-making processes. In this way, there is no resistance to any subsequent change because employees have been actively involved in the construction of the change. There is no disengagement from the project because employees are self-motivated toward ensuring the success of the change strategy they helped to create. Employees willingly invest in their work because they feel they belong and have purpose. As Figure 7.2 illustrates, the feedback loops between the leader and those they are leading grow the wisdom, intelligence, and knowledge of the leader and the employees. The employees are thriving because the culture is relational, supportive, fair, hospitable, and cooperative, thereby creating belonging and commitment which, in turn, results in discretionary effort, innovation, the sharing of information, knowledge, and wisdom. This is how an organization learns and grows; it is a far cry from the current performance management practices and time-wasting surveys, which only serve to delude leaders and starve the organization of its potential.

The Importance of Leadership Wisdom in Education

In this climate of globalization and international education, comparisons, evaluation, verification, and accountability within some form of school review have become key school issues in all developed countries. Hence, comprehensive school review processes, which incorporate a systematic, evaluative assessment of the conditions of work, working methods, and outcomes of the individual school, are now commonplace in most educational systems worldwide. Thus, the critical question is: Are today's principals able to do the best they can for their staff, students, and school community? There is little doubt that the exceedingly complex and never-ending challenges associated with these educational reforms require highly effective leadership—especially when we add in the normal daily responsibilities as well.

It is unsurprising, therefore, that Fullan (2001) claims that the school principal's role has become extraordinarily complex and challenging, which now encompasses not only direction-setting but also inspiring others to make the journey to a new and improved state in relation to the external expectations around student learning outcomes (Davies 2005). Johnson and Kardos (2002) point out that an effective leader is one who spends exorbitant amounts of time at school, focuses on teaching and learning processes, monitors classroom environments, regularly provides professional feedback, and provides personal and professional guidance. Moreover, King (2002) admits that the roles of educational leaders such as principals and senior assistants or superintendents have expanded during the past decade, which include a larger focus on teaching and learning, professional development, data-driven decision-making, and externally imposed accountability demands. In addition, there is strong and growing evidence that principals play a pivotal role in initiating and sustaining school improvement in terms of students' academic performance (Harris 2004). In other words, effective leadership capacity is the most important and essential skill the school leader must have because they are perceived to be the causal agent for the success or failure of the school's educational environment (Cheng 2010).

To be successful in such initiatives, principals must motivate and encourage teachers, students, parents, and other community members to join their efforts in creating positive and engaging school climates that increase the likelihood of improved academic achievement and other forms of students' performance (Hallinger and Heck 1997; Leithwood and Reihl 2005). It is now recognized that such leadership is not the provenance of one individual but teams of people, who provide leadership in the school and, by doing so, they support and inspire others to achieve the best for the students and for their own professional careers. In other words, today's school leadership is not set in isolation but is set in the context of organizations and the wider society (Quong and Walker 2010; Hofman and Hofman 2011). Bush (2011) states that the role of the principal is widely regarded as central for school improvement and enhanced student outcomes. The development and success of a school is in the hands of the school's principal, leader, or administrator. In this sense, whatever they offer in terms of leadership determines the level of success and accomplishment of the school.

Such effective leadership capacity includes appropriate interpersonal relationship competences, fitting educational and leadership knowledge and skills, influential communication skills, learning gained from past relevant experiences, the ability to understand and appreciate the local context, and emotional intelligence in order to remain positive and optimistic during extremely difficult times. Simply put, today's schools require wise leaders. Hairuddin (2012) posits that since leadership wisdom, in its wholeness, is intricately interconnected, interdependent, cocreative, and optimistic, it is an absolute necessity for school leaders. He adds that principals guided by leadership wisdom are naturally responsible but not blaming, engaging but not controlling, interested but not constricting, and influential but not suppressive. Sternberg (2002) states that when principals are guided by leadership wisdom, they can help the school community to realize deeper levels of educational understanding and can reveal much of what is needed to know to teach and learn more richly. He adds that wise leadership is able to achieve this because it is founded upon deep empathy, compassion, understanding, mutual aid, and collaborative problem-solving—qualities that are essential when leading people toward profoundly new, unfamiliar, and challenging outcomes. Moreover, these are foundational and integral leadership qualities as described and promoted in the Theory of Organizational Ecology.

This understanding is reinforced and extended by the views of Syed Othman and Aidit (1994) who declare that a school principal with leadership wisdom can deepen and boost their capacity by integrating reason, logic, and facts with intuition, body awareness, spiritual sensibilities, narrative intelligence, emotional intelligence, and other ways of apprehending the staff, students, and school community. The outcomes from this wisdom can also be actions, or knowledge, or statements, or solutions that arise from such understandings and envisioned outcomes (Saleh 2002). Saleh goes on to argue that educational leadership wisdom becomes accessible through reflective thought, atonement, conversation, understanding, and collaboration, which are essential factors for the success and high achievement of the school's educational performance. Cooperation and collaboration among staff and students are highly important in instilling inclusion and harmony and the rights of every individual in the school community (Al-Bureay 1990). Again, all of these views and propositions are restated and reinforced as the explicit outcomes generated by the Theory of Organizational Ecology.

Conclusion

The outcomes generated by any organization, be these productive and profitable or dysfunctional and inexpedient, are a reflection of the leader's capacity to lead. An organization that invariably functions productively, purposefully, and in harmony as a connected and collectively committed group of employees is established and maintained by the knowledge, intelligence, and wisdom of its leader. Arguably, however, for most of the past century our leadership theories have essentially focused on developing leadership knowledge. Our various theories have been applied with a view to tell our leaders how they should act and what specific behaviors constitute leadership. Thus, the support for the development of our leaders has focused mainly on episteme and techne knowledge. It has mostly ignored or underemphasized pathos and logos knowledge, thereby ill-preparing our leaders for knowing the social dynamics associated with how humans gather and the critical importance of belonging in human social relationships and human motivation.

Organizations are, and have always been, human gatherings albeit formed in a nonnatural way as described in Chapter 6. Moreover, this nonnatural gathering together of people into organizations greatly increases the need for our leaders to have deep knowledge of the social dynamic and human relationship consequences likely to be caused by this unusual coming together of a diverse array of people for a common purpose. In other words, for a leader, pathos and logos knowledge are integral and not optional.

But what this chapter has also emphasized is the awareness that knowledge in and of itself is drastically insufficient from a leadership perspective. The person first needs to have the capacity to appropriately apply the most suitable knowledge in the light of the circumstances being confronted. This necessitates intelligence. To be a leader the person needs to act with intelligence by applying the right knowledge at the right time. Furthermore, the leader needs to act wisely by seamlessly adapting and adopting the most applicably effective source of intelligence as required by the unfolding demands and characteristics of the situation. For example, should a wise leader be confronted with having to resolve a highly heated and emotionally contested interpersonal dispute then aspects of emotional intelligence helps create initial calmness, practical intelligence helps to create a suitably inclusive resolution process, analytical intelligence helps to ask the most insightful questions, and intuitive intelligence helps to understand and describe the most telling concerns and how these are to be constructively addressed. Echoing the claim made in this chapter, it is wisdom that needs to be guiding leadership practice in today's extensively globalized, highly competitive, and extraordinarily unpredictable organizational environment.

Moreover, wisdom must be guiding practice at all levels of leadership throughout the organization—executive, middle, department, team, and group—but it must start at the top level. It is the executive group or senior leadership team that must set the example for everyone else to follow and to firmly set the expectation that it will be happening throughout the organization. This becomes even more essential when the functioning of the organization is distributed across multiple sites. For example, with respect to an educational context there must be total consistency from the administrative authority (superintendent or educational ministry or executive director) to the principal to the senior staff, and so on. For far too long, schools have been expected to provide a leadership and cultural experience different from what they received from their administrative authority.

In an organizational ecology, there must be consistency in action and experience throughout the organization regardless of its structural challenges. The truth of this crucial understanding has come to the fore in 2020 as organizations around the world have struggled to cope with Covid-19 lockdowns. Contrary to beliefs that employee work quality and quantity is dependent upon closely monitored accountability and performance management processes, working-from-home opportunities have significantly improved productivity despite the absence of direct line-manager and leader controls. But what has also been found by international research is that countless organization leaders have lost a sense of purpose and role clarity during these arrangements. These leaders don't know what to do when they are unable to initiate command-, control-, and management-based strategies. The leaders who have functioned well, and whose organizations have flourished, have been those who have enacted wise leadership closely aligned with the principles and practices presented in our Theory of Organizational Ecology. These leaders sought and used all possible means of keeping in contact and supporting their employees as well as creating opportunities for regular online team and employee meetings. Also, these leaders developed both internal and external support processes to ensure no employee was adversely disadvantaged by the technological demands of having to work off-site or at home. Simply put, wise leadership is that which has been previously described in the chapters of this book as prioritizing trust, support, connectivity, collaboration, belonging, creativity, initiative, and networking even when close physical presence is not possible.

Hence, it can be clearly seen how the application of our Theory of Organizational Ecology can not only provide excellent leadership guidance under normal conditions but even more so in extremely abnormal conditions as those experienced during the Covid-19 pandemic. The application of our Theory of Organizational Ecology has a holistic organizational benefit. But it can also produce specific strategic benefits. In the concluding chapter we will vividly describe two critically important applications of the Theory of Organizational Ecology. Each application will be in a different context in order to illustrate its universality. The first application will describe the application of this theory to an extensive formal organizational review in an educational context, while the second application will describe the application of this theory to an organizational cultural alignment process in a corporate context.

Conclusion: Applications and Implications

Introduction

A commonly acknowledged truism is that *the proof of the pudding is in the eating*. When applied to a new theory this means that the true benefit of the proposed theory can only be plainly determined by the practical benefits gained from its application. By unambiguously studying an organization as an ecosystem, this book has not only presented the ecology of an organization but has also laid claim to have illustrated a new organizational theory—the Theory of Organizational Ecology. A simplified overview of this theory would highlight how it has offered a comprehensive study of the significant benefits to be gained from an organizational culture manifested through the nurturing of collaborative interpersonal relationships among the leader, the employees, and the teams. Thus, the challenge is to show how this theory, when applied in practice, can reap the proposed organizational rewards.

To this end, this concluding chapter will begin by describing two different but equally powerful ways that we have applied the Theory of Organizational Ecology. Moreover, in order to demonstrate the universality of this new theory, the respective context for each application will be different. The first application will describe how the theory was used to guide a large-scale school improvement project, while the second application will describe how the theory was used to facilitate an organizational culture alignment process in a corporation. The chapter then concludes with a brief summary of the key implications associated with this new theory.

Application #1—The Organizational Ecology Theory and a School Improvement Project

The introduction of comprehensive school review processes is usually justified by arguing that, as schools are now increasingly responsible for the quality of their work, they should undergo regular external reviews. These regular external reviews are intended to guarantee minimum standards for quality of processes. However, school reviews are not only introduced for monitoring purposes. Rather, the introduction of school reviews is linked to certain hopes and expectations, often encapsulated in the more palatable term, "improvement." Often, judgments about the degree of improvement are based on standardized criteria for evaluating good teaching and good schools according to normative expectations determined by administrative and/or government bodies. It is in this way that school reviews claim to represent an objective, data-based evaluation.

Despite these ideals, disappointing outcomes are being acknowledged in school review research data. According to Peck and Reitzug (2014), American empirical studies offer little evidence that school reviews or similar approaches to school improvement are an effective way to improve student academic performance. Similarly, research conducted by Altrichter and Kemethofer (2015), which gathered survey data from 2,300 school principals across seven European countries, found that the overall results from school reviews was far from conclusive as to the question of whether or not the review processes contributed to school improvement, while Australian research by Antoniou, Myburgh-Louw, and Gronn (2015) posits that there is very little research evidence supporting the view that current school review processes actually improve school effectiveness. Research-informed reasons for this lack of success include an incompatibility of combining accountability with improvement goals (Schildkamp and Visscher 2010), mission and identity confusion when there is an emphasis on evaluation, verification, and accountability (Vaz 2016), an absence of contextual specificity (Hallinger and Heck 2011), schools being seen as a simplistic rather than complex organizations (Jones and Harris 2013), a failure to consider the people dynamics (Murphy and Meyers 2009), and a failure to explore the invisible cultural dynamics (Brown et al. 2018). In effect, failing to consider the people and cultural aspects is absurd and dehumanizing and is based on ignorance. It ignores the fact that it is the people and the culture of a school that are the very elements creating the momentum and possibility of improvement for each person, student, and teacher, and therefore the school. The following case study provides an alternative perspective.

The case being illustrated as an application of the Theory of Organizational Ecology was a secondary school (student ages 12–18) with an enrolment of approximately one thousand students and eighty staff. Although this school had maintained a very positive reputation in its local community there was a growing perception among the staff, students, and parents that this was now under threat. Indeed, two main concerns were known: (1) a growing number of students were seeking to complete their final two years of secondary education at other available schools, and (2) many of those associated with the school community were concerned that the school's culture had become outdated. Essentially the view was that the school's culture, with an emphasis on senior academic achievements, the elite status of certain traditional subjects, and a very hierarchical and authoritarian administrative structure, no longer met the local community's needs. In short, the school community knew something was not working for them, but they were challenged in defining the problem and how to resolve it.

The serious challenge for this school community was twofold. The first serious challenge for the school was in determining whether or not this view was correctly naming the problem and, thereby, promoting the best solution. Then, the second serious challenge, if this view was correct, was in determining how to successfully change the culture. Without relevant data the leaders of this school community were not in a position to address either of these two serious challenges. The aim of the research was not only to address both of these serious challenges but also to provide some clear direction on how the school could overcome whatever unhelpful leadership and cultural issues that were present.

In general terms, this ecologically informed review began with an exploration, both in public documents and in the minds of those interviewed, of understandings in relation to the school's core purpose. This is in keeping with our ecological approach since it is founded upon (as explained in Chapter 2) the anthropological understanding of organizational culture where it is believed to emerge out of the individual interpretations and cognitions of those within the organization. Hence, it is concerned with understanding the culture from the subjective and objective views and justifications provided by those associated with the school. Thus, this review project investigated interviewee perceptions of the quality, diversity, and extent of belongingness and interconnectedness both within the school as well between the school and its community. During this investigation, judgments about belongingness and interconnectedness were developed based on data gathered pertaining to the presence or otherwise of the following elements within existing relationships:

• Compassion/care	• Harmony
• Information sharing	• Collaboration
• Commitment to mission	• Respect
• Responsibility to contextual character	• Shared values and beliefs

These elements were seen as the energy factors driving the school's processes for growing and developing its students. As described in Chapter 3, if this energy is significantly reduced through the presence of any disconnections, then this has a seriously detrimental impact on the beneficial outcomes for students. Where the energy flow is optimized through strong and extensive interconnectedness the beneficial outcomes for students are maximized.

More specifically, this ecological review of this school's culture occurred across five school days, which saw a total of seventy-seven persons—staff, students, parents, education system personnel, and key community stakeholders—being involved in an interview either individually or as a member of a focus group. In addition, 58 percent of the school staff completed the online survey. Data gathered in this way were then cross-referenced with that provided in official school documents including vision and mission statements, school prospectus, position descriptions, publicity brochures, school policies, strategic planning documents, and school newsletters.

As a result of the analysis procedures, data not only unequivocally substantiated the view that the school's culture was outdated with respect to local community needs but it also uncovered two serious concerns for the school. The first was the presence of serious disconnections among some of the parts/departments of the school. These disconnections were a result of academic bias and hierarchical power struggles, which created organizational disconnection laterally and horizontally. The critical area of disconnection was among the subject departments, where there was a constant battle for resources and where collaboration and support were not part of the culture. As such, it diminished the capacity of teachers and teams to the point that people were professionally and personally struggling at times. Figure C.1 illustrates the disconnect between heads of subject departments, leading to the diminished ability of teaching and outcomes for the school. Thus, the culture needed to be

Applications and Implications 181

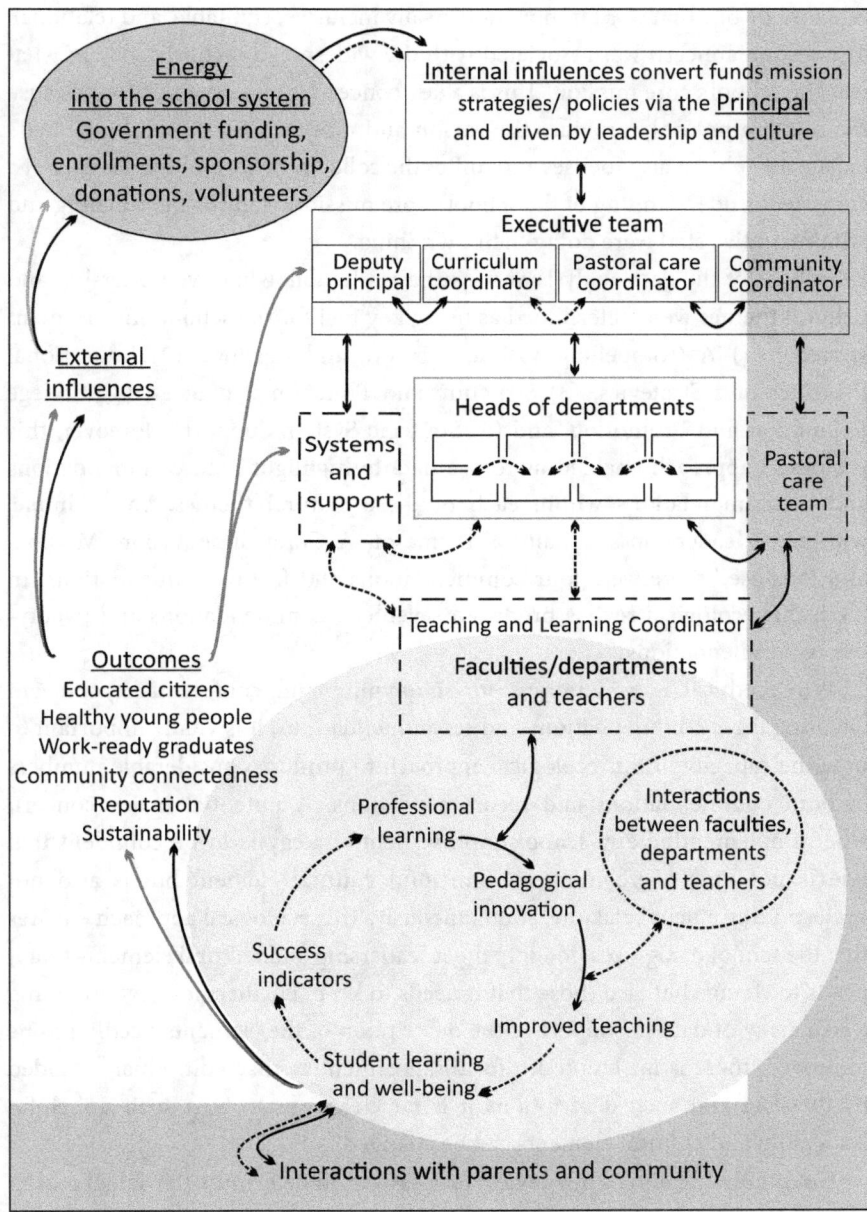

Figure C.1 A diagrammatical illustration of the case school's organizational ecology.

replaced by one that was far more holistically inclusive, equitable, and relational. The second concern was associated with the widespread inconsistency in what was the school's core mission. This is a key concern for an organization because the mission not only provides the reason and motivation for each individual's engagement but it also focuses and unites the collective effort. In the absence of a consistent understanding of the school's core mission many of the teaching and administrative staff were doing their own thing.

In light of the data analysis and synthesis, the following five leadership and cultural themes were determined as being key foci for the school improvement strategy: (1) A Compelling Vision, Mission, and Purpose, (2) Educational Priorities and Strategies, (3) Structure and Function Primacies, (4) College Reputation and Promotion, and (5) Strategic System Support. Moreover, this ecological approach enabled us to use data to highlight both commendations and recommendations within each of these cultural themes. For example, within the leadership and cultural theme of "A Compelling Vision, Mission, and Purpose," there were four commendations and five recommendations. In total, this ecological review produced seventeen commendations and twenty-five recommendations.

While ethical considerations for anonymity and confidentiality prevent detailing these commendations and recommendations, it is vitally important to note the capacity of this ecological approach to produce considerable numbers of both commendations and recommendations. A potential major concern when implementing any school improvement strategy is to be confident that one is not only overcoming an unhelpful cultural element but is also not undermining a beneficial one, simultaneously. This ecological approach ensures that the school recognizes not only those leadership and cultural elements that it needs to change but also those that it needs to keep. Furthermore, by providing a rich array of data in support of the description of the elements needing to be improved, there is far less room for disagreement or discredit. Finally, guided by the data and such descriptions it is far clearer as to how such unhelpful leadership and cultural elements can be changed.

Essentially, the aim of this review process was to determine the actual reason why students were leaving the school and how this enrolment decline could be turned around. What the ecological review process established was that the school's leadership and culture were deemed by a rapidly growing number of students and parents to be outdated and no longer suitable. Simply stated, the leadership and culture were considered often to be far too authoritarian, elitist, inequitable, and noninclusive. Indeed, the ecological review process was able to readily provide a rich array of data describing and supporting these perceptions. Moreover, because this data not only captured many participants' common impressions about the school's leadership and culture but also their reasons for having such impressions along with their views about what they would like to see changed, the ecological review process effectually developed a comprehensive list of both the highly beneficial and the decidedly constraining elements within the current leadership and culture.

In so doing, this ecological approach to this particular school review comprehensively addressed, and thereby readily overcame, the aforementioned limitations that are undermining school improvement processes worldwide. Clearly, this approach has an exploration and examination of the school's organizational culture as its foundation. Its inclusion of an intensive and extensive interview schedule effectively surfaces the breadth and depth of diverse personal and group values, beliefs, attitudes, interpretations, and meanings about the school, its leadership, its community, its past, and its future. Moreover, the genesis for these cultural artifacts gained from school and system leaders, teachers, students, parents, and relevant local community members was in how they described their everyday interpersonal relationships across the school community. Essentially, each interview provided individual and collective impressions pertaining to senses of belonging and connectivity, and how these influenced the construction of their judgments about the school and its leadership. That is, this approach sought to uncover impressions and justifications in relation to the qualities of coordination, coherence, and orchestration. In this way, this ecological approach recognized the organizational complexity of the school by gathering awareness of the diversity, rather than generality, of views and opinions. This acknowledges that there is never just one "truth" about the school, and any one view is an opinion based on personal interpretations of experiences and not facts, but within the described justification for commonly held or opposing views and opinions there is precious insight about the school, its leadership, and its culture.

Thus, this ecological approach is contextually specific—each school review is deemed to be unique. But does this mean that it fails to meet the evaluation, verification, and accountability demands? It is so that this ecological approach does not explicitly include any data-gathering process to address government or system-devised evaluation, verification, and accountability criteria. However, we argue that these criteria only gain prominence when school review processes are failing to generate clearly observable school improvement outcomes. Where school reviews are generating clearly observable school improvement outcomes, evaluation, verification, and accountability data become self-evident and do not need to be deliberately sourced through the school review process. The development from this ecological approach of a wide but focused array of strategically important commendations and recommendations for the school undoubtedly met both system and government accountability requirements. Having concrete guidelines and evidence of how the school can and is improving in its support of student growth and development is all that any school, system, or government is seeking, and this is what this ecological approach to school improvements provides in abundance.

Arguably, the extraordinary effectiveness of this unique ecological approach to school reviews in being able to provide comprehensive, clear, precise, and defensible school review commendations and recommendations is best proffered by the executive director of the authority tasked with overseeing the administration of this particular educational system. This person wrote that the Review Report

> captured the school culture very well. The detail and the elaboration provided was presented with great clarity. … Being comprehensive in nature, it has enabled a detailed Action Plan to be developed by the school in consultation with Office based staff. … The commendations and recommendations have been fully embraced by the school leadership and the Office based staff and have been the basis for the development of a strategic action plan to assist in driving the necessary improvements in the school culture. One key action is being undertaken in this first week of the new school year, with an external facilitator leading the staff in a process to reflect upon and renew their Vision/Mission/Values.

Application #2—The Organizational Ecology Theory and a Cultural Alignment Process

The fundamental purpose of this cultural alignment process is to establish a collectivist rather than individualistic organizational culture. Simply stated, this process creates the highly desired workplace environment where there is widespread, if not total, agreement about which behaviors throughout the organization are appropriate and necessary and which behaviors are not. But, in doing so, this process does not solely concentrate on desired behaviors but rather it delves much deeper into the invisible cultural antecedents, those of personal and group values and beliefs as highlighted in Chapter 2, that manifest as employee behaviors.

While the genesis of this process (see Branson 2008) was initially confined to an educational context, it is now being used in all contexts. It has universal application. Hence, this particular case describes its application in a corporate organization where the chief executive was struggling to create a collaborative, united effort in their rapidly growing organization. The chief executive was troubled about disunity, contestation, and self-interest among the executive team and, therefore, their capacity to work together in securing the future of the organization. The net result of the dysfunction of the executive team was an unsustainable high level in staff dissatisfaction, disengagement, and turnover. Essentially this was a team getting in its own way. Rather than focusing on the fundamental purpose of the organization and how they contributed to its achievement, the energy of this team was being consumed by personal defensiveness, protectionism, and non-responsibility.

In keeping with our ecological understanding of organizational culture, we argue that the key to positively influencing an employee's individual consciousness and behavior is in helping them to determine the most beneficial values for maximizing the achievement of the organization's core purpose and how best to apply these in order to create an appropriate and successful organizational culture. Each employee needs to be able to clearly see how these values are important to the organization's culture and how the application of these values can lead to a better and more successful organization. Furthermore, they need to be able to know and understand the antecedent forces that support the adoption of these preferred values. Also, they need to be able to see how the application of these values will be able to change the organization for the better. It is in this way that the employees are able to develop alignment between their personal values and the perceived strategic values of the organization.

To this end, the following model (Figure C.2) was created to help guide this essential values alignment process. Importantly, the crux of this process is about the inclusive, open, and transparent sharing of knowledge, views, attitudes, beliefs, and aspirations by all when discussing and arriving at consensus with each aspect of the model. It is described here generically in order to maintain ethical confidentiality. This process is carried out at a team level because it has at its core the fundamental purpose of the team, and this is particular to each team. In this example the alignment process was carried out with the executive team.

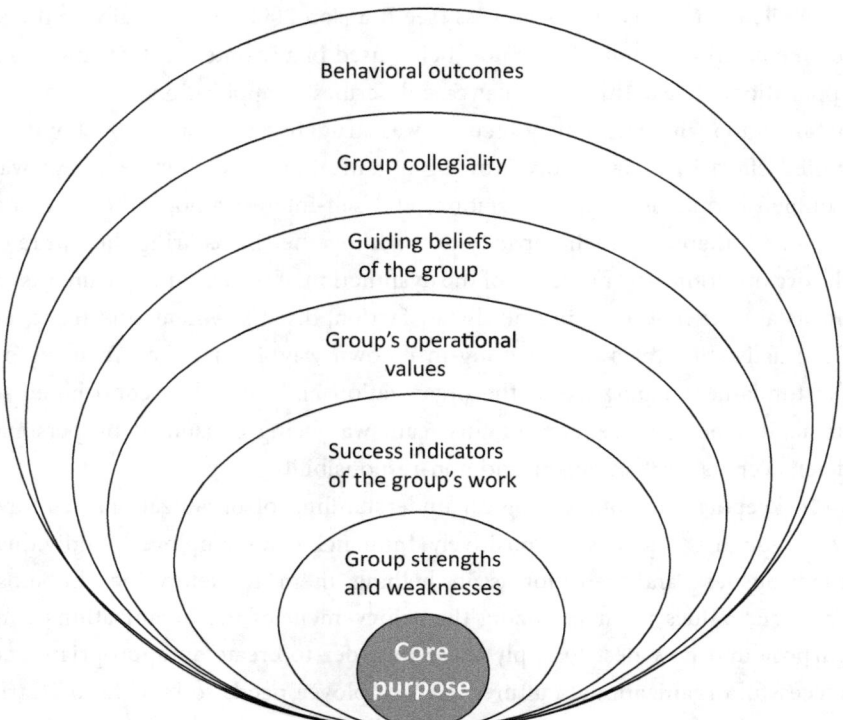

Figure C.2 A model showing the constituent aspects of a team's culture that are integral to the achievement of cultural alignment.
Source: Adapted from Branson (2008).

In this model, the respective understandings associated with each of these proposed constituent aspects of an organization's culture can be described as follows:

(a) Core Purpose is the collaboratively discerned controlling insight as to that which is at the very heart of what the group/team is striving to achieve in order to create long-term success for the organization. It describes what the group needs to do and, as such, it is distinct from, but related to, the organization's overall vision and mission statements. The Core Purpose is a single sentence that uses rich descriptive words to describe not only what is seen as the core business of the collective group but also the manner and means for achieving it. As a controlling insight, the Core Purpose must:
  • Apply across a wide range of situations;

- Succinctly describe what would result from the achievement of excellence; and
- Guide essential action.

In describing these outcomes, the Core Purpose becomes a source of potential organizational values in the mind of all those involved. Hence, these perceived values have meaning for those involved since each individual can readily understand the significance of these values and, therefore, is in a better position of being able to willingly support and adopt them.

(b) Group Strengths and Weaknesses—of the group, and each individual, with respect to the achievement of the Core Purpose. Discussion of these crucial ingredients enables the group to develop confidence in its ability to achieve its Core Purpose by either reinforcing its group and individual strengths or by overcoming its weaknesses through specifically targeted group or individual professional development. In this way, it affirms the existing talent and worth in the group and the individuals while also confirming the organization's commitment to its people through its support for strategic professional development. Again, this open and transparent process provides clarification as to what is valued and why it is valued. In this way, the meaningfulness of such values is reinforced in the minds of the group members.

(c) Success Indicators of the Group's Work are the perceived logical consequences that will be achieved if the group is able to achieve excellence in the way it goes about its Core Purpose. Getting the group to list the indicators of success that would naturally result if every group member was fully committed to the Core Purpose provides motivation and stimulus to each individual to become engaged and to provide his/her quality contribution to the group's activities. In this way, there is increased motivation for each individual to develop an affective organizational commitment and to adopt the group's nominated strategic values.

(d) Group's Operational Values are the nominated strategic values that appear as a natural consequence if each of the previous antecedent constituent parts of the organization's culture is to be achieved. However, since the reflection upon the stated Core Purpose, the acknowledged Strengths and Weaknesses, and the desired Success Indicators produces an abundance of nominated values, it is also essential that a secondary process is implemented that allows the group to prioritize the most important values up to a suggested maximum of ten values. This ensures that everyone is more likely to be concentrating on applying the same values to their work environment. Having too many values is more likely to diffuse the commitment as it would be difficult for every person to equally apply their self to a wide array of nominated organizational values.

(e) Guiding Beliefs of the Group are the agreed ways in which the application of each of the prioritized strategic values will produce a positive outcome for each person as well as the group, overall. The creation of such Guiding Beliefs is done simply by converting each prioritized strategic value to a belief by asking the group to complete the following sentence with each value:

"We value [*value*] because …"

Every time we have worked through this process with a group, the people have commented on how powerful the experience was. To see a group align with a single and unanimously agreed belief about a value is unifying and empowering. It also has an added benefit of being a wonderful team-building experience.

(f) Group Collegiality is the job satisfaction, outlook, and feelings of well-being the person has within their workplace setting. Great organizations generally have high morale. When morale is high, the employees tend to have more energy and greater focus on achieving the organization's goals. Conversely, when morale is low, employees seem to have less energy and spend more of their time complaining, looking for other jobs, and/or simply trying to protect themselves. In short, when morale suffers, performance suffers because employees devote far less time toward delivering results. By providing an opportunity for the group to openly compare thoughts and opinions about the impact of the achievement of the stated Core Purpose and its associated key values will have on their feelings about coming to, and being at, work provides a strong personal emotional engagement with and, thereby, commitment to the core purpose.

(g) Behavioral Outcomes are the behaviors that can be expected to be seen enacted by a person authentically living out these beliefs and values. The process so far has only developed a cognitive and emotional commitment to the nominated strategic values. By getting the group to publicly predetermine those behaviors that logically result from a person proactively living out the strategic values not only makes it quite clear what is expected from each person but also each person knows that others will be able to judge his/her personal commitment to these values by their behavior. In this way, it is more likely that each person will behaviorally commit to these beliefs and values as well.

It is argued that while each of these proposed constituent aspects of an organization's culture is able to provide a discrete and valuable contribution to the individual consciousness of the person, it is the synergistic affect achieved by working through each aspect as a contributing segment to the essential whole that achieves the most profound outcome. The full power and impact of this comprehensive cultural alignment process is only accomplished when each and every aspect is examined in the order suggested. In this way, an all-embracing understanding of the culture of the organization is gained. As a result, the individual is able to more easily align their personal values with the organization's nominated strategic values while also sensing heightened workplace belonging, meaningfulness, and fulfillment.

As promised, Figure C.3 (see below) illustrates the explicit outcomes generated by this cultural alignment process with the executive team.

The alignment process is a collective agreement of the members of a team. It is the re-setting, refreshing of the norms of the group to guide their actions and behaviors. It is the focusing on achieving the fundamental purpose of the team to achieving the strategic goals of the organization. An essential procedural requirement with this process is the integral but not controlling involvement of the leader and leadership team members. All involved have equal say, carry equal right to say what they truly think, and what they say carries equal sway. No one person's view is more or less important than any other view.

All in this executive team are now working in collaboration and the impact is being felt throughout the organization. People are now reporting that this organization is *a nice place to work*. All executive team members are living and working by the behavior charter that they each contributed in forming, developing, and implementing.

Although, due to publication limitations, only two applications of the Theory of Organizational Ecology can be comprehensively described, we posit that these applications address critically important issues in today's organizations. As previously highlighted in this book, organizational improvement and cultural change are notorious leadership stumbling blocks that persistently undermine employee performance and organizational productivity. Our strident position is that this untenable situation is due to a paucity in theoretical knowledge and practice associated with how to understand leadership, culture, and organizations. Our solution, therefore, is encompassed in the new Theory of Organizational Ecology along with the following implications.

> ***Our responsibility is our truth—***
> Our people and our clients depend on our ability to work together to guide our organization to success
>
> ## Our values
> **Cooperation** - we can and must work together
> **Unity** - we are one team with one focus
> **Support** - we are kind, care for, and support each other
> **Openness** - we share and discuss ideas openly with each other
> **Courage** - together we can make courageous decisions
> **Willingness** - to take on responsibilities when asked
> **Respect** - we speak and act with professionalism and collegiality
>
> ## If we are working to our values our organization would be....
> A place where people want to work ....
> ... which is a place where they feel belongingness
> ... which is a place where they feel appreciated and valued
> ... which is a place where they see they are making a contribution to something they believe in
> ... which is a place where they feel connected and can trust their colleagues
> ... so they build relationships and fully cooperate in teams
> ... so they are engaged and sharing ideas in their work
> ... and so see that working with others brings greater success
> ... and for all this to happen, **we the leaders must show the wisdom and intelligences to grow the culture and model the behaviors for the success of the organization and its people.**

Figure C.3 The organizational chart developed by the executive team as the explicit outcome from its cultural alignment process.

Implications of the Organizational Ecology Theory

Mostly, the focus, functioning, systems, and managerial practices widely applied in contemporary organizations are now very much at odds with society. Although these may well have been a reflection of society at some point last century, they are now simply out of kilter with contemporary ways of being. Consequently, employee disengagement is at plague proportions crippling organizations around the globe. Just 15 percent of people are fully engaged in their jobs. If these same data were applied to a viral pandemic, such as the world is currently experiencing since 2020, so that 85 percent of workers around the world were unwell, the response would be global outrage and an enormous endeavor to find a cure. So, why aren't the leaders of our organizations looking for new ways to solve the employee disengagement pandemic?

Interestingly though, disengagement is not only an organizational productivity issue, but also a health issue. Disengaged people often feel depressed at work and stressed about being there. It is an epidemic and the solution is obvious. It is time for organizations to ditch the destructive practices of managerialism and adopt a people-centric approach to culture and leadership whereby each of these is focused on relationships, connectivity, collaboration, and belonging. The surprising thing is that this is what our organizational literature is similarly urging, but without any clear message of how this can be achieved.

In contrast our Theory of Organizational Ecology offers a clear and practical solution. It provides a lens though which an organization can be modeled based on the six ecological principles of

1. *No organization, or parts of an organization, exists in isolation*: Organizations are open systems in which the incoming energy (e.g., funding, sales, fees, employee commitment) creates desired strategic outcomes/outputs through pivotal relationships, connectedness, and flow of information in both its external and internal environments.
2. *Organizational climate (how culture is experienced by the individual) shapes the level of individual, team, and departmental capacity, performance, and productivity*: Organizational culture is a collective of subcultures that may or may not be aligned to each other or to the core purpose of the organization. The organization's core purpose is achieved by the employees and not the strategy, and it is the organizational culture that shapes how committed the employees are toward achieving the core purpose and the full potential of the organization. Unless the leader constructively attends to the organization's culture it will trump the strategy and capacity, and employee performance and productivity will decline.
3. *Information and knowledge sharing are pivotal to organizational success*: The creation, gathering, utilization, and sharing of information and knowledge in an organization are fundamental to its success as these are the mechanisms for facilitating organizational unification, learning,

innovation, and the flow of energy: The energy provided to an organization must be able to move throughout the organization in order for it to address both the relationship needs as well as the production needs according to the organization's core purpose.
4. *Organizational success is greater than the sum of its parts*: Organizations are communities of departments, teams, and employees providing various contributions to the purpose of the organization. When these departments, teams, and individuals are all working together purposefully and collaboratively, the overall organizational output is enhanced significantly. Leaders who nurture organizational-wide interpersonal collaboration, and strong, purposeful teamwork, maximize the organization's productivity.
5. *Organizational change is constant*: Organizations exist in a dynamic metastable equilibrium whereby they must constantly change and adapt. Hence staying the same is not a strategy for success. Organizations that are able to readily cope with change have leaders who draw employees' attention to the constancy of change and continually build their capacity to learn, adapt, and thrive.
6. *Each person counts*: Each employee, regardless of their particular role, both consumes and creates some of the organizational energy. Whether or not this energy is lost or flows on to be used by others depends upon the levels of engagement and performance of each individual employee. The most successful organizations have leaders who are able to maximize the flow of energy throughout the organization because their relational approach brings out the best in each employee.

But just knowing and understanding these principles is unlikely to change our current underperforming organizational world. Now, more than ever before, we need wise organizational leaders regardless of the context. *Leadership wisdom* needs to be guiding today's leaders. In our vastly challenging organizational environments, we need wise leaders with high levels of analytical, practical, emotional, and intuitive intelligences so that they can confidently respond to today's organizational challenges, ambiguities, and paradoxes. As posited by Bolman and Deal (2008), only those leaders who are being guided by leadership wisdom have the "versatility in thinking that fosters flexibility in action, [the] capacity to act inconsistently when uniformity fails, diplomatically when emotions are raw, non-rationally when reason flags, politically in the face of vocal parochial self-interest, and playfully when fixating on task and purpose backfires" (435). Wise leadership is as much about understanding people as it is about knowing what to do.

In association with leadership wisdom, these organizational ecological principles manifest as an organization that is connected throughout by relationships among the employees and teams, which provides the conduit, the pathway for energy to flow throughout the organization. The energy flowing is that of information, knowledge, and ideas formed from creativity and innovation and brought to life through commitment, belongingness, collaboration, and harmony. This is the energy of the organization, and it is the culture that provides the matrix by which the organization operates, learns, grows, and succeeds.

The pivotal message here is that culture and leadership are inseparable and codependent in so far as organizational culture reflects the leaders' actions and priorities. A relational leader will create a relational culture within which individuals and teams reset their cultural norms to match. In this way, culture is the combination of the personal experiences and values that each person brings to the workplace, and which is coupled with the cultural norms of the team that guide the working practices and behaviors—all of which have been influenced and moderated by the expectations and behaviors of the leader and through interactions with the leader. When employees strongly feel that they can trust their leader, because the leader walks their own talk, they want to belong and perform their best for the organization.

Collaborative relationships and constructive connectivity are the heart and soul of the organization and gives life to the organization. Without such relationships and connectivity, the organization slowly loses energy and life, and decays from within. Diminished performance, disengagement, infighting, competition, favoritism, exclusion, depression, and stress are just some of the possible signs of organizational decay. In such sad circumstances the leadership is nothing more than rhetoric. The culture is rife with suspicion and mistrust. The flow of information and creativity is stifled. Regrettably, often the misguided and futile belief is that tough managerialism will solve the problem because it will lift engagement and performance through stringent control mechanisms. But the opposite has been proven to be true. When the energy required to fuel engagement, performance, and productivity has been depleted due to poor connectivity no amount of managerialism will ever rectify the problems. In such poor circumstances, the organization is at best reduced to the sum of its underperforming parts. But, the relational leader, who is able to connect the people and the teams to achieve a common purpose, who can foster new ideas, curiosity, and innovation, who can harness the collective energy, and who can instill in each employee a strong sense of belonging and a desire to do their best work, is the solution.

Doing the same thing and expecting different results is hardly a strategy for organizational success. That doing the same thing is imposing managerial practices on human endeavor and expecting people to like it and respond to it is not only deluded thinking but highly damaging to organizations and the people working in them. It's time that we once and for all accept that people are the organization—not structures, processes, reporting, or building. It's time that those who seem totally committed to imposing performance goals, KPIs, and other levels of performance accountabilities finally understand that these impositions actually limit the possibility of achieving desirable outcomes. Actually, the way to enhance employee performance is by setting them free to be the best they can be. Thus, it is time to ditch the old ways and recipes for success and focus on a relational approach from the leader and throughout the organization. The very best thing that governing bodies and leaders can do is to create, grow, and harness the energy of their people and organization. This takes a connected and relational organizational culture—a culture that is comprehensively captured by, and produced from, applying principles and implications of the Theory of Organizational Ecology.

References

Albrecht, K. (2003), *The Power of Minds at Work: Organizational Intelligence in Action*. New York: AMACOM.

Al-Bureay, M. A. (1990), *Management and Administration in Islam*. Dhaharan: King Fahd University of Petroleum and Minerals.

Altrichter, H., and D. Kemethofer (2015). "Does Accountability Pressure through School Inspections Promote School Improvement?," *School Effectiveness and School Improvement*, 26 (1): 32–56.

Amabile, T. (1996), "Creativity and Innovation in Organizations," Harvard Business School, January 5. Available online: https://edisciplinas.usp.br/pluginfile.php/4927750/mod_resource/content/0/Creativity%20and%20Innovation%20in%20Organizations.pdf (accessed November 10, 2020).

Anderson, H. J., J. E. Baur, J. A. Griffith, and M. R. Buckley (2017), "What Works for You May Not Work for (Gen)Me: Limitations of Present Leadership Theories for the New Generation," *Leadership Quarterly*, 28: 245–60.

Antoniou, P., J. Myburgh-Louw, and P. Gronn (2015), "School Self-Evaluation for School Improvement: Examining the Measuring Properties of the LEAD Surveys," *Australian Journal of Education*, 60 (3): 191–210.

Ardelt, M. (2004), "Wisdom as Expert Knowledge System: A Critical Review of a Contemporary Operationalization of an Ancient Concept," *Human Development*, 47: 257–85.

Asimov, I. (1978), "Foreword," in R. Holdstock (ed.), *The Encyclopaedia of Science Fiction*, n.p. Portland, ME: Irish Booksellers.

Bandura, A. (1997), *Self-Efficacy: The Exercise of Control*. New York: W. H. Freeman.

Bauman, Z. (1992), *Intimations of Postmodernity*. London: Routledge.

Baxter Healthcare (2020), Quoted in *Sydney Local Health District, Sydney Innovation*. Available online: https://www.slhd.nsw.gov.au/innovation/about.html (accessed October 5, 2020).

Bellinger, G., D. Castro, and A. Mills (2000), "Data, Information, Knowledge, and Wisdom Outsights." Available online: https://homepages.dcc.ufmg.br/~amendes/SistemasInformacaoTP/TextosBasicos/Data-Information-Knowledge.pdf (accessed April 29, 2021).

Bierly, P., E. Kessler, and E. Christensen (2000), "Organizational Learning Knowledge and Wisdom," *Journal of Organization Change*, 13 (6): 595–618.

Bolman, L. G., and T. E. Deal (2008), *Reframing Leadership: Artistry, Choice, and Leadership* (4th ed.). San Francisco: Jossey-Bass.

Branson, C. M. (2007), "The Effects of Structured Self-Reflection on the Development of Authentic Leadership Practices among Queensland Primary School Principals," *Educational Management Administration and Leadership Journal*, 35 (2): 227–48.
Branson, C. M. (2008), "Achieving Organizational Change through Values Alignment," *Journal of Educational Administration*, 46 (3): 376–95.
Branson, C. M. (2009), *Leadership for an Age of Wisdom*. Dordrecht: Springer Educational.
Branson, C. M. (2014), "The Power of Personal Values," in C. M. Branson and S. J. Gross (eds.), *Handbook of Ethical Educational Leadership*, 195–209. New York: Routledge.
Branson, C. M., M. Franken, and D. Penney (2016), "Reconceptualizing Middle Leadership in Higher Education: A Transrelational Approach," in J. McNiff (ed.), *Values and Virtues in Higher Education Research: Critical Perspectives*, 155–70. Abington: Routledge.
Branson, C. M., M. Marra, M. Franken, and D. Penney (2018), *Leadership in Higher Education from a Transrelational Perspective*. London: Bloomsbury Academic.
Brown, A. (1998), "Organizational Culture," *Financial Times*, May 22, 1998. Harlow, New York.
Brown, R., D. Heck, D. Pendergast, H. Kanasa, and A. Morgan (2018), "Developing a Profiling Tool Using a Values Approach to School Renewal," *Teachers College Record*, 120: 1–44.
Bryk, A., E. Camburn, and K. S. Louis (1999), "Professional Community in Chicago Elementary Schools: Facilitating Factors and Organizational Consequences," *Educational Administration Quarterly*, 35 (Supplement): 751–81.
Burns, J. M. (1978), *Leadership*. New York: Harper and Row.
Burns, J. M. (2010), *Leadership*. New York: HarperCollins.
Bush, T. (2011), "Becoming a School Principal: Exciting Opportunity or Daunting Challenge?," *Educational Management, Administration & Leadership*, 39 (5): 514–15. Available online: doi.org/10.1177/1741143211409506 (accessed January 5, 2021).
Cameron, K. S., and R. E. Quinn (2011), *Diagnosing and Changing Organizational Culture: Based on the Competing Values Framework* (3rd ed.). San Francisco: Jossey-Bass.
Cheng, Y. C. (2010), "A Topology of Three-Wave Models of Strategic Leadership in Education," *International Studies in Educational Administration*, 38 (1): 35–54.
Clayton, V. P. (1982), "Wisdom and Intelligence: The Nature and Function of Knowledge in the Later Years," *International Journal of Aging & Human Development*, 15 (4): 315–21.
Cockshaw, W. D., I. M. Shochet, and P. L. Obst (1993), "General Belongingness, Workplace Belongingness, and Depressive Symptoms," *Journal of Community & Applied Social Psychology*, 23: 240–51.
Commoner, B. (1971), *The Closing Circle: Nature, Man & Technology*. Mineola, NY: Dover.

Costa, A. C., C. A. Fulmer, and N. R. Anderson (2018), 'Trust in Work Teams: An Integrative Review, Multilevel Model and Future Directions," *Journal of Organizational Behavior*, 39: 169–84. Available online: doi.org/10.1002/job.2213 (accessed April 24, 2021).

Davies, B. (2005), *The Essentials of School Leadership*. London: Paul Chapman & Corwin Press.

De Smet, A., J. Lavoie, and E. S. Hioe (2012), "Developing Better Change Leaders," *McKinsey Quarterly*, April. Available online: http://www.mckinsey.com/business-functions/organization/our-insights/developing-better-change-leaders (accessed August 20, 2020).

Deci, E. L., and R. M. Ryan (2008), "Facilitating Optimal Motivation and Psychological Well-Being across Life's Domains," *Canadian Psychology*, 49 (3): 14–23.

Deloitte (2016), "The New Organization: Different by Design," *Global Human Capital Trends 2016*. Birmingham, AL: Deloitte University Press. Available online: https://www2.deloitte.com/content/dam/Deloitte/na/Documents/human-capital/BCTWF-2016/na_HC_Trends_2016_presentation_BCTWF_Launch.pdf (accessed April 29, 2021).

Deloitte (2019), "Leading the Social Enterprise: Reinvent with a Human Focus," *Global Human Capital Trends Report*, 1–106. Birmingham, AL: Deloitte University Press.

Deshpande, R., and F. E. Webster (1989), "Organizational Culture and Marketing: Defining the Research Agenda," *Journal of Marketing*, 53 (1): 3–15.

Disch, J. (2009), "Generative Leadership," *Creative Nursing*, 15 (4): 172–7.

Donate, M. J., and F. Guadamillas (2010), "The Effect of Organizational Culture on Knowledge Management Practices and Innovation," *Knowledge and Process Management*, 17 (2): 82–94.

Drucker, P. F. (1985), *Innovation and Entrepreneurship*. New York: Harper and Row.

Drucker, P. F. (1993), *Managing for Results*. New York: HarperCollins.

Ewenstein, B., W. Smith, and A. Sologar (2015), *Changing Change Management*, July 1. Available online: https://www.mckinsey.com/featured-insights/leadership/changing-change-management (accessed October 29, 2020).

Fay, D., H. Shipton, M. A. West, and M. Patterson (2015), "Teamwork and Organizational Innovation: The Moderating Role of the HRM Context," *Creativity and Innovation Management*, 24 (2): 261–77.

Frankl, V. E. (1959), *Man's Search for Meaning*. Boston: Beacon Press.

Fullan, M. (1998), "The Meaning of Educational Change: A Quarter of a Century of Learning," in A. Hargreaves, A. Lieberman, M. Fullan, and D. Hopkins (eds.), *International Handbook of Educational Change*, 214–30. Dordrecht: Kluwer Academic.

Fullan, M. (2001), *The New Meaning of Educational Change* (3rd ed.). New York: Teachers College Press.

Fullan, M. (2019), *Nuance: Why Some Leaders Succeed and Others Fail*. Thousand Oaks, CA: Corwin.

Fulmer, C. A., and M. J. Gelfand (2012), "At What Level (and in Whom) We Trust: Trust across Multiple Organizational Levels," *Journal of Management*, 38 (4): 1167–230.

Gallup (2019), *Perspective on Building a High-Development Culture through Your Employee Engagement Strategy*. Available online: https://www.gallup.com/workplace/267512/development-culture-engagement-paper-2019.aspx (accessed June 15, 2020).

Gao, Y. (2017), "Business Leader's Personal Values, Organizational Culture and Market Orientation," *Journal of Strategic Marketing*, 25 (1): 49–64.

Geertz, C. (1973), *The Interpretation of Cultures: Selected Essays*. New York: Basic Books.

Gigerenzer, G. (2007), *Gut Feelings: The Intelligence of the Unconscious*. New York: Viking.

Gino, F. (2018), "The Business Case for Curiosity," *Harvard Business Review*, October–November, 48–57. Available online: https://hbr.org/2018/09/the-business-case-for-curiosity (accessed October 5, 2020).

Gleeson, B. (2017), "One Reason Why Most Change Management Efforts Fail," *Forbes*, July 25. Available online: https://www.forbes.com/sites/brentgleeson/2017/07/25/1-reason-why-most-change-management-efforts-fail/#4f17d9c2546b (accessed August 27, 2020).

Goodburn, M. (2015), "What Is the Life Expectancy of Your Company?", *World Economic Forum*. Available online: https://www.weforum.org/agenda/2015/01/what-is-the-life-expectancy-of-your-company/ (accessed October 5, 2020).

Gottlieb, J., and P. L. Oudeyer (2018), "Towards a Neuroscience of Active Sampling and Curiosity," *Nature*, 19: 758–70.

Government of New Zealand (2020), Quoted in *Sydney Local Health District, Sydney Innovation*. Available online: https://www.slhd.nsw.gov.au/innovation/about.html (accessed October 5, 2020).

Gupta, R., and P. Banerjee (2016), "Antecedents of Organizational Creativity: A Multi-Level Approach," *Business: Theory and Practice*, 17 (2): 167–77.

Hagerty, B. M., J. Lynch-Sauer, K. L. Patusky, M. Bouwsema, and P. Collier (1992), "Sense of Belonging: A Vital Mental Health Concept," *Archives of Psychiatric Nursing*, 6 (3): 172–7.

Hagui, A., and J. Wright (2020), "When Data Creates Competitive Advantage," *Harvard Business Review*, January–February Issue. Available online: https://hbr.org/2020/01/when-data-creates-competitive-advantage (accessed February 25, 2020).

Hairuddin, M. A. (2012), "The Quest for Strategic Malaysian Quality National Primary School Leaders," *International Journal of Educational Management*, 26 (1): 83–98.

Hairuddin, M. A., and B. A. M. Muhamad (2010), *School Strategic Planning*. Selangor: PTS Professional.

Hallinger, P., and R. H. Heck (1997), "Exploring the Principal's Contribution to School Effectiveness," *School Effectiveness and School Improvement*, 8 (4): 1–35.

Hallinger, P., and R. H. Heck (2011), "Exploring the Journey of School Improvement: Classifying and Analyzing Patterns of Change in School Improvement Processes and Learning Outcomes," *School Effectiveness and School Improvement*, 22 (1): 1–27.

Handy, C. (1996), *Gods of Management, the Changing Work of Organizations*. Oxford: Oxford University Press.

Hargreaves, A. (2005), "Pushing the Boundaries of Educational Change," in A. Hargreaves (ed.), *Extending Educational Change: International Handbook of Educational Change*, 1–14. Dordrecht: Kluwer Academic.

Harris, A. (2004), "School Leadership and School Improvement: A Simple and Complex Relationship," *School Leadership & Management*, 24 (1). Available online: doi.org/10.1080/1363243042000172778 (accessed January 5, 2021).

Hartner, J. (2017), "Dismal Employee Engagement Is a Sign of Global Mismanagement," Blog Review of Gallup Report, *State of the Workplace*. Available online: https://www.gallup.com/workplace/231668/dismal-employee-engagement-sign-global-mismanagement.aspx (accessed August 12, 2000).

Hofman, W. H. A., and R. H. Hofman (2011), "Smart Management in Effective Schools: Effective Management Configurations in General and Vocational Education in the Netherlands," *Educational Administration Quarterly*, 47 (4): 620–45. Available online: doi.org/10.1177/0013161X11400186 (accessed January 9, 2020).

Hofstede, G. (1991), *Cultures and Organizations: Software of the Mind*. London: McGraw-Hill.

Holliday, S. G., and M. J. Chandler (1986), "Wisdom: Explorations in Adult Competence," *Contributions to Human Development*, 17: 1–96.

Homburg, C., and C. Pflesser (2000), "A Multiple-Layer Model of Market-Oriented Organizational Culture," *Journal of Marketing Research*, 37 (4): 449–62.

Hord, S. M. (1997), *Professional Learning Communities: Communities of Continuous Inquiry and Improvement*. Austin, TX: Southwest Educational Development Laboratory.

Hunt, E. (2020), "Blue Sky Thinking: Is It Time to Stop Work Taking Over Our Lives?" Available online: https://www.theguardian.com/money/2020/oct/04/blue-sky-thinking-is-it-time-to-stop-work-taking-over-our-lives (accessed January 9, 2021).

Isenman, L. (2013), "Understanding Unconscious Intelligence and Intuition: 'Blink' and Beyond," *Perspectives in Biology and Medicine*, 56 (1): 148–66.

Johnson, S. M., and S. M. Kardos (2002), "Keeping New Teachers in Mind," *Educational Leadership*, 59 (6): 12–16.

Johnson. G., K. Scholes, and R. Whittington (2008), *Exploring Corporate Strategy* (8th ed.). Harlow, NY: Prentice-Hall.

Jones, C. A. (2005), "Wisdom Paradigms for the Enhancement of Ethical and Profitable Business Practices," *Journal of Business Ethics*, 57 (4): 363–75.

Jones, M., and A. Harris (2013), "Principals Leading Successful Organizational Change: Building Social Capital through Disciplined Professional Collaboration," *Journal of Organizational Change Management*, 27 (3): 473–85.

Joost, M. (2018), "Gary Hamel's Powerful Speech: Highlight of the Drucker Forum." Available online: https://corporate-rebels.com/hamel-speech-drucker-forum/ (accessed November 25, 2020).

Kaine, G., and L. Cowan (2011), "Using General Systems Theory to Understand How Farmers Manage Variability," *Systems Research and Behavioral Science*, 28 (3): 231–44.

Kalkan, F. (2016), "The Relationship between Professional Learning Community, Bureaucratic Structure and Organizational Trust in Primary Education Schools," *Educational Sciences: Theory & Practice*, 16 (5): 1619–37.

Kasanoff, B. (2017), "Intuition Is the Highest Form of Intelligence," *Forbes*. Available online: https://kasanoff.com/blog/2020/5/18/intuition-is-the-highest-form-of-intelligence#:~:text=Although%20this%20may%20be%20a,and%20has%20forgotten%20the%20gift.%22 (accessed April 29, 2021).

Kashdan, T. B., and M. F. Steger (2007), "Curiosity and Pathways to Well-Being and Meaning in Life: Traits, States, and Everyday Behaviors," *Motivation and Emotion*, 31: 159–73. Available online: doi 10.1007/s11031-007-9068-7 (accessed January 9, 2021).

Keller, S., M. Kruyt, and J. Malan (2010), *How Do I Develop an Effective Top Team?* New York: McKinsey.

Khanghahi, M. E., and P. Jafari (2013), "A Model for Organizational Intelligence in Islamic Azad University," *Mathematics Education Trends and Research*, 2013 (2013): 1–10.

Kidd, C., and B. Y. Hayden (2015), "The Psychology and Neuroscience of Curiosity," *Neuron*, 88 (3): 449–60. Available online: doi.org/10.1016/j.neuron.2015.09.010 (accessed November 11, 2020).

King, D. (2002), "The Changing Shape of Leadership," *Educational Leadership*, 59 (8): 61–3.

Kujala, J., H. Lehtimäki, and R. Pučėtaitė (2016), "Trust and Distrust Constructing Unity and Fragmentation of Organizational Culture," *Journal of Business Ethics*, 139: 701–16.

Labouvie-Vief, G. (2000), "Affect Complexity and Views of the Transcendent," in P. Young-Eisendrath and M. E. Miller (eds.), *The Psychology of Mature Spirituality: Integrity, Wisdom, Transcendence*,103–19). London: Routledge.

Lam, L. W., and D. C. Lau (2012), "Feeling Lonely at Work: Investigating the Consequences of Unsatisfactory Workplace Relationships," *International Journal of Human Resource Management*, 23 (20): 4265–82.

Lawton, G. (2017), "Thoughtlessly Thoughtless," *New Scientist*, 236 (3156): 28–35.

Leithwood, K., and C. Riehl (2005), "What We Know about Successful School Leadership," in W. Firestone and C. Riehl (eds.), *A New Agenda: Directions for Research on Educational Leadership*, 22–47. New York: Teachers College Press.

Lemken, B., H. Kahler, and M. Rittenbruch (2000), "Sustained Knowledge Management by Organizational Culture," Proceedings of the 33rd Annual Hawaii International

Conference on Issue Date, January 4–7: vol. 2. Available online: doi: 10.1109/HICSS.2000.926701 (accessed November 10, 2020).

Lipman-Blumen, J. (2005), "Toxic Leadership: When Grand Illusions Masquerade as Noble Visions," *Leader to Leader*, Spring (March): 1–16. Available online: https://onlinelibrary.wiley.com/doi/pdf/10.1002/ltl.125 (accessed April 29, 2021).

Luppicini, R. (2012), *Ethical Impact of Technological Advancements and Applications in Society*. Hershey, PA: Information Science Reference.

MacDonald, A. (2020), "Eight Management Ideas to Embrace in the 2020s," *MIT Sloan Management Review*, January 15: 1–4.

Mandal, F. B. (2014), "Nonverbal Communication in Humans," *Journal of Human Behavior in the Social Environment*, 24 (4): 417–21.

Marra, M. J. (2013), "Pleistocene Beetles in New Zealand," in S. A. Elias (ed.), *Encyclopaedia of Quaternary Science* (2nd ed.), 244–54. London: Elsevier.

Martin, J. (2002), *Organizational Culture: Mapping the Terrain*. Thousand Oaks, CA: Sage.

McKenna, B., D. Rooney, and K. Boal (2009), "Wisdom Principles as a Meta-Theoretical Basis for Evaluating Leadership," *Leadership Quarterly*, 20: 177–90.

Methor, J. R., S. Melwani, and N. B. Rothman (2017), "The Space between Us: A Social-Functional Emotions View of Ambivalent and Indifferent Workplace Relationships," *Journal of Management*, 43 (6): 1789–819.

Meyerson, D., K. E. Weick, and R. M. Kramer (1996), "Swift Trust in Temporary Groups," in R. M. Kramer and T. R. Tyler (eds.), *Trust in Organizations: Frontiers of Theory and Research*, 166–95. Thousand Oaks, CA: Sage.

Michailova, S., and K. Husted (2003), "Knowledge-Sharing Hostility in Russian Firms," *California Management Review*, 45 (3): 59–77.

Minnaar, J. (2018), "Toxic Colleagues—A Bigger Problem Than You Think," *Corporate Rebels*, March: 1–3.

Moorman, C. (1995), "Organizational Market Information Processes: Cultural Antecedents and New Product Performance in Chinese Firms," *Journal of Product Innovation Management*, 21: 375–88.

Moynihan, A. B., E. R. Igou, and W. A. P. van Tilburg (2017), "Free, Connected, and Meaningful: Free Will Beliefs Promote Meaningfulness through Belongingness," *Personality and Individual Differences*, 107: 54–65.

Murphy, J., and C. V. Meyers (2009), "Rebuilding Organizational Capacity in Turnaround Schools," *Educational Management Administration & Leadership*, 37 (1): 9–27.

Nietzsche, F. W. (1966), *Beyond Good and Evil* (Walter Kaufmann, trans.). New York: Vintage.

Nilsen, D., and G. J. Curphy (2018), "Organizations That Get Teamwork Right," *People + Strategy*, 41 (2): 42–5.

O'Connor, M. I., M. W. Pennell, F. Altermatt, B. Mathews, C. J. Melian, and A. Ganzalez (2019), "Principles of Ecology Revisited: Integrating Information and Ecological

Theories for a More Unified Science," *Frontiers in Ecology and Evolution*, 7: 219. Available online: doi.org/10.3389/fevo.2019.00219 (accessed September 19, 2020).

O'Neill, T. A., and E. Salas (2018), "Creating High Performance Teamwork in Organizations," *Human Resource Management Review*, 28 (4): 325–31.

Obama B. (2007), "*Business Week's*," in subsection, 6. Available online: https://www.bizjournals.com/seattle/blog/techflash/2011/01/full-text-obamas-innovation-speech.html (accessed April 29, 2021).

Ogbeibu, S., A. Senadjki, and J. Gaskin (2018), "The Moderating Effect of Benevolence on the Impact of Organizational Culture on Employee Creativity," *Journal of Business Research*, 90: 334–46.

Peck, C., and U. C. Reitzug (2014), "School Turnaround Fever: The Paradoxes of a Historical Practice Promoted as New Reform," *Urban Education*, 49 (1): 8–38.

Pettigrew, A. M. (1979), "On Studying Organizational Cultures," *Administrative Science Quarterly*, 24 (4): 570–81.

Price Waterhouse Coopers (2020), *Workforce for the Future: The Competing Forces Shaping 2030*. Available online: https://www.pwc.com/gx/en/services/people-organisation/publications/workforce-of-the-future.html (accessed April 29, 2021).

Quong, T., and A. Walker (2010), "Seven Principles of Strategic Leadership," *International Studies in Educational Administration*, 38 (1): 22–34.

Ready, D. A., C. Cohen, D. Kiron, and B. Pring (2020), "The New Leadership Playbook for the Digital Age: Reimagining What It Takes to Lead," *MIT Sloan Management Review*, January 21. Available online: https://sloanreview.mit.edu/projects/the-new-leadership-playbook-for-the-digital-age/ (accessed June 15, 2020).

Rock, D., J. Davis, and B. Jones (2014), "Kill Your Performance Ratings," *Organizations & People*, August 2014 (76): 1–20. Available online: https://www.strategy-business.com/article/00275?gko=586a5 (accessed June 15, 2020).

Salas, E., T. L. Dickinson, S. A. Converse, and S. I. Tannenbaum (1992), "Toward an Understanding of Team Performance and Training," in R. W. Swezey and E. Salas (eds.), *Teams: Their Training and Performance*, 3–29. Norwood, NJ: Ablex.

Salas, E., D. E. Sims, and D. S. Burke (2005), "Is There a 'Big Five' in Teamwork?," *Small Group Research*, 36 (5): 555–99.

Salas, E., M. L. Shuffler, A. L. Thayer, W. L. Bedwell, and E. H. Lazzara (2015), "Understanding and Improving Teamwork in Organizations: A Scientifically Based Practical Guide," *Human Resource Management*, 54 (4): 599–622.

Saleh, A. M. J. (2002), *Educational Administration: An Islamic Perspective*. Kuala Lumpur: A. S. Nordeen.

Sapolsky, R. (2017), *Behave—the Biology of Humans at Our Best and Worst*. New York: Penguin Books.

Schein, E. H. (1985), *Organizational Culture and Leadership* (1st ed.). San Francisco: Jossey-Bass.

Schein, E. H. (2004), *Organizational Culture and Leadership* (3rd ed.). San Francisco: Jossey-Bass.

Schein, E. H. (2010), *Organizational Culture and Leadership* (4th ed.). San Francisco: Jossey-Bass.

Schein, E. H., and P. A. Schein (2019), "A New Era for Culture, Change, and Leadership," *MIT Sloan Management Review*, Summer edition: 52–8.

Schildkamp, K., and A. Visscher (2010), "The Use of Performance Feedback in School Improvement in Louisiana," *Teaching and Teacher Education*, 26: 1389–403.

Scott, W. R. (1981), *Organizations*. Englewood Cliffs, NJ: Prentice Hall.

Senge, P. (1990), *The Fifth Discipline: The Art & Practice of the Learning Organization*. Sydney, NSW: Random House.

Senge, P., R. Ross, B. Smith, C. Roberts, and A. Kleiner (1994), *The Fifth Discipline Fieldbook: Strategies and Tools for Building a Learning Organization*. London: Nicholas Brealey.

Small, M. W. (2004), "Wisdom and Now Managerial Wisdom: Do They Have a Place in Management Development Programs?," *Journal of Management Development*, 23 (8): 751–64.

Srivastva, S., and D. L. Cooperrider (1998), "An Invitation to Organizational Courage and Executive Wisdom," in S. Srivastva and D. L. Cooperrider (eds.), *Organizational Wisdom and Executive Courage*, 1–22. San Francisco: The New Lexington Press.

Sternberg, R. J. (2002), "Wisdom, Schooling and Society," *Keynote Presentation at the 2002 International Thinking Skills Conference*, Harrogate, UK.

Sternberg, R. J. (2007), "A System Model of Leadership," *American Psychologist*, 62 (1): 34–42.

Stoll, L., R. Bolam, A. McMahon, M. Wallace, and S. Thomas (2006), "Professional Learning Communities: A Review of the Literature," *Journal of Educational Change*, 7 (4): 221–58.

Syed Othman, A., and H. G. Aidit (1994), *Islamic Values and Management*. Kuala Lumpur: Institute of Islamic Understanding Malaysia.

Taylor, F. W. (1911), *The Principles of Scientific Management*. New York: Harper & Brothers.

Thomke, S. (2020), "Building a Culture of Experimentation," *Harvard Business Review*, March–April, 1–10. Available online: https://hbr.org/2020/03/building-a-culture-of-experimentation?ab=hero-main-image (accessed June 3, 2020).

Tschannen-Moran, M. (2004), *Trust Matters: Leadership of Successful Schools*. San Francisco: Jossey-Bass.

Van Rooij, B., and A. Fine (2018), "Toxic Corporate Culture: Assessing Organizational Processes of Deviancy," *Administrative Sciences*, 8 (23): 1–38.

Vaz, G. (2016), "The Identity and Mission of Catholic Schools in Evangelization of Asia." Pontifical Council for the Laity, *Proclaiming Jesus Christ in Asia*, conference paper. Available online: http://www.laici.va/content/dam/laici/documenti/aamm/proclaiming-jesus-christ-in-asia/conferences/identity-mission-catholic-schools.pdf (accessed January 9, 2021).

Weber, M. (1921/1968), *Economy and Society* (G. Roth and C. Wittich, eds., G. Roth and C. Wittich, trans.). New York: Bedminster Press.

Wei, Y. S., and N. A. Morgan (2004), "Supportiveness of Organizational Climate, Market Orientation, and New Product Performance in Chinese Firms." Available online: doi.org/10.1111/j.0737-6782.2004.00092.x (accessed November 13, 2020).

Wheatley, M. J. (2006), *Leadership and the New Science: Discovering Order in a Chaotic World*. San Francisco: Berrett-Koehler.

Whittington, R. (2010), *What Is Strategy—and Does It Matter?* (2nd ed.). London: Thomson Learning.

Yaniv, D. (2012), "Dynamics of Creativity and Empathy in Role Reversal: Contributions from Neuroscience," *American Psychological Association*, 16 (1): 70–7.

Zaidel, D. W. (2014), "Creativity, Brain and Art: Biological and Neurological Considerations," *Frontiers in Human Neuroscience*. Available online: doi: 10.3389/fnhum.2014.00389 (accessed June 3, 2020).

Zhao, Y., and W. Zhang (2013), "Organizational Theory: With Its Application in Biology and Ecology," *Network Biology*, 3 (1): 45–53.

Index

abnormal 2, 32, 38, 98, 176
acceptance 23, 52, 54, 58, 74, 145, 170–1
accepted 6, 10, 24, 27, 39, 40, 43, 47, 51, 58, 62, 79, 92, 110, 130–1, 136, 149, 154, 161, 164, 166, 170–1
accountability 15, 20, 27, 100, 171–2, 175, 178, 183–4
acknowledge 25, 27, 32, 50, 79, 81, 100, 104, 117, 120, 124, 130, 140, 148, 157, 164
adaptation 1, 36, 40, 114, 123, 136, 143, 150, 152
adaptive 36, 91, 96, 142
advancement 1, 134, 140
affirm 24–5, 27, 104
alignment 20, 22, 46–8, 55, 64, 79, 154–5, 176–7, 184–6, 189, 190
analytical 10, 40, 138, 164–6, 168, 174, 192
anthropology 40–1, 43–4, 48, 138, 151, 179
Aristotle 160, 166, 168–9
assumption 21, 26, 50, 85, 125, 156, 160–1
attitude 57, 106, 114
authentication 170–1
authenticity 24, 145
autonomy 20, 78, 80

behavior 19, 23, 26, 31, 37–40, 42, 45, 49, 54–5, 58, 61, 63–4, 73, 75, 85, 101, 119, 131, 136, 138, 141, 143, 160, 169, 185, 189
belief 50, 52, 67, 108, 134, 140, 143, 145, 150–1, 188, 193
belonging 5, 10, 12, 18, 25, 31, 51, 54, 60, 61, 65, 72, 98, 109, 128, 130, 152, 169, 170–1, 174–5, 183, 189, 191, 194
benefits 10, 13, 20, 31, 33, 46, 52, 55–6, 58–9, 65, 67–8, 76, 80–1, 85, 93–5, 98, 101, 112, 120, 122, 124, 127, 129–30, 135, 137, 140, 142, 147–8, 151, 156, 168, 176–7, 188

Branson 22–3, 29, 46–7, 52–3, 55, 62, 145–6, 167, 185–6
Burns 134, 137
business 2, 12, 15, 18, 28, 34, 66–7, 82, 98, 103, 105, 112, 115, 136, 186

Cameron 33–4, 40
capacity 2, 7–8, 12–13, 16–17, 21, 24, 33, 35, 65, 70, 78–81, 83–5, 91, 93–4, 100, 103, 105, 108, 114, 117–18, 120, 124–5, 128, 130, 137, 148–51, 162, 165, 167–8, 171–4, 180, 182, 185, 191, 192
championing 24–5, 104, 148–9
change
　failure 3, 34
　organic 114–15, 117, 142
　periodic 114–15, 117
　resistance 36, 82
chaos 120, 142, 144–5
classical theory 133, 135, 138, 141, 144, 152, 153
closed mindset 34
collaboration 5, 7, 9–10, 12, 21, 32–3, 68, 88, 93, 95–6, 100, 102, 106, 110, 127, 146, 151, 173, 175, 180, 189, 191–3
collectivism 31, 38, 88, 90, 95, 97, 100, 117, 122, 152, 184
collegiality 23, 83, 127, 130, 190
commitment 5, 13, 21–2, 25, 34, 36, 41, 46, 52, 55, 57, 60–1, 64, 67, 73–4, 80, 83–4, 90, 94–5, 97, 104, 106, 114, 117, 120, 123–5, 127, 129–30, 137, 145, 152, 164, 171, 187–8, 191, 193
Commoner 6, 67
communication 18–20, 36, 68–70, 73–4, 77, 85, 104, 109, 113, 121, 149, 161, 163, 165, 173
　verbal 74–5, 84
community 4–5, 14, 23, 26–7, 31, 63, 65–6, 89, 93–5, 98, 125–6, 172–3, 179–81, 183

competition 1, 11, 15, 20, 38, 63–4, 76, 90, 96–7, 99, 106, 114, 117, 123, 140, 193
complex adaptive system 1, 9, 130–2, 142, 143–5, 147–52, 156
complexity 2, 6, 8, 11, 21, 46, 50, 59, 77, 90, 99, 103, 110, 112, 130–2, 140–3, 153, 162–3, 183
concept 28–9, 32–3, 41–2, 44, 47, 50, 52–3, 55, 59, 66, 79–81, 91, 93, 102–3, 117–18, 125–7, 132, 140, 142, 147, 152, 161, 168
conflict 63, 72, 82, 105, 121
connected system 6
connectivity 8–12, 21, 26, 28, 51, 65–8, 70, 79–82, 84, 87–90, 95–7, 99–100, 103–8, 110, 116, 122, 124, 127–8, 147–8, 152–3, 170, 175, 183, 191, 193
consideration 36, 56, 68, 78, 134, 168
consistency 24, 75, 133, 145, 175
contemporary 1, 2, 6, 12, 14, 18, 28–9, 35, 45, 66, 71, 98, 100, 113, 123, 132, 156, 170, 190
contribution 12, 31, 41, 50, 52, 81, 105, 132, 144, 187, 189, 190
control 2, 15–16, 20, 39, 40–1, 48, 50–1, 60, 81, 91, 103–4, 111, 127, 131, 134, 137–8, 140, 143, 151, 170, 175, 193
cooperation 5, 23, 57, 65, 81, 94–7, 101, 107, 147, 151
core purpose 4, 7–9, 11, 13, 23, 46, 49–50, 52, 60–2, 65, 84, 87–8, 95, 132, 136, 148, 179, 185, 188, 191–2
creativity 3, 5, 10, 68, 83, 101, 110–12, 118–25, 127–8, 130, 142, 144, 163, 175, 193
culture 2–10, 12, 16–23, 25, 27–9, 31–52, 54–68, 75–6, 79, 84–5, 88, 90, 92–7, 101–3, 106, 109–12, 115–17, 121–4, 126–8, 130, 132–3, 135–41, 144, 150–1, 154–6, 161, 169–71, 177–87, 189–91, 193–4
  alignment 154–5, 176, 184, 186, 189, 190
  subculture 56–7
  toxic 38–9, 75
curiosity 9, 111–12, 117–21, 124–5, 127, 130, 143–4, 193

decision-making 16, 42, 53–5, 69, 73, 75–6, 78–9, 94, 120–1, 137, 163, 167, 171–2

Deloitte 15, 21, 91
department 57, 83, 97, 106, 108, 175
digital 19, 35, 119, 129, 139
discernment 109, 161
disconnection 3, 9, 38, 88, 90, 99, 107, 180
disengagement 3, 8, 15, 28, 38, 82–3, 90, 122, 145, 169, 171, 185, 191, 193
disorder 141, 144, 148
disturbance 113, 116, 123
disunity 88, 90, 99, 106, 185
diversity 2, 11, 13, 18, 38, 78, 82, 88, 99, 102–3, 121, 179, 183
division 63, 100, 145, 153
Drucker 77, 118
dynamic metastable equilibrium 7, 192

ecology 4–6, 8, 11, 59, 67, 103, 110, 116, 131–2, 140–1, 144, 152, 156, 175, 177, 179–85, 191, 193
ecosystem 4–7, 9–10, 12–14, 21, 26–9, 31–3, 66–8, 84, 90, 112–13, 131, 141, 145, 147, 150, 159, 177
education 12, 15, 21, 27, 42, 82, 92–4, 109, 129, 171, 179–80
emergence 23, 101, 128, 141–3, 145–6, 151, 163
employees 3–9, 12–15, 17–21, 23–6, 32, 34–9, 41–3, 46–7, 49–52, 54–7, 59–60, 62, 65, 68–70, 72–4, 76–80, 82, 85, 87–91, 98–101, 103–5, 107, 110–17, 121–24, 127–30, 133–40, 143–51, 153–6, 159, 169–71, 174–75, 177, 185, 188, 191–3
energy 5–10, 12–14, 65, 66–8, 78–84, 89–90, 96–7, 110, 123–4, 148, 180, 185, 188, 191–4
engagement 8, 15, 20, 23, 25, 47–8, 54, 68, 74, 95, 111, 116–17, 122, 128, 149, 152, 160, 168–9, 182, 188, 192–3
expectations 1, 15, 27, 32, 35, 40, 42, 45–7, 52–4, 57, 64, 70, 72–3, 79, 91, 94, 97, 101–3, 135, 141, 149, 151, 172, 178, 193
external 4, 7, 12–14, 21, 23, 25, 27, 36, 40, 56, 67, 69, 72, 80, 90, 109, 113–14, 116–17, 121, 126, 143–4, 170, 172, 175, 178, 184, 191

faculties 2, 11, 99
failure 3, 15, 34, 36, 49, 61, 66, 77, 115, 122, 172, 178

Index

feeling 43, 60, 72, 167
flexibility 58, 101, 116, 144, 161, 192
flow 3, 6–8, 10, 13–14, 27, 62, 65–70, 75–9, 82–5, 89, 90, 96–7, 111, 120–1, 123–4, 146, 148, 170, 180, 191, 192, 193
Forbes 115
friend 17, 46, 47
Fullan 15, 21, 22, 126, 172

Gallup 54, 82
general systems theory 136, 153
gossip 56, 76, 78
governance 18, 27
groups 12, 31–2, 35, 38, 41, 43, 46–7, 62, 92, 98, 149, 153
growth 5, 8, 14, 23, 26–7, 67–8, 79, 81, 83, 89, 96, 113, 117, 120, 122–3, 128, 131, 133, 135, 146, 152, 164, 184

Hargreaves 15
harmful 72, 88
harmony 10, 50, 67, 132, 137, 140, 173–4, 193
Harvard Business Review 18, 121
health 34, 51, 66, 84–5, 90, 157, 191
higher education 82
holistic 42, 140–1, 146, 159, 176
honesty 23, 94, 124
human 3, 8, 17–18, 20, 24, 31, 40, 44, 51–2, 57, 59, 62, 84, 97, 117–20, 122, 135, 142, 161–2, 167, 174, 194

inclusive 22, 25, 41, 43–4, 58, 60–1, 65, 84, 88, 102, 108–9, 121, 137, 144, 147, 150–1, 168, 170, 174, 182, 185
individualism 3, 7, 17, 20, 24–5, 37–8, 49, 51, 54–5, 60–2, 64, 67, 71, 75–6, 81, 91–100, 102, 109, 112, 120–1, 127–8, 131, 137, 142, 149, 187, 192, 193
industrial revolution 1, 15, 125
influence 7, 11, 13, 23–5, 32, 34, 36, 39, 41–2, 50, 52–3, 55, 58–61, 64, 66, 70–2, 76–7, 81–5, 102, 108, 127, 131, 134, 137–8, 146–7, 149, 151, 166
information 3, 5, 7–9, 13–14, 18, 20, 33, 57, 59, 60–1, 64, 67–77, 79, 82–5, 87, 89, 96–7, 102, 109, 120, 123–4, 143, 146–7, 149–50, 152, 163, 165, 167, 171, 191, 193

blockage 75
flow 7–8, 13, 68–9, 75–6, 82–5, 96–7, 124, 146, 191, 193
processing 75, 165, 167
sharing 124
innovation 1, 3, 5, 7, 9, 20, 23, 58, 68, 79, 110–12, 117–28, 130, 142, 171, 181, 192–3
integrity 16, 23, 105, 124
intelligence 1, 2, 16, 125, 163–8, 170–1, 173–4
analytical 165–6, 168, 174
artificial 1, 2, 16, 125
emotional 165–8, 173–4
intuitive 10, 165, 167–8, 174, 192
practical 165–6, 168, 174
interaction 4, 23, 47, 54, 70, 92, 103, 108, 116, 124, 140, 142–4, 147, 149, 151, 153
interdependence 4–5, 11, 13, 32, 59, 91, 101, 128, 173
internal 7, 12–13, 21, 23, 36–7, 40, 55, 67, 69, 80, 85, 113–14, 117, 142–3, 167, 175, 191
interpersonal 3, 7, 9, 16, 20–1, 23–4, 28, 31, 41, 50, 70–2, 75, 79, 81–2, 85, 87–8, 90, 92, 94–5, 99–104, 148, 163, 173–4, 177, 183, 192
collaboration 7, 9, 192
trust 101, 103–4
interpretation 41, 44, 54, 60, 70, 144, 147, 167, 168
inventive 120
isolationism 6, 7, 9, 11–13, 26, 28, 58, 76, 81, 84, 94, 96–8, 106, 120, 129, 172, 191

knowledge 5, 7–8, 10, 13–14, 18, 21–2, 26–7, 32–3, 36, 41, 46, 52, 57, 61–3, 67–8, 70, 77, 78, 79, 80–5, 87, 89, 91, 96, 98, 99, 102–5, 107–8, 110, 112, 117, 119–20, 125, 127, 129, 135–7, 140, 143, 145–7, 149–50, 152, 156–7, 160, 162–6, 168, 169–74, 185, 189, 191, 193
collective 171
explicit 150
sharing 5, 7–8, 14, 33, 36, 68, 77–9, 82, 85, 87, 105, 143, 147, 191
tacit 77, 150

leadership 1–6, 8–10, 12, 14–18, 20, 22–9, 33–5, 37, 45, 57, 62–6, 68, 73–6, 81, 87–8, 90, 94, 96–7, 100, 103, 105–8, 112, 114, 121–4, 127–8, 130, 132–4, 136–7, 139–41, 144–57, 159–61, 168–76, 179, 181–4, 189, 191–3
  leader 1–10, 12, 14–29, 32–3, 35, 37, 39, 44, 47–8, 50–1, 53–66, 69–71, 73–5, 77–9, 82, 84–5, 88, 90, 92, 95–7, 100–11, 113, 115–17, 120–1, 122, 124, 127–30, 132, 134–5, 137–40, 143–51, 153–4, 156–7, 159–62, 167–75, 177, 179, 183, 189–94
  middle leader 60, 62, 66, 108, 122
  practice 2–3, 9, 12, 16–18, 22, 26–8, 62, 68, 88, 100, 107, 112, 130, 132, 137, 147, 152, 159–60, 169–70, 175
  principal 27, 64–5, 109, 172–3, 175, 181
  relational 100
  transactional 134, 137
  transformational 137, 140
  transrelational 28, 146
  wisdom 10, 157, 159, 161, 163, 165–71, 173, 175, 192, 193
learning 1, 5, 7, 10, 14, 16–19, 21, 25, 27–8, 33, 43, 46, 49, 61, 63–5, 67–8, 79–80, 83–4, 89–95, 104–5, 107–8, 111, 114, 117–27, 129, 137, 143–4, 146–7, 150, 152, 159–60, 164–5, 172–3, 181, 191–2
  organization 18, 91, 93
life experience 10, 58, 78, 99, 121, 162, 167
living systems 7, 79
loneliness 72–3, 94
loyalty 34, 55

manager 54, 59–60, 62, 139, 144, 147, 169, 175
  managerial 2, 18–19, 39, 65, 88, 134, 139, 153, 160, 190, 194
  managerialism 2, 38–9, 105–6, 108, 123, 127, 159, 191, 193
manifest 8, 23, 40, 50, 99, 110, 127, 132, 169, 184, 193
market 5, 14, 34, 89, 113–14, 160
Marra 116
McKinsey 15, 92, 115
meaning-making 23, 40–1, 52, 54, 60, 74, 80, 82, 120, 142, 146, 166, 187

mission 5, 14, 25, 63, 80, 89, 91, 94, 178, 180–2, 186
MIT Sloan 16, 18–19
modulate 116–17, 123, 130, 152
morale 34, 36, 94, 188
motivation 34, 37, 51, 60, 74, 80–1, 90, 93, 104, 118–19, 125, 172, 174, 182, 187
  external 80
  intrinsic 60, 80–1, 118
mutuality 33, 71
mutually beneficial 6, 20, 23–4, 62, 81, 100, 105

natural 11–12, 41, 44, 66–7, 80, 84, 100, 113, 131, 142, 148, 187
network 4, 13, 25, 141–2, 144, 147
norms 11, 19–20, 31–5, 37–8, 40, 43–6, 49, 55–8, 61, 64, 71, 98, 121, 124, 160, 189, 193

objective 40, 41, 56, 91, 138, 160, 165–6, 178–9
open mindset 115
open system 7, 12–13, 136, 191
openness 5, 23, 57–8, 94, 96, 124, 161, 168
order 2, 6–7, 12–13, 17–23, 25–8, 32–3, 37, 40–1, 52, 55–6, 58, 77–9, 81, 84–5, 88, 91, 93, 95, 102–4, 113, 123, 126–8, 130–1, 134, 136–8, 140–2, 144–5, 148, 150–1, 160–1, 163, 165–6, 173, 176–7, 185–6, 189, 192
organization
  change 3, 9, 15, 32, 34, 36, 112, 113, 117, 130, 138, 143, 148, 150, 151, 160
  climate 7, 8, 65, 94, 167, 171, 191
  culture 3, 7–9, 16–20, 22, 29, 32–7, 39–42, 44, 45, 48–52, 54–9, 63–6, 68, 79, 84, 110–11, 116–17, 122–4, 127–8, 130, 132–3, 135, 137–8, 140, 151, 155, 169, 177, 179, 183–5, 191, 193–4
  dysfunction 90
  ecology 6, 131–2, 144, 181
  energy 8, 65, 79, 81–2, 192
  growth 68
  success 79, 13, 36, 41, 77, 85, 137, 191, 194

past experience 5, 14, 46, 57, 89, 99, 102, 110, 154
people 2, 4–5, 7–8, 11, 13–14, 16–17, 19–20, 23–4, 26, 27–8, 31–2, 37–8,

42–8, 50, 52–4, 57, 60–2, 67–9, 72, 74–5, 77, 79–80, 89–92, 97–102, 108, 110–11, 116–20, 122–3, 127–30, 137, 154, 157, 163, 166, 170–4, 178, 180, 181, 187–8, 190–1, 193–4
performance 2–3, 6–8, 14–16, 20, 23, 34–5, 37, 42, 48, 51–2, 54, 60, 68–9, 74, 80–2, 85, 87–8, 95–6, 98, 100, 103–5, 109, 111, 118, 120–2, 128, 133–7, 139, 142, 144, 148–9, 169, 171–3, 175, 178, 188–9, 191–4
  management 15, 98, 100, 171, 175
person 2, 8–10, 18, 21–2, 24, 35, 38, 41, 46–7, 50–5, 58, 60, 64, 69, 70–3, 76, 78, 80–1, 84–5, 97, 99, 102, 110, 117–18, 121, 143, 146, 148, 156, 159, 160–8, 170, 171, 174, 179, 184, 188–9, 192, 193
personality 36, 63, 119, 162
perspective 3, 5, 8–9, 13, 23, 28–9, 33, 37, 40–1, 44, 48, 51, 56, 58, 66–7, 69, 73–4, 83–4, 101, 103, 118, 120, 134–8, 140–3, 148–9, 150–1, 160, 165, 174, 179
perturbation 113–14
phenomenon 8, 23, 29, 31, 44–6, 50, 58, 145, 161, 163–5
Plato 119, 162
policies 16, 37, 42–3, 49, 55–6, 63, 68, 77, 116, 122, 134, 150, 159, 169–70, 180–1
power 2, 27, 32, 34, 41–2, 51, 57, 76–7, 82, 109, 138, 146, 162, 180, 189
predictability 16, 20, 23–4, 127, 141–3, 145, 175
Price Waterhouse Coopers 16
problem 8, 22, 27, 32, 34, 37, 39, 50, 57–8, 60, 63, 69, 78, 90, 97, 100, 102–3, 106, 115, 118, 125, 127, 129, 151, 154, 156, 159, 169, 173, 179, 193
problem solving 34
processes 13, 15–16, 18, 21, 25, 37, 42, 48–9, 55–6, 62–3, 68–9, 77, 88, 91, 97, 109, 112–13, 115–17, 122, 134, 137, 143, 147, 150, 159, 170–2, 175, 178, 180, 183, 194
productivity 2, 5, 7–8, 13–14, 33–4, 65, 67, 80, 82, 87–91, 96, 102, 111, 116, 131, 133, 139–40, 148, 153, 175, 189, 191–3

professional 18, 27, 61, 63–4, 82–3, 90, 92–5, 105, 107–9, 115, 121, 125–6, 155, 160, 165, 172, 187
professional learning community 93–5, 125–6
promotion 20, 43, 52, 102, 106, 112, 151
protectionism 12, 185
purpose 4–5, 7–9, 11–14, 23, 26, 33, 35, 45–6, 49–50, 52, 54, 57, 60–2, 64–5, 67, 69–70, 78–81, 83–4, 87, 88–90, 94–8, 101–2, 104–6, 120–2, 126, 129, 132–3, 136, 146–9, 171, 174–5, 179, 184–5, 188–9, 191–3

reciprocity 12, 32, 54, 95, 101, 105, 128
relatedness 71, 80
relationship 2, 7, 19, 20, 22, 24, 47, 52, 70–2, 84, 90, 99, 101, 105, 124, 138, 145, 146, 173–4, 192
research 2–3, 10, 15–16, 18–19, 21, 28, 32–4, 36–7, 47, 50–1, 70–4, 83, 92–6, 101, 103, 112, 115, 118, 121, 124, 160, 162, 175, 178–9
resilience 53, 71, 94, 116, 128
resources 13, 23, 49, 52, 55, 61, 63–4, 73, 93, 96–7, 104, 105–7, 122, 124, 126–9, 134, 141, 169, 180
restructuring 38, 91, 138–40, 144, 154, 162
role 8–12, 16, 20–1, 23, 27–8, 33, 49, 53–8, 69, 73, 75–8, 84–5, 90, 95, 97, 101, 102, 127–8, 131, 138–40, 143, 145–9, 151, 155, 166, 169, 172, 175, 192

Sapolsky 54, 98–9
Schein 19, 37, 39–44, 50, 56–7, 135
school 15–16, 26–8, 63–5, 83–4, 92–5, 97–8, 107–9, 126–9, 171–3, 175, 177–84
section 13, 22, 39, 57, 101, 104, 144, 150, 161, 163, 168
self-concept 52, 53, 55
Senge 91, 93
shared meanings 149
skills 16–18, 22, 43, 46, 58, 69, 72, 78, 80–1, 92, 96, 99, 104–5, 110, 114, 116–17, 120, 127, 129, 133, 135–7, 140, 143, 145, 147, 156, 163–6, 170, 173
social
  categorization 102
  clique 99

connection 72, 85
network 90
ordering 31
socializing 98
sociological 40-2, 44, 138, 140, 151
socio-relational 2-3, 95, 98, 101, 103
stakeholders 12, 18, 33, 36, 43, 104-5, 126, 149, 180
stories 49, 61, 129, 150, 152, 168
storytelling 149
strategy 1, 5, 7, 14, 34, 35-6, 38, 72, 89, 98, 125, 145, 154, 171, 182, 191-2, 194
   strategic thinking 45
   strategic vision 25
strengths 25, 146, 148, 187
structures 37, 42, 56, 63, 65, 85, 113, 116, 120, 130, 141-2, 146, 170, 194
subjective 41, 44, 165-6, 179
success 4, 7-9, 13, 18-19, 21, 26, 31-2, 34, 36, 41, 46, 49, 51, 56-7, 61, 67-8, 74, 77, 79-81, 83, 85, 88-9, 91, 94-6, 98, 100, 110, 120, 122-4, 129-31, 136-7, 171-3, 178, 186-7, 190-2, 194
support 5-6, 10, 14, 19, 24, 55, 60-1, 63-5, 67-8, 73-5, 82, 83, 88-9, 92-3, 95, 100, 107, 109, 112, 124, 127, 130-1, 138, 146-51, 156, 168, 170, 172, 174-5, 180-2, 184-5, 187, 190
survival 32, 38, 45, 51, 98, 111, 118, 120
   survival instinct 51
sustainability 13, 16, 23, 31, 44, 84, 131, 135, 137, 144
symbols 43, 49, 63
synchronicity 10-11, 132, 137, 140
systems 4, 6-7, 11-13, 15, 21, 26, 42, 67, 79, 88, 91-4, 97, 109, 112, 125-7, 133, 136, 141-2, 170-1, 190, 191
   systems theory 136, 141

task 22, 27, 29, 56, 58, 66, 75, 78, 84-5, 88, 92, 95-6, 103, 133, 135, 137, 148, 162, 167, 192
Taylor 133
teacher 63-4, 93, 94-5, 107-8, 125-6, 179
teams 3, 5-9, 11-14, 20-1, 24-5, 31, 35, 37-8, 42-3, 45, 47, 49-50, 56-8, 60-1, 64, 67-9, 73, 75-8, 81-3, 85, 87-111, 116-17, 120-4, 126, 127-9, 131, 135, 137, 139, 142, 147-9, 151, 155, 159, 172, 175, 177, 180-1, 185-6, 188-93
   team membership 109, 139
teamwork 7, 9, 22-3, 38, 68, 75, 81, 88, 90-2, 94, 95-6, 101, 108-10, 121, 126, 137, 151, 192
tension 45, 100
thrive 2-3, 7, 13, 18-19, 90, 170, 192
transparency 21, 23
tribal 98
trust 5, 9-10, 20-1, 23-5, 33, 36, 39, 64, 67, 71, 74, 76, 88, 90, 94, 96-7, 100-5, 112, 122, 124, 145, 148, 170, 175, 190, 193
   mistrust 193
   propensity 102, 105
   swift trust 102-4
trustworthy 24, 145

uncertainty 1, 21, 35, 70, 93, 100, 105, 114, 132, 142, 162, 167
unity 11, 50, 70, 90, 97, 106, 108

values 11, 19, 20, 23, 34-5, 37, 40-3, 45-50, 53, 56-7, 61, 63-5, 68, 80, 85, 124, 133, 135, 140, 155, 159, 163, 167, 180, 183-5, 187-90, 193
vision 17, 23, 25, 50, 63, 74, 78, 127-8, 149, 180, 186

whole 4, 6, 12-13, 20, 42, 50, 64, 66, 76, 82, 89, 96, 104, 106, 109-10, 115, 136, 141-3, 148, 189
willingness 47, 59, 74, 83, 89, 102-3, 122, 124, 130, 162, 164
wisdom 7-8, 10, 26-7, 84, 110, 115, 150, 157, 159-75, 190-3
wise 8, 10, 26-8, 46, 65, 157, 159-64, 166, 168, 170-1, 173-5, 192
workplace 4, 8, 11, 16, 28, 37, 39, 47, 52-4, 65, 67, 68-73, 75, 77, 79, 81, 85, 88, 90, 99-101, 112, 121-2, 128-9, 135, 137, 147, 154-5, 166, 184, 188-9, 193
   knowledge 68, 77, 79, 99

www.ingramcontent.com/pod-product-compliance
Lightning Source LLC
Chambersburg PA
CBHW062228300426
44115CB00012BA/2258